Rise of the Partisan House of Representatives

by

Karl Gerard Brandt

Foreword

Wright Patman of Texas, Bob Poage of Texas, and Felix Edward "Eddie" Hebert of Louisiana all entered the House in 1929, 1937, and 1941, respectively, and during much of their careers, the House operated under a distinct set of ideas and practices that featured party leaders with limited powers, autonomous committee chairmen, seniority, traditional House customs, significant regional and ideological blocs, weak party discipline, and cooperation across partisan and ideological lines. All three men rose to power through the seniority system; the seniority system was the well-respected custom of awarding the chairmanship of a committee to the member of the majority party with the longest service on that committee. Patman became chairman of the Banking and Currency Committee; he sought to restrain large concentrations of economic power, oppose corruption, and promote opportunities for ordinary working Americans. Poage became chairman of the Agriculture Committee; he sought to use the federal government to strengthen the agriculture sector and to improve the standard of living for people who worked in agriculture or who lived in rural areas. Hebert became chairman of the Armed Services Committee; he sought to promote a strong national defense and an assertive foreign policy during the era of the Vietnam War. During their careers, all three men found themselves in controversies and made political enemies.

Over time, the nation changed, and the House changed, too. A Congressional reform movement emerged, and liberal Democrats from the North and the West composed the bulk of the movement. The movement used the Democratic Study Group (DSG) as the primary means of advancing its goals of stronger party authority and weaker committee chairmen. The movement believed the chairmen, who frequently were Southern conservatives, impeded progressive legislation and acted autocratically. The Congressional reform movement succeeded in gradually reforming House and Democratic Party rules. By the early 1970s, the power structure of the House had been reformed, and a method of popular election for committee chairmen was created. Yet, the reforms had not been fully utilized. The same chairmen held power, and many of the older ideas and practices remained. The Watergate Crisis greatly impacted the nation, and one of the results was a new demand for accountability. The elections of 1974 featured the election of seventy-five freshmen House Democrats who collectively possessed a strong desire to challenge the status quo and advance some type of reform. They focused their attention on the committee chairmen and the issue of autocratic management of the committees. In 1975, the political enemies of these three chairmen, the Congressional reform movement, and the freshmen Democrats formed a coalition that removed Patman, Poage, and Hebert from their chairmanships by popular vote in the House Democratic Caucus. No other incumbent chairmen were removed.

The careers of Patman, Poage, and Hebert concluded within a few years, but the ramifications of their removal affected the entire House and the nation's politics. The removal proved that the reforms would be fully utilized, and the seniority system was overturned both in the rules and in actual practice. The removal marked the decline of the set of ideas and practices that had earlier governed the House. The reforms promoted by the Congressional reform movement became entrenched and facilitated the rise of a much more partisan

House characterized by stronger party leaders and institutions, a greater stress on party unity and discipline, greater uniformity among party members regarding ideology and voting, and a more partisan approach towards the work of the House. This trend began after the 1975 removal, accelerated in the 1980s, solidified in the 1990s, and became institutionalized in the twenty-first century.

Table of Contents

Chapter 1 - The Bipartisan House System 1
Chapter 2 - Wright Patman 27
Chapter 3 - Bob Poage 49
Chapter 4 - Felix Edward "Eddie" Hebert 77
Chapter 5 - The Stirrings of Reform 100
Chapter 6 - The Demand for Accountability 135
Chapter 7 - The Coalition Assembled 151
Chapter 8 - The Removal 178
Chapter 9 - The Legacy 231
Bibliography 273
Index 281

Chapter 1 - The Bipartisan House System

From the 1920s through the 1970s, the U. S. House of Representatives consistently managed itself according to a specific system, the Bipartisan House System. This system evolved from the House's earlier systems of centralized management based on either a strong Speaker or a strong Caucus in the early 1900s. There never was an official definition of the Bipartisan House System, but it displayed salient characteristics that clearly distinguished it from the systems of centralized management of the early 1900s and the system of centralized management that arose in the House since the middle of the 1970s. Some of the salient characteristics of this Bipartisan House System included party leaders with limited powers, autonomous committee chairmen, seniority, traditional House customs, significant regional and ideological blocs, weak party discipline, and cooperation across partisan and ideological lines. The system's bipartisanship enabled it to work effectively and served as a defining characteristic. For this reason, this system can be called the Bipartisan House System. The Bipartisan House System endured until the removal of the triumvirate of committee chairmen Wright Patman, Bob Poage, and Felix Edward Hebert in 1975.

In the early 1900s, the House employed two systems of centralized management based on either a strong Speaker or a strong Caucus. The Speaker had developed great power prior to 1910. The Speaker could appoint members of standing committees, appoint the committee chairmen, serve as chair of the Rules Committee, and use unlimited power of recognition. In 1910, Joseph Cannon of Illinois was Speaker, but opposition had emerged against his system of centralized management based on a strong Speaker. On March 16, 1910, a coalition of dissident Republicans and Democrats forced a major change in House rules. The changes removed the Speaker from the Rules Committee, deprived the Speaker of the power to make committee assignments and choose committee chairs, limited the Speaker's power of recognition regarding members seeking to address the House, and set up a new means to choose the Rules Committee. The resolution making the rules changes was passed on March 19, 1910. The changes became accepted and normative.[1] From 1910-1920, the party caucus exercised dominant authority in the House, and both parties relied on the caucus. In 1911, after capturing the majority in the 1910 elections, the Democrats established a system of centralized management based on a strong Caucus. Stress was placed on party discipline exercised through the Caucus, and Caucus authority was used on legislation and House organization. This system was nicknamed "King Caucus."[2] After World War I, the House changed. Party caucuses declined in power. Party discipline became weaker. Party government was superseded by coalitions of different blocs.[3] In the 1920s, House leadership was diffused and exercised by several people.[4]

Following these systems of centralized management, the Bipartisan House System arose. It avoided the excesses of Cannon's system and King Caucus, and these systems of

---

1. George B. Galloway, *History of the United States House of Representatives* (Washington, D. C.: U. S. Government Printing Office, 1965), 50-53.
2. Galloway, *History House*, 123-125.
3. Galloway, *History House*, 127.
4. Galloway, *History House*, 128.

centralized management became reference points describing excessive or unfair exercise of power. There never was an official definition of the Bipartisan House System, but it displayed salient characteristics that clearly distinguished it from the systems of centralized management of the early 1900s and the system of centralized management that arose in the House since the middle of the 1970s.

The Bipartisan House System existed during the decades of momentous events and highly significant issues for the U. S. The nation experienced the Great Depression, the New Deal, World War II, the Cold War, the Korean War, the Vietnam War, the Civil Rights Movement, the Women's Liberation Movement, the Great Society, the post-war economic boom and decline, racial conflict, changes in social mores, the Watergate Crisis, and many other events and issues all within a few decades. The Bipartisan House System helped shape the policies that the nation implemented to address all of these events and issues, and all of these events and issues provided the conditions in which the Bipartisan House System existed, thrived, and fell.

The Bipartisan House System requires description. The Constitution identifies the Speaker of the House in Article I, Section 2, but few details are provided. Although the Speaker of the House held the preeminent position in the House in the Bipartisan House System, the Speaker had limited authority and had to rely on personal influence. The opinions of several members illustrated the Speaker's predicament. Richard Bolling of Missouri, a member with ties to the House Democratic Leadership and House reformers, described the actual authority of the Speaker in these terms: "A modern Democratic Speaker is something like a feudal king--he is first in the land;

he receives elaborate homage and respect; but he is dependent on the powerful lords, usually committee chairmen, who are basically hostile to the objectives of the national Democratic party and the Speaker."[5] Joseph Martin of Massachusetts, the long-time Republican House leader and Speaker in two Congresses, stressed this same theme. The Speaker could facilitate or impede the progress of legislation or prolong or end debate. The Speaker possessed the authority to recognize a member to address the House and also to ignore a member and prevent him or her from addressing the House. Despite such authority, the Speaker needed to display fairness in order to serve effectively because the House could override or oppose the Speaker.[6] Martin explained that as Speaker he relied on persuasion. Unless it was critically necessary, he never asked a member to vote his (Martin's) preference if that vote would cause the member problems in his or her district. He could ask the member for support on another vote.[7] Carl Albert of Oklahoma, a Democratic Speaker, stressed the limited authority of the Speaker. The Leadership could not compel members to vote for or against something and instead could only try to persuade them. Persuasion tactics included employing a regional whip or influential member to talk with members, enlisting the legendary Speaker Sam Rayburn of Texas to influence members, and establishing good relations with members in general. Albert wrote: "Once in Congress, he could stay and rise in the House without toeing any party line.

---

5. Richard Bolling, *House Out of Order* (New York: E. P. Dutton & Co., Inc.,1965), 70.

6. Joe Martin and Robert J. Donovan, *My First Fifty Years in Politics* (New York: McGraw-Hill Book Company, Inc., 1960), 181.

7. Martin, *First Fifty*, 183.

No whip, no leader, no one could make a single member vote against his own wishes."[8]

Sam Rayburn exercised great influence over the House during his many years as Speaker, and his personal influence became a standard by which people judged other Speakers. Yet, the Bipartisan House System limited and conditioned Rayburn's influence. Albert wrote that Rayburn's influence stemmed primarily from his personal qualities and record (knowledge, character, good judgment, performance of favors) rather than institutional or formal authority: "The power that Sam Rayburn exercised over the House was the power of his being Sam Rayburn."[9] Bolling explained that Rayburn established good relations with other members and performed favors for them, including political opponents. He treated these favors as debts and used them as the means to lobby and persuade other members. On issues critical to a member, Rayburn could avoid pressure if that member might seriously hurt his or her reelection prospects. If there were poor prospects of success on an issue, Rayburn avoided conflicts over that issue.[10] Bolling wrote that Rayburn amassed great personal authority and used it to advance his goals and views on issues. Yet, the official power of the Speaker was weak, and Rayburn did not seek reform of the Speaker's authority.[11] Bolling claimed that Rayburn did not promote ideas or reforms that could have changed the decentralized system of the House or the House Democratic Party: "He believed so much in the

---

8. Carl Albert and Danney Goble, *Little Giant: The Life and Times of Speaker Carl Albert* (Norman, OK: University of Oklahoma Press, 1990), 205-206.
9. Albert, *Giant*, 172.
10. Bolling, *House Out of Order*, 68-69.
11. Bolling, *House Out of Order*, 64-67.

'system' that he refused to support those very changes that would have strengthened him as Speaker and would have put down the committee chairmen."[12]

The Board of Education served as a critical part of Rayburn's Speakership. Tip O'Neill of Massachusetts, a junior member during Rayburn's era and later a Democratic Speaker, recalled the Board of Education. The Board of Education began under Speaker Nicholas Longworth of Ohio and his Democratic counterpart John Nance Garner of Texas, also a Speaker. These two men referred to drinking alcohol together as "striking a blow for liberty," and the slogan became popular in the House. There was a special room on the first floor of the Capitol located behind the members' dining room. The name "Board of Education" originated from the fact that Longworth and Garner learned much from the guests they invited to this special room. Garner continued the Board of Education as Speaker, and Rayburn later continued it, too. When Rayburn served as Speaker, the House Democratic Leadership frequently gathered in the room every afternoon at approximately 4:30 or 5:00. The room was unmarked, and a guard was posted outside the door. Rayburn did not particularly like the name "Board of Education." He just referred to the room as "downstairs." Under Rayburn, the Board of Education "was more like a club, with admission by invitation only." The regular attendees included persons such as John McCormack of Massachusetts (a later Democratic Speaker), Albert, Hale Boggs of Louisiana (a later Democratic Majority Leader), Homer Thornberry (a representative from Texas), Wright

---

12. Richard Bolling, *Power in the House: A History of the Leadership of the House of Representatives* (New York: E. P. Dutton & Co., Inc., 1968), 194-195.

Patman, Lewis Deschler (the House Parliamentarian), Bolling, and Lyndon Johnson. Regular attendees sometimes brought guests, and O'Neill accompanied McCormack sometimes. Bourbon was served, and the room had black leather chairs and a long black leather sofa with red pillows. Rayburn asked the guests about politics in their home state and city, and Republicans were sometimes invited to facilitate the passage of legislation.[13]

Albert also described the Board of Education and stressed its importance. He recalled that the Board of Education met in Room H-118 which was 12 x 20 feet. The House had designated the room for the Speaker's use for decades, and Rayburn furnished it according to his own preferences. It had a persian carpet, framed political cartoons, signed photographs, and a few portraits. Eight chairs surrounded Rayburn's desk, and there was a couch along one wall. He wrote that receiving an invitation from Rayburn was a big honor and a sign of advancement in the House hierarchy. Rayburn invited Albert in his first term often, and afterwards, Albert had a standing invitation. The regular attendees included Texans, Rayburn's long-time friends, and junior members with potential. Rayburn used the conversations in the Board of Education as a means to collect information from the members for use in House work. The Board of Education gatherings generally ended at approximately 7:00 p.m.[14]

In the Bipartisan House System, the Caucus still existed but exercised only a small amount of authority. For several

13. Tip O'Neill and William Novak, *Man of the House: The Life and Political Memoirs of Speaker Tip O'Neill* (New York: Random House, 1987), 126-128.
14. Albert, *Giant*, 171-172.

decades after World War I, the Caucus rarely met except when a new Congress convened. The Caucus nominated House officers and approved committee assignments. The Party leadership could not bind members on votes and did not, typically, punish members by removing them from committees.[15] Albert recalled that Rayburn did not trust the Caucus, and McCormack also did not trust the Caucus.[16] Jim Wright of Texas, a future Democratic Speaker, recalled that Rayburn and McCormack had typically allowed only one meeting of the House Democratic Caucus every two years. The Caucus nominated the Speaker, chose the Majority Leader and House officers, and readopted the rules for the new Congress.[17] Bolling wrote that the Democratic Caucus was predominantly used at the start of a new Congress for nominations of party leaders and organizational work.[18]

In the Bipartisan House System, the House conducted its work through the system of standing committees. The House made reforms at different times to reorganize the committees and reduce their numbers. In 1946, the House consolidated forty-eight standing committees into nineteen standing committees.[19]

The method of making committee assignments showed continuity through much of the Bipartisan House System. The Republican Conference (the official name of the Republican's caucus) chose a Committee on Committees, and the

---

15. Galloway, *History House*, 103.
16. Albert, *Giant*, 311.
17. Jim Wright, *Balance of Power: Presidents and Congress from the Era of McCarthy to the Age of Gingrich* (Atlanta: Turner Publishing, Inc., 1996), 188.
18. Bolling, *Power in the House*, 39.
19. Galloway, *History House*, 59.

Democratic members of the Ways and Means Committee served as a Committee on Committees. Each Committee on Committees prepared committee membership lists. The lists were ratified by the party caucuses, separately and respectively by each party, and then passed by the House. House members typically used the seniority system to determine committee chairmanships, but there were a few rare and special instances when the seniority system was not followed.[20] The Democratic members of the Ways and Means Committee represented the regions of the nation. Typically, a Democratic member solicited the Ways and Means Committee member from his or her region for assistance in obtaining committee assignments. If someone left the Ways and Means Committee, then another member from that region would fill that vacancy.[21]

The committee chairmen were the pillars of the standing committee system. The authority of standing committee chairmen evolved throughout the history of the House and was not formally and officially stated in one single source; the authority was based on several sources such as the official House rules, the individual committee's standing orders, and actual U. S. law.[22] The chairmen obtained their positions through the seniority system. Members of a committee were ranked in order of their length of service on that particular committee. The House followed a custom that awarded the chairmanship to the member possessing the longest

---

20. Galloway, *History House*, 61-62.

21. Jeffrey R. Biggs and Thomas S. Foley, *Honor in the House: Speaker Tom Foley* (Pullman, WA: Washington State University Press, 1999), 28.

22. Galloway, *History House*, 63.

continuous service among the members of the majority party on that committee.[23]

In the Bipartisan House System, the chairmen possessed great autonomy. Bolling described the authority of the committee chairmen using a feudal analogy; the committee chair was similar to "a legislative baron with supreme power over his fief."[24] Albert characterized the committees as the primary forum for the House's work. Committees drafted bills, proposed the amendments for bills, and chose the length of time for debate. Committee chairmen dominated their committees, and as a group, they dominated Congress.[25] Bolling explained that the committee chairmen set the committees' agendas, appointed subcommittee chairs, determined if bills would be referred to subcommittees, determined when to hold committee meetings, appointed committee staff, and approved witness lists for hearings.[26] Tom Foley of the state of Washington, a future Democratic Speaker, wrote that many committees lacked written rules and instead were managed simply by the chairman.[27] Albert wrote that Rayburn intervened in a committee chair's work only on rare occasions and highly significant items using his personal influence.[28] Bolling wrote that Rayburn had clashes with committee chairs and sometimes even lost to them because

---

23. Wright Patman, *Our American Government and How It Works*, 7th ed. (New York: Barnes & Noble, 1974), 60.
24. Bolling, *House Out of Order*, 37.
25. Albert, *Giant*, 218-219.
26. Bolling, *House Out of Order*, 37.
27. Biggs, *Honor in the House*, 35.
28. Albert, *Giant*, 231.

the chairmen possessed autonomy over their own committees.[29]

The Rules Committee exercised great power by controlling the schedule for House consideration of legislation; it became infamous for its autonomy because of its encounters with the Civil Rights Movement. Howard Smith of Virginia chaired the Rules Committee for many years and used it to obstruct liberal legislation. Smith was conservative, and the Committee's conservative Democrats and Republicans often controlled the Committee.[30] O'Neill described Howard Smith and his efforts to block civil rights legislation. On one occasion, he held an unusually large number of hearings, and sometimes, he refused to even schedule a hearing. Less often, he left Washington and returned to his farm in Virginia to prevent the Committee from meeting and working. In one instance, he left after informing members that a barn owned by him had caught fire and burnt.[31]

Traditional House customs shaped relations among members and the work of the House in the Bipartisan House System, and beyond the specific seniority system, the general idea of seniority affected many customs of the House including selections for leadership positions. Jim Wright wrote that the House filled leadership positions in a predictable manner in the mid-twentieth century. For several decades after the creation of the Majority Leader position in the early twentieth century, every Speaker was succeeded by the Majority Leader provided

---

29. Bolling, *House Out of Order*, 70-72.
30. Bolling, *House Out of Order*, 71.
31. O'Neill, *Man of the House*, 138-139.

that their party maintained the House majority. Also, the habit developed for the Whip to succeed the Majority Leader.[32]

Due to the general idea of seniority, it was traditional for senior members to lead and for junior members to follow. O'Neill's entry into the House reflected these customs. He described the attitude regarding freshmen when he entered Congress in the 1950s in these terms: "In those days, new members, like children, were expected to be seen and not heard. Our job was simple and basic: learn the ropes, follow the party line, and pay attention to what's going on around you."[33] In January 1953, the freshmen Democrats (including O'Neill) participated in an orientation luncheon in the Speaker's dining room. Rayburn told them to wait patiently and to learn about their job. Rayburn counseled them with his famous line about advancement in the House: "'If you want to get along, go along.'"[34] Foley had a similar experience during his entry into the House in 1965 as a freshman. McCormack explained to the freshmen that members would not receive respect or responsibility until their second term. Michael Kirwan, a senior member of the Appropriations Committee, warned the freshmen against the worst danger for a freshman, thinking for one's self. Instead, freshmen should follow their leaders such as the subcommittee chairs, the committee chairs, the Caucus chair, the Whip, the Majority Leader, and the Speaker.[35]

The general idea of seniority affected even minor customs, too. Morris Udall of Arizona explained that seniority influenced not only committee assignments but also office

---

32. Wright, *Balance of Power*, 258-259.
33. O'Neill, *Man of the House*, 117.
34. O'Neill, *Man of the House*, 130.
35. Biggs, *Honor in the House*, 36.

locations, parking space locations, and the speed of service in the Members' Dining Room. Udall wrote that he authored a letter to Rayburn a few weeks after arriving in Washington. His letter suggested that Congress find a means to obtain a balanced budget every year and that Rayburn appoint a committee to study the seniority system. He offered to meet Rayburn to discuss these matters at any time. Udall never received a response.[36] Joseph Martin wrote that in 1925, when he entered the House, there was a large round table in the House restaurant reserved for the Speaker, the committee chairmen, and maybe a few senior members of the Rules Committee. Martin served in the House for three years before he ever sat there.[37] Bolling described one salient encounter with a committee chair. When Bolling was a new member, he informed the chair of a committee of his intention to offer an amendment to a bill sponsored by the chair. The bill was on the floor. When the reading clerk began the section of the bill relevant to Bolling's amendment, other members of the committee then distracted Bolling. The reading clerk completed the section before Bolling was recognized to offer the amendment.[38]

The general idea of seniority was expressed among senior members and junior members in the custom of the mentor-protege relationship, and Albert's career illustrated this custom. Albert was a protege of Rayburn. Albert wrote that Rayburn looked for junior Democrats with great potential, especially ones from his own region. Rayburn knew about

---

36. Morris K. Udall, Bob Neuman, and Randy Udall, *Too Funny to Be President* (New York: Henry Holt and Company, 1988), 106.

37. Martin, *First Fifty*, 47.

38. Bolling, *House Out of Order*, 86.

Albert and his background, but Albert's deep interest in and appreciation for Congress struck Rayburn as noteworthy. He sometimes asked Albert to predict the outcome of a vote or to identify a member, and through this interaction, Albert became close to Rayburn.[39] As a freshman, Albert wrote to the Democrats' Committee on Committees about his preferences for committee assignments. Each freshman could list three preferences, and Albert listed the Rules Committee, the Appropriations Committee, and the Ways and Means Committee. He subsequently offered to serve on the Public Works Committee. Instead, he was assigned to the Post Office Committee and the Civil Service Committee.[40] In 1949, Albert obtained a seat on the Agriculture Committee through Rayburn's influence. Later, several members advised Albert to seek a vacant seat on the Ways and Means Committee. Rayburn advised against this action because Albert had good career prospects in the House, and service on the Ways and Means Committee, a controversial assignment, could hurt his prospects.[41] Rayburn was correct, and Albert rose through the House Democratic Leadership and eventually became Speaker. After Albert acquired greater status and influence, he became a liaison between Congressional leaders and junior members, and junior members frequently asked him for assistance and advice. He offered advice, campaigned in their districts for them, and facilitated the progress of their legislative projects.[42]

---

39. Albert, *Giant*, 170-171.
40. Albert, *Giant*, 151-153.
41. Albert, *Giant*, 173.
42. Albert, *Giant*, 206.

O'Neill's career also illustrated the custom of the mentor-protege relationship; he was a protege of John McCormack. When O'Neill entered Congress, John Kennedy advised him to be nice to John McCormack because McCormack could provide or withhold favors and assistance.[43] O'Neill became a regular attendee at McCormack's table for breakfast in the House dining room, and the number of persons at McCormack's table ranged from a few to a couple of dozen. McCormack received invitations to many events because of his position in the House Democratic Leadership. He often took O'Neill to these events, and O'Neill met many prominent people and made valuable political connections.[44] In January 1955 (the start of O'Neill's second term), Rayburn asked O'Neill to serve on the Rules Committee (a very important assignment, especially for a junior member). Rayburn explained that he learned about O'Neill from McCormack and that he knew that O'Neill respected party loyalty. Rayburn told O'Neill that he was selected to serve as a supporter for the Party's position on the Rules Committee in order to facilitate the progress of the Party's position.[45]

Jim Wright experienced the custom of the mentor-protege relationship. Jim Wright wrote that Rayburn picked proteges from the junior members. Rayburn liked to help Texans but also helped non-Texans such as Hale Boggs and Richard Bolling.[46] Jim Wright wrote about his first encounter with the Board of Education. Wright visited Washington in 1954 prior to his election to the House when he was still just the

---

43. O'Neill, *Man of the House*, 117-120.
44. O'Neill, *Man of the House*, 120-121.
45. O'Neill, *Man of the House*, 134-135.
46. Wright, *Balance of Power*, 54-55.

Democratic nominee. Rayburn invited Wright to join him and some other members for drinks in the Board of Education and for dinner at a local restaurant. Wright and Rayburn rode together to dinner in Rayburn's private car which included just them and the driver. Wright believed that Rayburn took the opportunity to evaluate him.[47]

The seniority system, the autonomy of the committee chair, the general idea of seniority, and the custom of the mentor-protege relationship found expression in the management of the Agriculture Committee by one of its chairs, Harold Cooley of North Carolina. Bob Poage wrote that, "When he was present, Harold ran the committee with an iron hand." Cooley called Democratic Committee members to his office and instructed them on voting, and most of them followed the instructions. At Committee hearings, he recognized the senior member first and then followed the Committee roster in order of seniority until the hearing ended. As a result, junior members often were never recognized to speak. When they objected, Cooley explained that they could learn all relevant information about a bill by listening to the senior members.[48] Tom Foley, also a future Agriculture Committee chair, had similar recollections. On his first day on the Committee, Cooley told the new Committee members that he disliked the interruption of senior members by junior members regardless of party affiliation. He argued that new members needed months or years to gain the information and experience necessary to

---

47. Wright, *Balance of Power*, 17-18.
48. W. R. Poage, *My First 85 Years* (Waco, TX: Baylor University Press, 1985), 90-91.

contribute to the Committee's work. Therefore, new members should be silent and pay attention.[49]

In the Bipartisan House System, both parties contained significant regional and ideological blocs, but overall, the Democrats possessed greater diversity than the Republicans. The Democrats held the majority in the House for most of the Bipartisan House System, and therefore, their diversity played a critical role in shaping the affairs of the House, the policies of the government, and the fate of the nation. Southern Democrats were arguably the most important bloc in the Bipartisan House System. As a bloc, they exerted the greatest influence and received the most benefits.

Bolling described the ideological composition of the House membership in 1963-1964 in general terms. There were approximately 175 liberals; they included approximately 15 Republicans, approximately 12 Southern Democrats, and approximately 145 Democrats from urban areas of the East, the Midwest, and the West. There were approximately 185 solid conservatives. They included 45 Southern Democrats, and the remainder of this group were Republicans. These descriptions accounted for approximately 360 members. The remaining 75 members did not fit into either category. Both liberals and conservatives could assemble majority coalitions depending on the issue, and coalitions were sometimes formed between liberals and conservatives. Also, there were many exceptions to these general descriptions, and liberals sometimes took conservative positions while conservatives sometimes took liberal positions.[50] Bolling argued that the conservative Southern Democrats possessed great influence because of the

---

49. Biggs, *Honor in the House*, 37.
50. Bolling, *House Out of Order*, 50-51.

seniority system, the process of making committee assignments, their legislative skills, and the liberals' lack of legislative skills.[51]

Albert understood the diversity of the House Democrats and their regional and ideological blocs. Albert described the House Democrats of the 1950s in terms of three distinct blocs based on region and ideology. There were the members from the urban machines in the Northeast or Midwest; they were well-organized. There were the liberals from the North and the West; they were generally younger than other members and lacked organization and unity. There were the Southerners, the most powerful bloc of all. Because of Democratic dominance in the South, the Southerners typically included a large number of members, experienced long careers, and accumulated great seniority. The Southerners possessed a disproportionately large number of committee chairmanships, and frequently, the second-ranking members in seniority on many committees were Southerners who chaired subcommittees. Albert recognized the strength of the Southern bloc using agriculture in 1955 as an example: "It was the South, then, not Ezra Taft Benson, not Dwight Eisenhower, not the Democratic National Committee, and not some outside advisory group, that wrote America's agricultural legislation. It also was southern committee chairmen, none of these others, who decided what the Democratic House of Representatives would do."[52] Albert explained that from the 1930s until the 1970s, a coalition of Southerners and urban Northerners essentially ran the House Democratic Party. The Majority Leader contest in 1971 exemplified this coalition's longevity. Hale Boggs was the

---

51. Bolling, *House Out of Order*, 60-61.
52. Albert, *Giant*, 215-221.

leading candidate/favorite for the position, but several men ran for the position. Nonetheless, Boggs won, and he was the choice of Albert and the House Democratic leaders.[53]

Bolling noted the great influence of Southerners in the House. They exerted great influence through the chairmanships and the seniority rankings. On powerful committees such as the Ways and Means Committee and the Rules Committee, Democrats from the South held a disproportionately large number of seats. The second-ranking Democrat on many committees was also a Southerner.[54] Bolling wrote that in 1955, there were five vacant seats on the Democratic portion of the Ways and Means Committee. Southerners received three of the vacant seats. Overall, Southerners possessed seven of the fifteen Democratic seats on the Ways and Means Committee, including the chairmanship.[55]

Democrats from different regional and ideological blocs cooperated in many ways, and the long-time House Doorkeeper, William "Fishbait" Miller, described a sensational example of cooperation between Vito Marcantonio, an "ultraliberal" Democrat from New York, and William Colmer, an "ultraconservative" Democrat from Mississippi. The duo arranged a phony conflict in which they vehemently denounced each other in speeches on the House floor. People believed that there was a long-term feud, and the press eagerly reported on their clashes. Information was leaked to the press indicating that another clash between the two was imminent, and the press prepared to report on it. After the spectacle on the House

---

53. Albert, *Giant*, 325-326.
54. Bolling, *House Out of Order*, 106-107.
55. Bolling, *Power in the House*, 195-196.

floor, the duo retired to the Democratic cloakroom and celebrated their performances.[56]

Among the Southern states, the state of Texas exercised extraordinary influence during this era. Texas possessed many of the characteristics of the other Southern states, and therefore, its House delegation operated very similar to other Southern delegations. Texas had one of the largest populations in the Union and one of the largest House delegations. For a long time, the Texas House delegation was composed mostly of Democrats. Three Texans served as Speaker of the House during the twentieth century: John Nance Garner, Sam Rayburn, and Jim Wright. A disproportionately large number of committee chairmen were Texans. In the Ninetieth Congress (1967 and 1968), Texas claimed five chairmen of standing committees: Bob Poage on Agriculture, George Mahon on Appropriations, Wright Patman on Banking and Currency, Omar Burleson on House Administration, and Olin Teague on Veterans' Affairs. There were only twenty standing committees in the House.[57]

In addition, Jim Wright explained another reason for Texas' influence. He wrote that the Texas delegation was "one of the most cohesive in Congress." When Congress was in session, the Texas delegation, every Wednesday at noon, met for lunch in the Speaker's dining room. They all assumed that each member owed assistance to other Texas members whose districts had relevant issues/interests before his/her committee. Therefore, junior members had advocates for issues/interests

---

56. William "Fishbait" Miller and Frances Spatz Leighton, *Fishbait: The Memoirs of the Congressional Doorkeeper* (Englewood Cliffs, NJ: Prentice-Hall, Inc., 1977), 162.

important to their districts. Ideology was not relevant to this cooperation. Other state delegations and regional blocs lacked this extreme cohesion.[58] The Texas delegation Wednesday luncheons were held in private and allowed for a free exchange of ideas and information.[59]

Bolling noted the ideological diversity of the House Democratic Party and its implications for cooperation across partisan and ideological lines. The "national-party 'program' Democrats" supported the national party's positions on domestic matters and constituted a majority of the House Democratic Caucus. They came from all regions, including the South, and included moderates and liberals. Conservative Democrats frequently opposed the national party's positions and the Democratic majority's positions in the House. They came mostly from the South.[60] Party affiliation masked the real power of conservative Democrats and conservatives in general in the House. The House Democrats included a bloc of "strong conservatives," but there were few liberal Republicans. The bulk of the Republicans plus the conservative Democrats could assemble a bipartisan majority.[61]

Cooperation across partisan and ideological lines was a constant feature of the House for decades, and the bipartisan cooperation between conservative Democrats and Republicans illustrated this feature. Albert wrote that conservative Southern Democrats met regarding legislation, and they were sometimes called the Southern caucus in this context. The participants

---

57. "House Committees," *Congressional Quarterly Weekly Report*, February 3, 1967, 167-170.
58. Wright, *Balance of Power*, 42-43.
59. Wright, *Balance of Power*, 55.
60. Bolling, *Power in the House*, 21-22.
61. Bolling, *Power in the House*, 207.

formulated a strategy for a bill regarding its debate and vote. Howard Smith was a leader among conservative Democrats and cooperated with the Republican House leader.[62] Joseph Martin wrote that he consulted Howard Smith or Eugene Cox of Georgia and inquired about Democratic support regarding a bill. Martin considered Cox to have been the de facto leader of Southerners in the House, and Martin and Cox served as the primary liaisons between Northern Republicans and conservative Southern Democrats.[63]

This bipartisan cooperation also existed within a committee as seen in the history of the Rules Committee. Beginning in 1937, the role of the Rules Committee changed. A coalition of Southern Democrats and North-Central Republicans dominated the Rules Committee and used it to oppose the Democratic majority, the House Democratic Leadership, and the Roosevelt administration on certain occasions regarding the progress of legislation to the House floor.[64] On some occasions, Rayburn used his personal influence over both Democrats and Republicans to prevent the coalition from obstructing liberal legislation.[65] Furthermore, Bolling claimed that Southern Democrats had equaled or outnumbered Democrats from other regions of the U. S. between 1931 and 1967. In 1933, three of the six Democrats on the Committee were Southerners. Combined with four or five Republicans on the Committee, these Southern Democrats could control the Rules Committee. New England did not receive a Democratic seat on the Rules Committee until the

---

62. Albert, *Giant*, 227-230.
63. Martin, *First Fifty*, 84-85.
64. Galloway, *History House*, 135-136.
65. Albert, *Giant*, 223-227.

1950s, and California did not receive a Democratic seat on the Rules Committee until 1963.[66]

Bipartisan cooperation was measured statistically. Congressional Quarterly defined the Conservative Coalition as a voting phenomenon which pitted Southern Democrats and Republicans against Northern Democrats. The Conservative Coalition appeared when a majority of voting Southern Democrats and a majority of voting Republicans opposed the majority of voting Northern Democrats. The Southern states included the former Confederate states plus Oklahoma and Kentucky, and all other states qualified as Northern. The Conservative Coalition's frequency and success varied across the years. For example, in the Eighty-eighth Congress (1963 and 1964), the Conservative Coalition appeared twenty-seven times.[67] In the Ninetieth Congress (1967 and 1968), it appeared on 105 roll call votes in the House (22% of total roll calls) and won 70 times in the House (approximately 67% of the total number of appearances).[68] Several committee chairs strongly supported the Conservative Coalition when it appeared, but their support was not absolute or uniform as seen in their Conservative Coalition support and opposition scores in the Ninetieth Congress. These scores measured the frequency that a member supported or opposed the Conservative Coalition when it appeared. Southern chairmen showed a diversity of scores: Poage of Agriculture, 78% support, 10% opposition; South Carolina's L. M. Rivers of Armed Services, 70% support,

---

66. Bolling, *Power in the House*, 137-138.

67. "'Conservative Coalition' Appeared on 15% of Roll Calls," *Congressional Quarterly Weekly Report*, November 27, 1964, 2741-2750.

68. "Conservative Coalition Shaped Major 1968 Bills," *Congressional Quarterly Weekly Report*, November 1, 1968, 2983-2990.

9% opposition; Patman of Banking and Currency, 26% support, 52% opposition; Arkansas' Wilbur Mills of Ways and Means, 74% support, 13% opposition; Mississippi's William Colmer of Rules, 85% support, 2% opposition; Mahon of Appropriations, 65% support, 34% opposition; and Teague of Veterans Affairs, 52% support, 15% opposition.[69]

The highest leaders in the House practiced bipartisan cooperation. Jim Wright described the bipartisanship of the 1950s. Rayburn, Senator Lyndon Johnson, and President Dwight Eisenhower all worked well with one another and treated each other with respect. On many issues and instances, they agreed and supported the same position.[70] Martin described the relationship between him and Rayburn regarding their roles as Speaker and Minority Leader. In 1947, Martin became Speaker due to the election of a Republican majority in the House, but the Texas flag still hung in the Speaker's room. Some of Martin's Massachusetts associates wanted him to replace it. He refused because of political reasons and friendship with Rayburn. In 1955, upon returning as Speaker, Rayburn suggested to Martin that they not switch offices because of uncertainty about future election prospects. Rayburn, as Speaker, kept the Minority Leader's office, and Martin, as Minority Leader, kept the Speaker's office.[71]

The Bipartisan House System had its distinctive features, both advantages and disadvantages, but the creation of the atomic bomb in World War II revealed the great effectiveness of the Bipartisan House System. The House

---

69. "Political Orientation of Committee Chairmen," *Congressional Quarterly Weekly Report*, February 7, 1969, 226-227.
70. Wright, *Balance of Power*, 36-37.
71. Martin, *First Fifty*, 227-228.

played a critical role in the creation of the atomic bomb. Martin wrote that one morning Rayburn called and requested that he come to his office. He arrived and discovered that Secretary of War Henry L. Stimson, General George C. Marshall, and John McCormack were present with Rayburn. Stimson and Marshall described the Manhattan Project and explained that it required an extra $1.6 billion. Stimson and Marshall asked that the House appropriate the money with no explanation about the purpose, and Rayburn, McCormack, and Martin agreed. Rayburn and McCormack convinced Appropriations Committee Chairman Clarence Cannon of Missouri to cooperate, and Martin convinced the ranking Republican on the Committee, John Taber of New York, to cooperate. The House approved the appropriation without loss of secrecy.[72]

In a collection of letters, Rayburn and McCormack discussed the atomic bomb meeting, and their letters corroborated the published account of Martin. In a 1955 letter, Rayburn wrote that a meeting took place involving Stimson and Marshall in World War II concerning the atomic bomb, its appropriations, and the secrecy of it. Rayburn and McCormack were present at the meeting.[73] In a 1955 letter, McCormack discussed the atomic bomb meeting, and his letter corroborated the accounts of Martin and Rayburn.[74]

---

72. Martin, *First Fifty*, 100-101.

73. Rayburn to McCormack, October 1, 1955, Folder: McCormack, John W. Correspondence with Sam Rayburn 1953-, Box SRH 3U110, Sam Rayburn Papers, Dolph Briscoe Center for American History, University of Texas at Austin, Austin, TX.

74. McCormack to Rayburn, October 11, 1955, Folder: McCormack, John W. Correspondence with Sam Rayburn 1953-, Box 3U110, Rayburn Papers.

The Bipartisan House System emerged as a reaction against the excesses of the earlier systems and enjoyed a long period of existence. Its characteristics distinguished it from the systems before and after it, and supporters could point to a record of success. Its existence corresponded to the era when the U. S. experienced phenomenal growth and reform domestically and exercised unequaled influence across the world. It is within this system that Wright Patman, Bob Poage, and Felix Edward Hebert rose to power and conducted most of their careers.

Chapter 2 - Wright Patman

John William Wright Patman, better known simply as Wright Patman, had significant influence on many areas of public policy and had roles in some of the major controversies and crises of the twentieth century. Patman followed an ideology that stressed fighting concentrations of economic power and improving the economic lot of ordinary Americans. His ideology was outside the mainstream of American thought in the twentieth century, but he left a solid record of achievements and great credentials as a reformer. Patman's ideology, his record of achievements, and his credentials as a reformer also contributed to his removal. He used the Banking and Currency Committee to advance his preferred policies and to address issues of concern to him; these actions divided the Committee and alienated other members who did not also share his ideology.

John William Wright Patman saw many changes in America during his life and career. He was born at Patman's Switch near Hughes Springs, Cass County in Texas in 1893. He attended public schools and graduated from Hughes Springs High School in 1912. He then graduated from the law department at Cumberland University in Lebanon, Tennessee in 1916. His professional experience included practicing law, serving as assistant county attorney in Cass County (1916-1917), serving as a private and a machinegun officer in the U. S. Army in World War I, serving in the Texas House of Representatives (1921-1924), and serving as district attorney of the Fifth Texas Judicial District (1924-1929). He won election as a Democrat to the Seventy-first Congress and served in the U. S. House of Representatives from 1929 until his death in

1976.[1] By the mid-1970s, his district, the First District of Texas, was centered in the far northeastern corner of the state.[2]

In the House of Representatives, Patman acquired great authority. He served as chairman of the Select Committee on Small Business (Eighty-first, Eighty-second, and Eighty-fourth through Eighty-seventh Congresses) and the Committee on Banking and Currency (Eighty-eighth through Ninety-third Congresses). He also served as chairman of the Joint Economic Committee and the Joint Committee on Defense Production on several occasions.[3] Poage explained that Patman made a sincere effort to be helpful to other members of Congress and to work with them, and this effort gained Patman respect and credibility. Patman represented his district well and provided it with real, tangible benefits.[4]

In his book, *Bankerteering, Bonuseering, Melloneering*, Patman discussed salient issues of the Great Depression Era and revealed much about his ideology. He argued that the economic elites, whom he called the "'MONEY CHANGERS,'" enriched themselves at the expense of the public good and the interests of the working people and attempted to manipulate the government through corruption. In order to ensure future prosperity for the working people, the government needed to assert its authority over the economic elites and the money

---

1. Duane Nystrom, ed., *Biographical Directory of the United States Congress, 1774-1989*, Bicentennial Edition (Washington, D. C.: United States Government Printing Office, 1989), 1616.
2. Charles B. Brownson, *1975 Congressional Staff Directory* (Alexandria, VA: The Congressional Staff Directory, 1975), 102.
3. Nystrom, *Biographical Directory*, 1616.
4. "Oral Memoirs of William Robert 'Bob' Poage," volume 5, p. 87-89, Poage Papers, Baylor Collections of Political Materials, W. R. Poage Legislative Library Center, Baylor University, Waco, TX.

supply. Through the efforts of Franklin Roosevelt and the New Deal, Patman believed this task was being advanced. [5]

Historians and colleagues stressed Patman's ideology in their descriptions of him. Nancy Beck Young's biography, *Wright Patman: Populism, Liberalism, & the American Dream*, argued that Patman's ideology centered on preserving local ownership, small business, and economic opportunity for rural and small-town Americans. Because of this viewpoint, Patman often stood outside the political mainstream.[6] Jim Wright wrote that Patman wanted "to disperse and broaden the base of economic power, whose concentration in too few hands he saw as a major cause of the Great Depression." He also wrote that, "Patman opposed bullies throughout his life."[7] Felix Edward "Eddie" Hebert wrote that Patman fought against the financial elites, banks, and high interest rates.[8] Patman's successor as chairman of the Banking and Currency Committee, Henry Reuss of Wisconsin, compared Patman to Huey Long because: "like Huey Long, he liked to pick enemies, and in Huey Long's case it was the chain stores, and to a degree, Patman had the same enemies."[9] Richard Bolling wrote that, "His constant

---

5. Wright Patman, *Bankerteering, Bonuseering, Melloneering* (Paris, TX: Peerless Printing, 1934), 3-4.

6. Nancy Beck Young, *Wright Patman: Populism, Liberalism, & the American Dream* (Dallas: Southern Methodist University Press, 2000), xi-xii.

7. Wright, *Balance of Power*, 44.

8. F. Edward Hebert and John McMillan, *Last of the Titans: The Life and Times of Congressman F. Edward Hebert of Louisiana* (Lafayette, LA: Center for Louisiana Studies, The University of Southwestern Louisiana, 1976), 440.

9. Henry Reuss, interview by author, January 27, 2000, telephone tape recording, T. Harry Williams Center for Oral History, Louisiana State University, Baton Rouge, LA.

repetition of certain of his unorthodox views on money and banking has lost him influence in the House."[10]

Although no one single label can describe it precisely, Patman's ideology distinguished him from his colleagues in the House and shaped his career. His ideology focused on fighting concentrations of economic power and improving the economic lot of ordinary Americans. Patman was frequently separated from the mainstream of political thought. He frequently interpreted complex economic issues in terms of a perennial struggle between two sides with starkly different viewpoints, interests, and goals. For Patman, the government could play a constructive role in society by restraining the powerful special economic interests and advancing the interests of ordinary Americans. Patman's rhetoric stressed the idea of struggle. Yet, he displayed an optimistic view of the future and seemed to believe that the nation was making progress; he, and others who agreed, could cooperate to immediately achieve great results for the nation. Even if Patman's ideology might be considered extreme, the policies he advanced helped ordinary Americans, and he established a record of achievements and credentials as a reformer.

Patman's first significant achievement on the national political scene concerned Andrew Mellon, Secretary of the Treasury from 1921 to 1932. On January 6, 1932, Patman spoke in the House against Mellon, "On my own responsibility as Member of this House, I impeach Andrew William Mellon, Secretary of The Treasury of the United States, for high crimes and misdemeanors, and offer the following resolution." The resolution argued that Mellon violated a U. S. law which

---

10. Bolling, *House Out of Order*, 94.

restricted the business activities of the Secretary of the Treasury. The relevant law was section 243 of title 5 of the Code of Laws of the United States, and the resolution listed the offenses. The articles of impeachment were referred to the Committee on the Judiciary by a vote of the House.[11] Section 243 of title 5 of the Code of Laws of the United States prohibited the Secretary of the Treasury from engaging in certain forms of commercial activity. Mellon had extensive business interests, and his office, Secretary of the Treasury, had authority over regulation of some of these business interests. Mellon held regulatory authority over his own business interests or violated other laws in several instances. He owned ships subject to Coast Guard inspection, imported items into the nation, owned sea vessels, owned significant shares of corporations which received significant tax refunds, owned stock in banking institutions, profited from the sale of distilled whiskey from 1921 to 1928, used the government to promote the Aluminum Company of America of which he was a principal owner, and owned a part of a company that did business with the Soviet Union, a nation suspected of exporting items made by convict labor.[12] The impeachment ended prematurely. On February 3, 1932, Mellon accepted President Hoover's offer to become ambassador to Great Britain. According to Hoover, Mellon was superbly qualified to handle

---

11. *Impeachment of Andrew W. Mellon, Secretary of the Treasury,* 72nd Cong., 1st sess., *Congressional Record* 75 (January 6, 1932): 1400-1401.

12. U. S. Congress, House, Committee on the Judiciary, *Charges of Hon. Wright Patman Against the Secretary of the Treasury: Hearings Before the Committee on the Judiciary,* 72nd Cong., 1st sess., January 13, 14, 15, 18, 19, 1932, 1-4.

the international economic crisis.[13] Meanwhile, the impeachment resolution introduced by Patman was under consideration by a House subcommittee. Patman compared the appointment to a presidential pardon issued during a trial.[14] Patman claimed that some powerful Congressmen did not want Mellon impeached for fear that they would be criticized by their constituents for not addressing Mellon's conduct earlier. He thought this sentiment might have contributed to Mellon's confirmation by the Senate for the ambassadorship.[15]

The Great Depression featured an intense conflict over a payment to World War I veterans called the adjusted-service certificates, but this payment became widely known as the bonus. A federal law planned to pay it to the veterans by 1945. Due to the hardships of the Great Depression, support for immediate payment grew. Patman, a World War I veteran concerned with the economic lot of ordinary Americans, became a prominent figure in the fight for the bonus, a fight that the veterans and Congress waged against two presidents.

As the Great Depression continued, the fight for the bonus became more intense. In May 1932, World War I veterans began demonstrations to support the payment of the bonus. A group of veterans set up camp at Anacostia Flats in Washington, D. C. to demonstrate in support of a bill, sponsored by Patman, to pay the bonus immediately. The group numbered approximately 20,000 in June 1932 and

13. Lawrence Sullivan, "Mellon Has Accepted Post of London Envoy, President Announces," *Washington Post*, February 4, 1932, 1, 4.
14. "Hoover Names Mills To Take Mellon's Post," *Washington Post*, February 5, 1932, 1, 5.
15. Patman, *Bankerteering*, 137-138.

became known as the Bonus Expeditionary Force (B. E. F.).[16] On July 28, President Hoover ordered General Douglas MacArthur to disperse the B. E. F. using federal troops. Under his command, the troops destroyed the veterans' camps, chased men, women, and children from their positions, physically attacked some of these people, and caused the death of an eleven-week old baby. MacArthur took pride in the action and personally commanded the assault.[17]

Congress resolved the conflict, and Patman was involved. For Congress, the issue centered on HR 9870, the Vinson-Patman-McCormack bill, a bill to pay the full amount of the adjusted-service certificates in cash to the 3.5 million World War I veterans. The bill was an authorization for payment and did not specify a method of payment. Patman delivered a speech at the start of debate on the rule for the bill and explained that many people in Congress worked cooperatively, including himself, to advance this legislation. In 1924, Congress passed, over a presidential veto, a law to issue adjusted-service certificates to veterans of the World War. In 1929, he introduced a bill for full and immediate cash payment of the certificates. Bills for payment were defeated in 1929, 1932, 1934, and 1935. Patman was assisted by many other members, and he stated that over 150 House members deserved to be considered as joint authors of the bill. Patman identified several reasons to pass the bill (provided that his specific plan for payment was passed). The bill would save the government money over twelve years and save the government money in administration costs. It would pay a debt to the

---

16. Arthur M. Schlesinger, Jr., *The Age of Roosevelt: The Crisis of the Old Order, 1919-1933* (Boston: Houghton Mifflin, 1957), 256-259.
17. Schlesinger, *Old Order*, 262-265.

veterans for their services and allow veterans to receive new currency from a government obligation in the same way enjoyed by the Federal Reserve Banks. Veterans who borrowed money based on the adjusted-service certificates would be freed from making compound interest payments on those loans to the government and banks. The bill was a preexisting debt and required repayment eventually. Congress' constitutional duty to issue money would be reaffirmed, and the bill would expand the public's purchasing power in a fair way capable of stimulating the economy.[18] On January 10, 1936, the bill on the adjusted-service certificates was passed by the House, 356-59.[19]

Yet, President Franklin Roosevelt vetoed the bill, and the conflict continued. On January 24, 1936, the House voted on the presidential veto override of HR 9870; the vote was 326-61. The veto was overridden.[20] On January 27, 1936, the Senate voted on the presidential veto override of HR 9870; the vote was 76-19. The veto was overridden.[21] Throughout his career, Patman proudly noted that he was the author of this bill.[22]

Patman fought against price discrimination, a problem once found in society. On May 28, 1936, the House began debate on HR 8442, a bill with the purpose of "making it

---

18. *Payment of Adjusted-Service Certificates*, 74th Cong., 2nd sess., *Congressional Record* 80 (January 9, 1936): 219-233.

19. *Payment of Adjusted-Service Certificates*, 74th Cong., 2nd sess., *Congressional Record* 80 (January 10, 1936): 292.

20. *Payment of Adjusted-Service Certificates (H. Doc. No. 398)*, 74th Cong., 2nd sess., *Congressional Record* 80 (January 24, 1936): 975-977.

21. *Payment of Adjusted-Service Certificates--Veto*, 74th Cong., 2nd sess., *Congressional Record* 80 (January 27, 1936): 1015.

unlawful for any person engaged in commerce to discriminate in price or terms of sale between purchasers of commodities of like grade and quality, ... and to protect the independent merchant, the public whom he serves, and the manufacturer from whom he buys, from exploitation by unfair competitors."[23] On May 28, 1936, the House passed HR 8442 on a vote of 290-16.[24] On June 15, 1936, the House began consideration of the conference report on HR 8442.[25] Patman addressed the House and argued that the bill would simply promote equal opportunity and fairness and would not directly harm anyone's interests. It would benefit farmers, wage earners, and consumers. He stated that, "This bill grants each and every one the opportunity to do an honest, legitimate business, and protects him from cheaters and racketeers." The House passed the conference report; there was no recorded vote.[26]

Patman authored a book to explain the legislation's impact and significance in practical terms called *The Robinson-Patman Act: What You Can and Cannot Do Under This Law.* The book discussed ordinary issues faced by business and legal issues involving the Act; the book contained the text of the Act itself, Congressional reports on the Act during its preparation, and selections from the *Congressional Record*

---

22. "Background on Congressman Wright Patman First District of Texas," 19 March 1973, untitled folder, Box 388, Papers of Wright Patman, Lyndon Baines Johnson Library, Austin, TX.

23. *Prevention of Sales Discrimination*, 74th Cong., 2nd sess., *Congressional Record* 80 (May 28, 1936): 8223.

24. *Prevention of Sales Discrimination*, 74th Cong., 2nd sess., *Congressional Record* 80 (May 28, 1936): 8242.

25. *Price Discrimination*, 74th Cong., 2nd sess., *Congressional Record* 80 (June 15, 1936): 9413.

26. *Price Discrimination*, 74th Cong., 2nd sess., *Congressional Record* 80 (June 15, 1936): 9422.

relevant to the Act.[27] Patman and Senator Joseph Robinson of Arkansas were co-authors of the Act. In his book, Patman wrote that the book was a result of the "more than a thousand requests" for information that came from people in business. Many questions were repetitions of the same concern or issue, and there was great misunderstanding about the Act. The Act concerned only a minority of businesses because most businesses operated in accord with the Act's provisions. This minority of businesses violated ethics and were a "'bandit fringe,'" and the Act was consistent with ethics codes that businesses voluntarily adopted. Patman wrote that, "It is not a 'reform bill,' but rather a long forward step toward the arming of business with effective weapons against the relatively few outlaws who will not play fair."[28]

Patman had an interest in small business and tried to support it and its work through the government's management of World War II. On December 4, 1941, Adolph Sabath of Illinois introduced HR 294 to authorize an investigation of the national-defense program and its relation to small business. Sabath referred to Patman as the proponent of the resolution.[29] Patman discussed the resolution and explained that there would be a select committee appointed by the Speaker of the House. The purpose of the committee would be "to study and investigate whether or not the potentialities of small business in the national-defense program have been adequately

---

27. Wright Patman, *The Robinson-Patman Act: What You Can and Cannot Do Under This Law* (New York: The Ronald Press Company, 1938), vii-viii.

28. Patman, *Robinson-Patman Act*, iii-v.

29. *Select Committee to Study Relationship of Defense Program to Small Business*, 77th Cong., 1st sess., *Congressional Record* 87 (December 4, 1941): 9418-9419.

developed, and if not, why not, whether or not adequate consideration has been given to the needs of small business engaged in nondefense activities or engaged in the transition from non-defense to defense activity, and whether or not small business is being treated fairly in regard to allocations and allotments."[30] The House passed the resolution; there was no recorded vote.[31]

Patman's support for small business continued. On May 25, 1942, the House began debate on S 2250, a bill to "mobilize the productive facilities of small business" for the war effort. A select committee, which included Patman, produced a study, and he introduced a bill. The provisions of the Patman bill were inserted into the Senate bill in place of the Senate provisions. The bill proposed the creation of the Smaller War Plants Corporation, and its directors would be sympathetic to small business. The institution would make loans or advances that would enable small businesses to prepare themselves for government war contracts for military needs or civilian essentials. The institution could also arrange government contracts with small businesses to provide war-related necessities.[32] Patman addressed the House and argued that the bill would make it easier for small businesses to receive government contracts by streamlining the bureaucratic process

---

30. *Select Committee to Study Relationship of Defense Program to Small Business*, 77th Cong., 1st sess., *Congressional Record* 87 (December 4, 1941): 9425.

31. *Select Committee to Study Relationship of Defense Program to Small Business*, 77th Cong., 1st sess., *Congressional Record* 87 (December 4, 1941): 9428.

32. *Promotion of Small Business*, 77th Cong., 2nd sess., *Congressional Record* 88 (May 25, 1942): 4501-4502.

for contracts of government work.[33] On May 26, 1942, the House passed S 2250 by a vote of 346-0.[34]

Throughout his career, Patman strongly opposed the Federal Reserve System and large private banks. Early in his career, he expressed his ideology regarding these subjects in *Bankerteering, Bonuseering, Melloneering*. Patman argued that Congress failed to exercise its Constitutional power to issue and to regulate money and instead delegated its power to private parties.[35] In his view, private corporations composed of individuals controlled the Federal Reserve Banks, and the federal government did not own or benefit from these banks.[36] Patman believed that these banks dominated almost all large corporations (manufacturing, transportation, natural resource extraction, commerce) and also exerted an indirect control over small businesses. Small banks, such as local banks in small communities, were not the problem and were also dominated by the banking system.[37] Patman advocated that the federal government seize control of the Federal Reserve System's regional banks, increase the money supply in circulation, and extend credit to all parties in the nation. Profits would be deposited in the Treasury.[38]

Patman succinctly expressed his view of the Federal Reserve System and large banks in his speech, "The A B C's of America's Money System" from August 3, 1964, during special

---

33. *Promotion of Small Business*, 77th Cong., 2nd sess., *Congressional Record* 88 (May 25, 1942): 4503-4504.

34. *Promotion of Small Business*, 77th Cong., 2nd sess., *Congressional Record* 88 (May 26, 1942): 4577-4578.

35. Patman, *Bankerteering*, 7.

36. Patman, *Bankerteering*, 24.

37. Patman, *Bankerteering*, 14.

38. Patman, *Bankerteering*, 35-36.

orders in the House. Patman's subject was the Federal Reserve System and the commercial banks. According to him, they abused their authority given to them by Congress through management of the money supply (its size, interest rates, availability of credit).[39] Patman argued that the Federal Reserve System and the banking system endangered the U. S. by contributing to a growing national debt and impeding economic growth. They were unconstitutional; the Constitution placed authority in Congress and the President but did not provide for an independent Federal Reserve System. Using secret meetings, the Open Market Committee (composed of the seven members of the Federal Reserve Board and the twelve presidents of the Federal Reserve banks) ran the Federal Reserve System and the nation's banks by setting monetary policy (size of money supply, ease of credit, interest rates).[40]

According to Patman, great authority was concentrated in a few people. Patman argued that a small group of people controlled the Federal Reserve System and the banks due to the Federal Reserve Act of 1913, cooperation among the leading bankers, the Glass-Steagall Act of 1935, and the weakening of most of the regional banks of the Federal Reserve System. He believed that interest rates were maintained at high levels by the "moneylenders" or "moneylending lobby" through illegitimate excuses: "Such hobgoblins have fortunately been laid to rest, but the next time you hear them remember that they are part of the designed fraud put forth by the moneylending lobby--the American

---

39. *The A B C's of America's Money System*, 88th Cong., 2nd sess., *Congressional Record* 110 (August 3, 1964): 17837-17844.

40. *The A B C's of America's Money System*, 88th Cong., 2nd sess., *Congressional Record* 110 (August 3, 1964): 17837-17844.

Bankers Association particularly--to make higher interest rates palatable to the American people." Patman saw the current issues in a larger historical context, and in the past, the issues centered around or included Nicholas Biddle, John Pierpont Morgan, Andrew Mellon, the Morgan-Aldrich-Rockefeller group, and the Giannini Bank of America. Patman characterized the American Bankers Association as a powerful, self-interested lobbying group similar to other lobbying groups which worked for powerful banking interests.[41]

Patman proposed reforms. The Domestic Finance Subcommittee of the Banking and Currency Committee investigated the Federal Reserve System, and the Democrats on the Committee issued a set of reform proposals for the Federal Reserve System. They proposed that the term of the Chairman of the Board of Governors of the Federal Reserve System should be coterminous with the term of the U. S. President. They proposed that the number of Governors of the Board should be reduced to five. They proposed reducing the terms of office to five years and permitting reappointments. They proposed making only integrity and devotion to the public interest be the requirements for appointment as Governors. They proposed conducting an audit, by the Comptroller General, of the Board and the Reserve Banks. They proposed the retirement of the Federal Reserve stock. They proposed requiring that all capital gains and interest received by the Federal Reserve System from U. S. government securities be covered into the Treasury as receipts and that all capital losses be covered by the Treasury. They proposed requiring the President to better address monetary policy including its

---

41. *The A B C's of America's Money System*, 88th Cong., 2nd sess., *Congressional Record* 110 (August 3, 1964): 17837-17844.

connection to maximizing employment and production and purchasing power. They proposed that Congress pass a sense of the Congress resolution stating that the Federal Reserve Board should work in the open market to support the enactment of the President's monetary policy. If the Federal Reserve System's views and actions differed from the President's views and actions, it must file, to the President and Congress, a statement explaining the reasons for the difference. They proposed that the Federal Reserve System focus on monetary policy by reassigning its bank supervisory work to the Comptroller of the Currency, the FDIC, or to a new federal authority.[42]

In response to Patman's speech, the American Bankers Association (ABA) published a pamphlet highlighting errors in Patman's speech. The ABA believed that Patman wanted to place monetary policy under control of the politicians.[43] The pamphlet argued that the Federal Reserve System was a creation of the federal government and was accountable to it, and the Federal Reserve System worked independently within the federal government on monetary policy in order to prevent political pressure from affecting monetary policy managed on a daily basis.[44] Many of the "moneylenders" who benefitted from interest payments included average Americans possessing savings accounts, savings bonds, or deposits in banks or credit unions.[45]

---

42. *The A B C's of America's Money System*, 88th Cong., 2nd sess., *Congressional Record* 110 (August 3, 1964): 17837-17844.

43. The American Bankers Association, *Comments on Mr. Patman's ABC's of Money* (New York: privately printed, n.d.), preface.

44. Bankers, *Comments*, 2-3.

45. Bankers, *Comments*, 6-7.

Patman succeeded in achieving some regulation on large banks. On February 8, 1966, the House began debate on HR 12173, amendments to the Bank Merger Act of 1960. Patman addressed the House and explained that the bill would establish a standard to be used by both courts and government agencies for the approval and adjudication of bank mergers before their consummation. The bill would maintain the application of the antitrust laws to bank mergers, and the effect on competition would be the preeminent factor for the evaluation of a proposed merger. The bill would impede the trend of concentration in the banking sector, and the bill was needed because the federal banking agencies failed to enforce the Bank Merger Act of 1960 which was intended to halt bank mergers and to impede concentration in the banking sector. Patman claimed that concentration increased since 1960 and that the three federal bank supervisory agencies approved over 90% of bank merger applications.[46] The House replaced the text of S 1698 with the text of HR 12173. The House then passed S 1698 by a vote of 372-17.[47] The specific provisions of the bill included a prohibition on federal bank regulatory agencies' approval for bank mergers which possessed or could possess anticompetitive effects unless the effects were balanced by positive effects for the public. Section 2 of the Sherman Act prohibited monopolization. All proposed mergers that violated Section 2 of the Sherman Antitrust Act were to be prohibited.[48]

---

46. *Bank Merger Act Amendment*, 89th Cong., 2nd sess., *Congressional Record* 112 (February 8, 1966): 2440-2442.
47. *Bank Merger Act Amendment*, 89th Cong., 2nd sess., *Congressional Record* 112 (February 8, 1966) 2465-2467.
48. "Bank Mergers," *Congressional Quarterly Weekly Report*, February 11, 1966, 357-359.

In 1969, Patman oversaw another legislative victory for bank regulation. On November 4, 1969, the House began debate on HR 6778, a bill addressing regulation of one-bank holding companies. Patman gave a speech and stated that he was the original author of the bill. He explained that the issue and bill were connected to events in the 1930s. In that decade, the nation embraced the policy of separation of banking from other business activities, but this policy was not uniformly applied. The Bank Holding Company Act of 1956 contained exemptions and exempted one-bank holding companies because they were generally small. Therefore, powerful banking interests took advantage of the exemptions and engaged in nonbanking activities otherwise prohibited to them. Powerful banking interests spurred a large growth in one-bank holding companies. These one-bank holding companies enjoyed an unfair competitive advantage by controlling credit, needed by the people and the economy, while also engaging in nonbanking business activities in that same economy against those same people. Some banks abused this dual power of controlling credit and engaging in nonbanking business activities. Many one-bank holding companies engaged in nonbanking business activities such as insurance, real estate, credit and finance, retail, and manufacturing. Patman summarized the bill's intent: "Our economy cannot function properly without a sound, efficient, and objective banking system which will allocate credit and provide other banking services on a fair and equitable basis. Therefore, it is imperative that we continue to maintain the separation of banking activities from other businesses that has existed in

Federal law since 1933."[49] On November 5, 1969, HR 6778 was passed by a vote of 352-24.[50] Specifically, the bill extended the Bank Holding Company Act of 1956 to one-bank holding companies; prohibited bank holding companies from engaging in certain types of business activities such as securities, insurance, and accounting; required one-bank holding companies created after May 9, 1956 to divest themselves of nonbanking business activities; and established a definition of a bank holding company (a company which controls a bank).[51]

As the years passed, Patman faced challenges on the Committee. The Committee voted, on January 31, 1967, 19-13, to deprive from Patman and to award to the whole Committee the authority to set up special subcommittees. Thomas L. Ashley of Ohio led the anti-Patman movement; it included all Republicans on the Committee and four junior Democrats. Control of the Committee staff (Patman or the whole Committee) was a major concern, and critics claimed that the staff served Patman and was not responsive to other Committee members.[52] The Committee on March 1, 1967, passed a set of rules transferring some authority from Patman to the whole Committee. The new rules required that a majority of the Committee approve Patman's staff appointments and

49. *Bank Holding Companies*, 91st Cong., 1st sess., *Congressional Record* 115 (November 4, 1969): 32893-32898.

50. *Bank Holding Companies*, 91st Cong., 1st sess., *Congressional Record* 115 (November 5, 1969): 33153-33154.

51. "Bank Holding Companies," *Congressional Quarterly Weekly Report*, November 7, 1969, 2177.

52. Richard Lyons, "Banking Committee Chips Away Some of Patman's Authority," *Washington Post*, February 1, 1967, A6.

that the Committee receive at least five days' notice before the start of investigations and before the release of reports.[53]

Henry Reuss observed Patman on the Committee for several years. Reuss argued that Patman's ideology was outside mainstream thought and counterproductive. Reuss stated that Patman stood alone on his position that the Federal Reserve System should be less independent and more regulated. The other members of the Banking and Currency Committee did not accept Patman's position. His ideology prevented the Committee from effectively addressing issues and limited the influence of other members who did not accept his ideology. Reuss stated that, "But in fact, he didn't do the big interests any particular harm because his rhetoric was so, so insane, that nobody paid much attention to him."[54] In addition, Reuss added that Patman's management of the Committee hurt its effectiveness: "His heart was in the right place, but his arbitrary practices quickly divided the committee into warring factions; the financial lobbies with the largest purses were able to exercise decisive power."[55]

Early in his career, Patman challenged the Hoover administration, and towards the end of his career, Patman challenged the Nixon administration with a similar intensity. The long-time House Doorkeeper William "Fishbait" Miller wrote that Patman told him in 1971 that Nixon was dangerous and that Nixon was trying to secretly consolidate power for himself. The

---

53. "House Group Cuts Power of Patman," *Washington Post*, March 2, 1967, A31.

54. Henry Reuss, interview by author, January 27, 2000, telephone tape recording, T. Harry Williams Center for Oral History, Louisiana State University, Baton Rouge, LA.

55. Henry S. Reuss, *When Government Was Good: Memories of a Life in Politics* (Madison, WI: University of Wisconsin Press, 1999), 101.

problem originated with Nixon's choice not to spend money appropriated by Congress.[56]

Regardless of the ideological differences, Patman exercised a critical role in the Watergate Crisis, and the narrative of the Watergate Crisis is well-known. On June 17, 1972, a burglary occurred at the Democratic National Committee headquarters in Washington, D. C. Based on ties between the burglars and the Committee to Re-elect the President (CREEP), separate investigations began in the judicial system under U. S. District Court Judge John J. Sirica and in Congress. Ultimately, these investigations exposed the Nixon administration's corruption, and public discontent increased.

After the start of the Watergate Crisis, Patman began investigating the Nixon administration but faced obstacles. The House Banking and Currency Committee voted, 20-15, on October 3, 1972 to not hold public hearings on the emerging Watergate Crisis and Nixon's reelection campaign finances. Six Democrats and fourteen Republicans voted against the hearings. The six Democrats were Robert Stephens of Georgia, Richard Hanna of California, Tom Gettys of South Carolina, Charles Griffin of Mississippi, Frank Brasco of New York, and Bill Chappell of Florida.[57] Patman tried to start another investigation of the Watergate Crisis and failed. On October 12, he failed to assemble a quorum at two meetings of the Committee.[58]

---

56. Miller, *Fishbait*, 291.

57. "Watergate Investigation," *Congressional Quarterly Weekly Report*, October 7, 1972, 2600.

58. "Presidential Campaign: More Watergate Disclosures," *Congressional Quarterly Weekly Report*, October 14, 1972, 2639-2642.

Patman's efforts provided the groundwork for later Congressional investigation and the fall of the Nixon administration. Patman allowed Senator Sam Ervin of North Carolina and the Senate Select Committee that investigated campaign finances of the 1972 campaign to use the files from his investigation. Patman also advised Ervin to question Watergate conspirator John Dean about the coverup.[59] John Dean attached great significance to the termination of Patman's Committee hearings. The termination prompted Senator Edward Kennedy to begin an investigation resulting in the creation of the Ervin Committee.[60]

The most salient aspects of Patman's career concerned fighting concentrations of economic power and improving the economic lot of ordinary Americans, but the issue of civil rights was a highly significant issue during the decades of his career. Overall, Patman followed the typical White Southern position on the major civil rights legislation. The House passed the Civil Rights Act of 1964 on February 10, 1964 by a vote of 290-130. The vote displayed both partisan and regional divisions: Republicans, 138-34; Democrats, 152-96; Northern Democrats, 141-4; and Southern Democrats, 11-92. Patman voted against it.[61] The House passed the final version of the Civil Rights Act of 1964 on July 2, 1964 by a vote of 289-126. The vote fell along these lines: Republicans, 136-35; Democrats, 153-91; Northern Democrats, 141-3; Southern Democrats, 12-88.

---

59. Stanley I. Kutler, *The Wars of Watergate: The Last Crisis of Richard Nixon* (New York: Alfred A. Knopf, 1990), 235.

60. John W. Dean, III, *Lost Honor* (Los Angeles: Stratford Press, 1982), 202.

61. *Congressional Quarterly Weekly Report*, February 14, 1964, 334-335.

Patman voted against it.[62] The House passed the Voting Rights Act of 1965 by a vote of 333-85 on July 9, 1965. The vote breakdown was as follows: Republicans, 112-24; Democrats, 221-61; Northern Democrats, 188-1; and Southern Democrats, 33-60. Patman voted against it.[63] The House passed the conference report on the Voting Rights Act of 1965 on August 3, 1965 by a vote of 328-74. The vote divided as follows: Republicans, 111-20; Democrats, 217-54; Northern Democrats, 180-0, and Southern Democrats, 37-54. Patman voted for it.[64]

Undoubtedly, Patman influenced public policy and major events in the twentieth century and exemplified the autonomy of committee chairmen in the Bipartisan House System. He became a center of power in his own right and could be seen as part of the status quo. Late in his career, he could be seen by some people as an obstacle to progress. The American people accepted large concentrations of economic power as normal for the modern age. Much of Patman's achievements and credentials concerned issues from an earlier era that were less relevant in the 1970s or were accepted as normal by the 1970s. In addition, Patman practiced a traditional management style for his Committee. Other people, even members of his own Committee, resented his management style, his ideology, and his use of the Committee to advance his ideology. Ironically, by the 1970s, people considered Patman, the old reformer, as part of the problem and a target of reform.

---

62. *Congressional Quarterly Weekly Report*, July 3, 1964, 1414-1415.
63. *Congressional Quarterly Weekly Report*, July 16, 1965, 1402-1403.
64. *Congressional Quarterly Weekly Report*, August 6, 1965, 1588-1589.

Chapter 3 - Bob Poage

William Robert "Bob" Poage of Texas never received great national attention but significantly influenced U. S. agriculture policy and American life. His early life centered in Texas and was shaped by the rural life and agriculture, but he expanded his horizons and entered the urban life, the legal profession, and politics. As a member of the U. S. House of Representatives, he worked for the interests of rural America and the agriculture sector and rose to become chairman of the House Committee on Agriculture. Poage's political ideology defied easy characterization, and his beliefs and his record expressed both conservatism and progressivism. Although Poage felt that he consistently maintained his political ideology, the nation changed, and other people's notions changed, too. Late in his career, Poage was caught in a broader liberal-conservative ideological conflict that increasingly characterized politics and left fewer opportunities for traditional conservative Democrats.

Bob Poage has not been the subject of scholarly attention despite the large amount of primary source materials. Poage participated in twenty-six interviews for an oral history project prepared by Baylor University. The interviews were conducted from 1971 through 1983 and were compiled in a five-volume collection, the "Oral Memoirs of William Robert 'Bob' Poage." Poage also wrote an autobiography, *My First 85 Years*, and four books on Texas History: *After the Pioneers: Recollections of W. R. Poage*, *Politics—Texas Style*, *How We Lived*, and *McLennan County Before 1980*.

Poage's early life featured both the rural life and the urban life of Texas. He was born in Waco in 1899, but in 1901, his family moved to Throckmorton County and settled near Woodson. He attended the local public schools.[1] Years later, Poage's family returned to Waco, but he opposed the decision and preferred the rural/ranch life to which he was accustomed. At the time, he thought that he should find a ranch job and not relocate.[2] While in high school, he wanted to enter the ranching business and even threatened to quit school and take a ranch job, but his father wanted him to get an education instead. At the time, he had no interest in teaching school or practicing law.[3] Poage stated that he had been interested in politics since the time he was a child. His father was involved in local politics when he was a child, and Poage's family frequently discussed politics at home. As a boy, Poage stated that he had an opinion on most subjects and picked his own preferred candidates in elections. Often, his choices differed from the choices of his father.[4]

Poage pursued an education, and a political career soon followed. He graduated from Waco High School in 1918, earned an A.B. from Baylor University in 1921, and earned an LL.B. from Baylor University in 1924.[5] Poage developed an interest in practicing law because he wanted to become a member of a community, and a law practice allowed a person to become a member of a community. He studied geology and valued it because it helped a person understand the land. Yet, he did not want to work as a professional geologist because

1. Nystrom, *Biographical Directory*, 1656.
2. "Oral Memoirs Poage," volume 1, p. 31-36, Poage Papers.
3. "Oral Memoirs Poage," volume 1, p. 41-42, Poage Papers.
4. "Oral Memoirs Poage," volume 1, p. 89-93, Poage Papers.
5. Poage biography, Baylor Collections of Political Materials website, accessed March 8, 2007,
http://www3.baylor.edu/Library/BCPM/Poage/poage_biography.html.

geologists moved frequently.[6] Despite his earlier sentiments, Poage taught geology at Baylor (1922-1924), served as a law instructor at Baylor (1924-1928), and practiced law in Waco. He served in the Texas House of Representatives (1925-1929) and in the Texas Senate (1931-1937). He was elected as a Democrat to the Seventy-fifth Congress and served in the U. S. House of Representatives from 1937 until 1978.[7] By the mid-1970s, Poage's Eleventh District of Texas centered on the central area of the state surrounding Waco and Temple.[8]

Poage's political career illustrated many of the typical ideas and practices of Texas politics in the 1920s and 1930s. Poage explained that in the 1920s, the typical practice in campaigns for local elections and state legislature elections was to introduce one's self as a candidate and to ask people for their support. There was no mention of issues or ideas.[9] Candidates such as himself tried to avoid connections to the national party, overt party activities, and overt intra-party squabbles.[10] Some places such as Milam County and Bell County held rallies in which the county chairman would invite the candidates to address the public, and Poage attended these events. Poage and other politicians gave cards to the voters that identified the candidate, and many voters placed great value on receiving cards. Candidates, including Poage, even distributed cards at high school graduation ceremonies.[11] Poage announced his candidacy for the State Legislature while he was a student at Baylor Law School; he graduated in 1924

---

6. "Oral Memoirs Poage," volume 1, p. 67-68, Poage Papers.
7. Nystrom, *Biographical Directory*, 1656.
8. Brownson, *1975 Staff Directory*, 104.
9. "Oral Memoirs Poage," volume 1, p. 127, Poage Papers.
10. "Oral Memoirs Poage," volume 1, p. 159, Poage Papers.
11. Poage, *85 Years*, 56.

and was also elected in 1924.[12] In his first race in 1924, he did not have a campaign platform.[13]

Poage prepared for the U. S. House of Representatives. Poage stated that a general sentiment in the public emerged in the mid-1930s that Oliver Harlan Cross did not provide the Eleventh District adequate representation. Cross seemed to vote based on loyalty to Roosevelt without any reasons of his own.[14] Poage admitted that he had ambitions for Congress but did not have an exact long-range plan of when to run. In March 1934, Poage and a group of people met and agreed that someone should challenge Cross for the House; there was no consensus on the challenger. Poage suggested one man should run for the House, but this same man suggested that Poage should run for the House. Poage chose to run shortly before the filing date closed because no one else announced a candidacy. His total expenditures in the race were approximately $650.00. Few people loaned money to candidates at that time, but his brother loaned him $250.00. Poage's largest campaign contribution was $25.00 in 1934. Poage traveled the district, met people, and attended events; he promoted his candidacy with cards, folders, and posters. Radio played little role in campaigning. He visited local newspaper editors to explain that he did not place an announcement of his candidacy in their papers because he could not afford the $10-$25 cost of such an announcement.[15] In this contest in 1934, Poage challenged Cross in the

12. "Oral Memoirs Poage," volume 1, p. 120-121, Poage Papers.
13. "Oral Memoirs Poage," volume 1, p. 78, Poage Papers.
14. "Oral Memoirs Poage," volume 1, p. 299-300, Poage Papers.
15. Poage, *85 Years*, 55.

Democratic primary. Poage lost this contest, but he voted for Cross in the general election in accord with the party pledge.[16]

In 1936, Poage was elected to the House. Poage stated that after his 1934 defeat, he refrained from substantive campaign work until the 1936 election was very near.[17] Poage stated that in 1936 in Texas most candidates supported Roosevelt, and Poage and most folks in Central Texas approved of Roosevelt's performance as President.[18] There were few substantive issues between Poage and his most formidable opponent in 1936, and personalities again played a large role in the campaign.[19] In 1936, Poage spent a little over $2500, and Cross chose not to run for reelection but supported Frank Tirey, a former district attorney and lawyer. A Mr. Sherman, a retired businessman, also ran. All three candidates supported the New Deal.[20] Poage learned that people in rural areas appreciated candidates who actually made the effort to talk to them. Poage traveled the six-county district and tried to meet people in the more isolated areas. Poage also used loudspeakers that announced from a moving vehicle that he would make a campaign stop. He would speak to maybe a few people or a crowd.[21]

The 1936 campaign was one of Poage's more sensational campaigns. A political rally at Nolanville, Texas proved to be critical to the campaign. Tirey attended but did not expect Poage to attend, but Poage arrived just before Tirey's speech. Tirey claimed that he was a farmer, was close to the

---

16. Poage, *85 Years*, 55-57.
17. "Oral Memoirs Poage," volume 1, p. 343-344, Poage Papers.
18. "Oral Memoirs Poage," volume 2, p. 379-380, Poage Papers.
19. "Oral Memoirs Poage," volume 1, p. 356, Poage Papers.
20. Poage, *85 Years*, 57.
21. Poage, *85 Years*, 57-58.

land, and could pick 400 pounds of cotton. The local chairman who presided over the rally refused to let Poage speak because he was a Tirey supporter. The meeting officially ended, but Poage began a speech in which he exposed the falsehoods of Tirey's claims. He explained that Tirey and he (although coming from agriculture backgrounds) made their careers in non-agriculture work and worked in offices with electric fans. Poage expressed his doubts that Tirey could pick 400 pounds of cotton a day and challenged him to a contest. If Tirey could pick 400 pounds of cotton a day, he (Poage) would end his candidacy and support Tirey. If Tirey could not pick 400 pounds of cotton a day, then Tirey should end his candidacy and support Poage.[22] Word of the challenge over cotton spread across the district, and Poage thought it became more important than the substantive issues. He believed that the challenge over cotton was more crucial to his election victory than his positions on the issues.[23]

The 1936 campaign included accusations between the candidates over their business practices. At this time, the government had initiated payments to farmers as part of the New Deal's agriculture policy. Poage managed the farms owned by his mother in Throckmorton County and provided his tenant farmers with their fair share of the payments. Poage received affidavits from his tenants declaring that he never took the tenant shares of the payments. Tirey managed several farms for his father-in-law and took these payments. Tirey's tenants claimed that he took the tenant shares, came to Poage's office and related their story, and signed affidavits concerning Tirey's actions. Poage published all the affidavits

22. Poage, *85 Years*, 57-58.
23. "Oral Memoirs Poage," volume 1, p. 366-369, Poage Papers.

and distributed folders to the public about this controversy. People actually read the folders which were distributed in large numbers, and Poage received strong support among tenant farmers in 1936.[24]

Texas was part of the Democratic Solid South, and Poage's description of Texas and his district exhibited many of the characteristics of the Democratic Solid South for a very long time. Poage explained that in the 1920s the Republican Party in Texas existed only for patronage from the federal government when the Republicans held power: "It was made up of postmasters, would-be postmasters. The Republican party existed in Texas for revenue only for a long time. And it recognized itself that way, whether the public recognized it or not."[25] He wrote that during the 1930s, the Republican Party ran a ticket (a group of candidates) in the general election, but most people thought that the Democratic primary concluded the substantive campaigning.[26] Poage's district in Central Texas continued to follow some of the characteristics of the Democratic Solid South even in later decades when national and Southern politics had greatly changed. Poage faced Republican opponents in his Congressional campaigns only four times: 1964, 1966, 1974, and 1976.[27] Late in his life, Poage described his district: "Our district up until rather recent years has been one of the strongest Democratic districts in the

---

24. "Oral Memoirs Poage," volume 1, p. 373-375, Poage Papers.

25. "Oral Memoirs Poage," volume 1, p. 155, Poage Papers.

26. Poage, *85 Years*, 58.

27. Poage biography, Baylor Collections of Political Materials website, accessed March 8, 2007,

http://www3.baylor.edu/Library/BCPM/Poage/poage_biography.html.

state; this district and de la Garza's Rio Grande Valley district have been the two that have remained up until recently."[28]

Poage possessed a strong belief in party loyalty throughout his political career. He believed that he qualified as a yellow dog Democrat and had always supported the nominees of his Party. He lost in the Democratic primary on two occasions yet still voted for his primary opponent, who defeated him, in the general election on both occasions.[29] Concerning the pledge which accompanied the Democratic Party primary, he said that, "But if he's going to take part in the nominating process, then I think that he has an obligation to go along and accept the decision of his peers in making that nomination just the same as I."[30]

Poage possessed a strong record of party loyalty. Poage voted for the Democratic presidential candidate Al Smith, a Catholic, in the 1928 presidential election, but because of religious prejudice, Republican Herbert Hoover won Texas. A Republican presidential candidate had not won Texas since Reconstruction.[31] Poage explained that he ideologically agreed with the Dixiecrats of 1948 in some instances but did not think their disagreement with Harry Truman and the Democratic Party merited division: "No, I don't want to condemn their viewpoint, but I didn't think that it justified them quitting the party and seeking to establish another one."[32] In addition, he stated that, "I always felt that they should have stayed with the party and tried to reform the party rather than trying to defeat the party. It's sort of like quitting the church because you didn't

---

28. "Oral Memoirs Poage," volume 3, p. 802, Poage Papers.
29. Poage, *85 Years*, 143-145.
30. "Oral Memoirs Poage," volume 3, p. 939, Poage Papers.
31. "Oral Memoirs Poage," volume 1, p. 161-163, Poage Papers.

like the preacher, anyways, it seems to me."[33] In 1952, Democrat Adlai Stevenson angered many Texans by advocating federal government ownership of the tidelands claimed by Texas, and Texas Governor Allan Shivers led a lot of Texas Democrats to support Republican Dwight Eisenhower in the presidential election. Poage supported Stevenson in the election because of party loyalty.[34] Poage believed Texan John Connally's transformation from Democrat to Republican was motivated by self-interest and his desire for the presidency: "Because I think he figured that he could go in on the Republican ticket. I think he figured the Republicans would give him more than the Democrats could--or would." Poage said, "I think he made some terrible mistakes politically."[35] Poage even voted for Democrat George McGovern in the 1972 presidential election.[36]

Poage's belief in party loyalty was connected to a general respect for the two-party system. In a 1978 constituent newsletter, Poage argued that the two-party system screened candidates, restricted the power of wealth to influence elections with heavy advertising, and allowed for national policy since elected officials would have similar ideas. He wrote, "I accept the will of the majority both in my Country and in my Party." He also wrote, "Without two well-organized political parties we could not make our system work."[37] Poage opposed split-ticket voting and the practice of voting in one party's primary and then

---

32. "Oral Memoirs Poage," volume 3, p. 802, Poage Papers.
33. "Oral Memoirs Poage," volume 3, p. 801, Poage Papers.
34. "Oral Memoirs Poage," volume 3, p. 979-981, Poage Papers.
35. "Oral Memoirs Poage," volume 4, p. 1326, Poage Papers.
36. Poage, *85 Years*, 143-145.
37. Constituent newsletter, October 27, 1978, Poage Papers.

voting for the other party's candidates in the general election.[38] Poage felt that the misuse of the primaries carried great consequences: "I think there is a moral sanction there, and we should be aware of it. I think it invites destruction of our whole system of government to allow individuals to participate in the selection of party candidates and then to jump out and oppose the ones that they selected."[39] Poage thought that the Texas Democrats who supported Eisenhower permanently weakened the Party in Texas and deemphasized the oath on the primary ballot which stated that one was a Democrat and pledged to support the nominees of the Party. Poage explained that, "Because I believe that the two-party system is essential to the welfare of the nation. I don't think our government can function without two responsible parties. I think that you have to accept the will of the majority. And just as I think that you have to accept the will of the majority in governmental affairs, I think that in party affairs you have to accept the will of the majority. You don't have to join the Democratic party, but if you do, you should support it."[40]

Based on his statements and record, Poage's ideology seemed to be based on conservatism but tempered by progressivism, and Poage believed government action in the economy was justifiable when it served the public interest or facilitated a person or entity in their own efforts to better themselves or their circumstances. He considered himself to be "'conservative'" but stressed that he supported innovative policies and government action in some cases. He conceded

38. Poage, *85 Years*, 143-145.
39. "Oral Memoirs Poage," volume 1, p. 160, Poage Papers.
40. "Oral Memoirs Poage," volume 3, p. 938, Poage Papers.

that his voting record might have been inconsistent.[41] Poage stated that when he first entered Congress, he considered himself to be "progressive" and meant that: "I was trying to use it as something less than an extreme radical--something less than the liberal but not as reactionary as the true conservative." In the 1930s, he was uncomfortable with some of the New Deal policies but did not significantly oppose them.[42] Poage recognized that his ideology was hard to characterize: "Philosophically, I think you can--if you could class people: he's always conservative and he's always liberal, that's not--that's not true. Very few of us are 100 percent pure on our philosophy of government. Most of us agree--most of the conservatives, I should say, will agree that government shouldn't engage in a great many activities, but if they find that the government is engaging in them, they want to receive any of the benefits that anybody else is going to get from them."[43] Notions of liberal and conservative change over time, and Poage's ideology, at least compared to others, seemed to change over time, too. Poage's Party Unity and Opposition to Party scores (percentage of party unity roll calls in which one votes in agreement or disagreement with a majority of his/her party) revealed a significant change. In the Eighty-eighth Congress (1963-1964), Poage's scores were Party Unity, 70%, and Opposition to Party, 27%.[44] In the Ninety-fourth Congress

---

41. Poage, *85 Years*, 137-142.

42. "Oral Memoirs Poage," volume 2, p. 417-418, Poage Papers.

43. "Oral Memoirs Poage," volume 3, p. 1033-1034, Poage Papers.

44. "Party Majorities Split on 40.9% of Roll Calls in 1964," *Congressional Quarterly Weekly Report*, October 30, 1964, 2588-2592.

(1975-1976), Poage's scores were Party Unity, 21%, and Opposition to Party, 75%.[45]

In the House, Poage focused on advancing the interests of rural America and the agriculture sector, and the Agriculture Committee became the primary venue for Poage's work. Poage saw his interest in the Agriculture Committee as a logical result of his background. He spent his early years in rural areas, had a great respect for rural people, and served as chair of the Agriculture Committee in the Texas State Senate. When he entered the House in 1937, the majority of the residents of the Eleventh District were economically connected to agriculture.[46] As a freshman representative, Poage requested a seat on the Agriculture Committee and a seat on the Interstate and Foreign Commerce Committee. Instead, he received four other committee assignments: Claims, War Claims, Naturalization, and Census. He later received a seat on the District of Columbia Committee because no one else wanted it. In the next session, he received a seat on the Flood Control Committee, an assignment that he wanted. At the start of his third term, he received a seat on the Agriculture Committee, relinquished his other committee assignments, and never accepted another committee assignment; Poage believed that a representative should be an expert in one subject. If a member served on multiple committees, it became difficult to learn all the relevant information for each committee and to attend the meetings for each committee.[47] Jim Wright wrote

45. "Partisan Voting Shows Election-Year Drop," *Congressional Quarterly Weekly Report*," November 13, 1976, 3173-3177.

46. Poage, *85 Years*, 89.

47. Poage, *85 Years*, 63-64.

that Poage was, "Congress's most knowledgeable member on Agriculture."[48]

Poage described his daily schedule. He reviewed the mail and performed other necessary tasks in his office for approximately two hours. The Agriculture Committee met for business from 10:00 a.m. until 12:00 p.m. In the afternoon, he joined the other members when the House convened or managed other business. The House adjourned at inconsistent times, maybe 1:00 p.m. or 1:00 a.m., throughout his career.[49]

Poage's work on the Agriculture Committee involved many issues and showcased both his conservatism and progressivism. Early in his career, the New Deal's agriculture policies were significant issues in the U. S., and Poage stated that he generally supported the agriculture policies of the New Deal. For example, he opposed the intentional destruction of crops and livestock but supported the encouragement of farmers to refrain from producing a surplus.[50] In his early years on the Agriculture Committee, he worked to improve the standard of living of rural residents through programs for rural electricity, rural telephone service, and rural water systems. As chairman in later years, he focused on maintaining a degree of parity between farm income and non-farm income because non-farm income had increased at a faster rate than farm income.[51] The federal government was deeply involved with American agriculture through regulation and support, and Poage justified the federal government's involvement in agriculture. The federal government assisted many

---

48. Wright, *Balance of Power*, 44.
49. Poage, *85 Years*, 84.
50. "Oral Memoirs Poage," volume 2, p. 509, Poage Papers.
51. Poage, *85 Years*, 131-132.

constituencies and interests in society, and some of this assistance for them, such as the minimum wage and tariffs, unintentionally hurt agricultural producers. Therefore, the federal government needed to assist agricultural producers because of fairness.[52] In addition, Poage believed the federal government's involvement with agriculture produced other benefits. If the federal government allowed economic forces to operate freely, the number of producers would decline and cause a great increase in prices for consumers. The federal government thought agricultural production needed to be reasonably profitable for producers, and so, the federal government established policies to maintain prices and income for agricultural producers.[53] Poage ranked bills for rural telephone service and rural water systems as his most significant legislative accomplishments.[54]

Rural telephone service was an important issue to many Americans. Poage recalled that in the late 1940s only approximately 20% of the rural homes in the U. S. had telephone service. Rural electrification proceeded well, and it seemed logical to expand telephone service with assistance similar to the assistance extended to rural electrification. Power companies and telephone companies initially opposed the bill for rural telephone service.[55]

Poage helped provide telephone service to rural areas. On July 12, 1949, the House began general debate on HR 2960 which amended the Rural Electrification Act to provide for

---

52. "Oral Memoirs Poage," volume 3, p. 984-986, Poage Papers.
53. "Oral Memoirs Poage," volume 4, p. 1286-1290, Poage Papers.
54. Poage, *85 Years*, 92-93.
55. "Oral Memoirs Poage," volume 3, p. 859-867, Poage Papers.

rural telephone service. Poage was the author of the bill.[56] Poage addressed the House and stated that the bill was approved unanimously by the full Agriculture Committee. During his address, he was asked if there was any socialism in the bill. Poage replied that there was nothing socialistic about the bill, and the bill would actually help prevent America from becoming socialist. If the demand for phone service was not met, the demand would persist and eventually lead to government ownership of telephone service and the telephone system. By providing adequate and reasonable phone service (through private ownership), then people would not promote the idea of public ownership. Poage explained that the bill provided for the Rural Electrification Administration to make loans for rural telephone service on the same terms and conditions that it made for the extension of electrical service. The bill did not direct the government to enter the telephone business.[57] The House passed HR 2960 by a vote of 282-109.[58]

Poage helped expand access to clean water. The House began general debate on HR 10232 which sought to amend the Consolidated Farmers Home Administration Act of 1961 to provide loans for water supply, water systems, and waste disposal systems in rural areas and to provide grants for the facilitation of rural community development.[59] Poage addressed the House and explained that the Farmers Home

---

56. *Rural Telephone Service*, 81st Cong., 1st sess., *Congressional Record* 95 (July 12, 1949): 9309.

57. *Rural Telephone Service*, 81st Cong., 1st sess., *Congressional Record* 95 (July 12, 1949): 9312-9313.

58. *Rural Telephone Service*, 81st Cong., 1st sess., *Congressional Record* 95 (July 13, 1949): 9402-9403.

59. *Rural Water and Sanitation Facilities*, 89th Cong., 1st sess., *Congressional Record* 111 (September 23, 1965): 24948.

Administration had a loan program for water facilities in rural areas, but the program was underfunded. The Senate delayed addressing this issue, but the House addressed it. The Senate finally took action, and the House Agriculture Committee revised a bill passed by the Senate. The revised bill would equalize the treatment of urban areas and rural areas regarding water and waste disposal loans and grants. Until the revision, urban areas possessed advantages that rural areas did not possess. Under the revised bill, the Farmers Home Administration was authorized to extend loans or grants to nonprofit public organizations for water and waste disposal systems for rural areas and communities of 5,500 or less.[60] Cooley spoke and stated that Poage was the chair of the Subcommittee on Conservation and Credit which managed the bill. Cooley said that over 30,000 communities in the U. S. could benefit from the bill.[61] The House passed HR 10232 by a vote of 326-10, reconciled the House and Senate bills, and approved the final version.[62]

Poage's progressivism shaped some of the early legislation regarding animal rights. In 1958, the federal government passed the humane slaughter bill in response to criticism about slaughter methods as unnecessarily cruel. The act prohibited federal agencies from purchasing meat, after June 30, 1960, from plants that failed to meet certain standards. Animals had to be rendered insensible to pain by gunshot or some other method before slaughter. No penalties

60. *Rural Water and Sanitation Facilities*, 89th Cong., 1st sess., *Congressional Record* 111 (September 23, 1965): 24949.

61. *Rural Water and Sanitation Facilities*, 89th Cong., 1st sess., *Congressional Record* 111 (September 23, 1965): 24957.

62. *Rural Water and Sanitation Facilities*, 89th Cong., 1st sess., *Congressional Record* 111 (September 23, 1965): 24965-24967.

were provided for non-compliance except loss of government business.[63] In 1966, Poage sponsored an act intended to regulate the treatment of research animals and to protect pet owners' pets.[64] Reports emerged that many of the 1 million to 2 million dogs and cats used in research each year were pets stolen from residences and from the streets and then sold to animal dealers for transfer to research institutions. The animals received poor treatment from the dealers and researchers. The Agriculture Committee held hearings on the matter and prepared legislation.[65] The Congress completed work on the bill in August 1966. The bill authorized the Agriculture Department to regulate the transportation, sale, and handling in interstate commerce of dogs, cats, and certain other animals intended for research. The legislation required the Agriculture Department to set up humane standards for the care, treatment, and transportation of animals by dealers and research facilities except for the time when the animals were actually used in research or experiments. The standards covered guinea pigs, monkeys, rabbits, hamsters, dogs, and cats. The act required laboratories to buy dogs and cats only from licensed dealers with the exception of selected sources such as farmers, pet owners, and municipal pounds. The bill provided both civil and criminal penalties for violators.[66]

---

63. "Slaughtering Bill Becomes U.S. Law," *New York Times*, August 28, 1958, 3.

64. "Research Animals," *Congressional Quarterly Weekly Report*, May 6, 1966, 910.

65. "Humane Groups Split on 'Dognapping' Bill," *Congressional Quarterly Weekly Report*, July 22, 1966, 1609-1611.

66. "Research Animals," *Congressional Quarterly Weekly Report*, August 26, 1966, 1834-1835.

Even late in his career, Poage still sought to use the federal government to assist rural America and the agriculture sector. The House began consideration of the Rural Development Act of 1972, HR 12931.[67] Poage spoke at the beginning of general debate and delivered a speech that illustrated much about his view of rural America and agriculture in the modern economy. Poage pointed out that people in previous decades settled in rural areas and small towns, but the trend became for people to concentrate in large metropolitan areas. He believed the reasons for this change and trend were a decline in economic opportunities in rural areas. Agriculture incomes failed to keep pace with incomes in the other sectors of the economy which experienced significant growth in income. Farm prices changed little over the previous twenty years; in some cases, prices actually declined for some commodities. Incomes in other sectors of the economy rose dramatically in the last twenty years. Improved agriculture techniques and mechanization also reduced the demand for agricultural labor. The number of farmers declined because of economic pressures, and their local economies also suffered as a result. People left rural areas for urban areas to find work, but many encountered poverty and hardships in urban areas. As a result, problems in the urban areas grew. The Rural Development Act of 1972 would address all of these problems. The Act would use the Farmers Home Administration and the Soil Conservation Service (both in the Department of Agriculture), and together, these two agencies had approximately 4,700 offices all across America. The Farmers Home Administration would gain authority to make loans to

---

67. *Rural Development Act of 1972*, 92nd Cong., 2nd sess., *Congressional Record* 118 (February 23, 1972): 5187.

rural people to establish and to operate small businesses in rural areas and to make loans to industry to set up operations in rural areas. Loans would also be available for community facilities and services such as civic centers and fire and ambulance services. Grants to public bodies would also be permitted, and loans and grants for anti-pollution efforts would also be permitted. The loans would come from private lending institutions and would only be guaranteed by the federal government; the loans would not come from federal government appropriations.[68] The House passed the bill; there was no recorded vote.[69]

The food stamp program emerged as a salient political issue in the 1960s and fell under the jurisdiction of the Agriculture Committee. In the early 1960s, the federal government had two food programs to assist needy people. There was an older direct distribution program in which the federal government provided select commodities to the states for distribution, and there was a newer pilot food stamp program that began in 1961.[70] In 1964, Congress passed legislation that authorized $375 million for fiscal years 1965-1967 to expand and to make permanent the pilot food stamp program.[71] Under the guidelines of the bill, a member of an eligible household would apply for stamps and buy stamps from the federal government possessing a larger dollar value when

68. *Rural Development Act of 1972*, 92nd Cong., 2nd sess., *Congressional Record* 118 (February 23, 1972): 5188-5190.

69. *Rural Development Act of 1972*, 92nd Cong., 2nd sess., *Congressional Record* 118 (February 23, 1972): 5226.

70. "Food Stamp Program," *Congressional Quarterly Weekly Report*, April 10, 1964, 680-681.

71. "Food Stamp Program," *Congressional Quarterly Weekly Report*, August 14, 1964, 1737.

used to purchase eligible foods at approved stores. Southern Democrats supported the food stamp bill, favored by Northern Democrats, in exchange for Northern Democratic support of the wheat-cotton bill, favored by Southern Democrats. Both bills passed. The food stamp bill passed by a vote of 229 to 189. Democrats voted 216-26, and Republicans voted 13-163.[72] Poage defended the food stamp program in a February 1964 constituent newsletter. He argued that it was superior to the direct distribution program, provided needy people a healthier diet, and assisted business. He wrote that, "Basically the Food Stamp program is probably the most direct and effective approach to the problem of poverty which has been presented to us."[73]

The wheat-cotton bill addressed another salient issue for agriculture, agriculture subsidies. The bill provided a federal government subsidy to cotton mills allowing them to continue using cotton without significantly cutting cotton price supports. At the time, cotton was more expensive per pound than U. S. rayon or foreign cotton in the U.S. market. In addition, the bill included a voluntary program that guaranteed price supports for wheat for farmers complying with their acreage allotments. The bill passed on a vote of 211-203. Democrats voted 201-36, and Republicans voted 10-167.[74]

Over the years, the food stamp program expanded in size and in political significance and joined other agriculture programs as perennial parts of the budget, and the agriculture

---

72. "Food Stamp Program," *Congressional Quarterly Weekly Report*," April 10, 1964, 680-681.

73. Constituent newsletter, February 7, 1964, File 7, Box 1258, Poage Papers.

74. "House Passes Administration's Wheat-Cotton Bill," *Congressional Quarterly Weekly Report*, April 10, 1964, 679.

bills of 1973 illustrated this transformation. The agriculture authorization bill of 1973 extended price supports for cotton, wheat, and feed grains for four years; continued the food stamp and Food for Peace programs; and expanded the eligibility for food stamps. Most farm-state Democrats and liberal Democrats liked the bill, but Republicans generally did not like the bill.[75] The federal government provided a $9.9 billion appropriation for fiscal year 1974 for the Department of Agriculture. This sum included $3.6 billion for price support subsidies for agriculture commodities, $2.5 billion for food stamps, and money for several rural and agricultural programs. The programs for rural water and sewer grants amounted to $120 million.[76]

Poage eventually criticized the food stamp program and became part of a broader liberal-conservative ideological conflict. In 1969, it was reported that Poage expressed frustration with the food stamp program. The Agriculture Committee had been holding hearings on food stamps. Poage was concerned with the difference between assisting people truly in need and people who would not work but wanted government assistance. He thought someone who chose not to work, but could work, should not receive government assistance.[77]

Tom Foley, who succeeded Poage as chairman of the Agriculture Committee, explained the complex political significance of the food stamp program. Agriculture Committee bills included assistance for agricultural producers and

75. "Congress Passes Farm Bill, Drops Anti-Strikers Clause," *Congressional Quarterly Weekly Report,* August 11, 1973, 2219-2221.

76. "Funds for Agriculture Dept." *Congressional Quarterly Weekly Report*, October 13, 1973, 2746-2747.

77. "'He Who Will Not Work...,'" *Congressional Quarterly Weekly Report*, September 19, 1969, 1722.

assistance for needy people. Northern liberal Democrats generally were uncomfortable with the costs of federal farm programs that were important to conservative Southern Democrats and Midwest Republicans. Foley tried to persuade liberals that their support for these farm programs was important because agriculture bills contained many items. The liberals typically directed their general opposition to farm programs towards Poage, but Foley stressed that, "Mr. Poage had a bark that was much worse than his bite, and an image that was much more conservative and unfriendly than the reality of his performance as committee chairman."[78]

Fowler West worked as an assistant for Poage's Congressional office and the Agriculture Committee for several years. He stressed the political significance of the food stamp program and its significance to Poage's image. Advocates of the food stamp program and the critics of the food stamp program (who sometimes favored agricultural producers) fought for their respective priorities in the Agriculture Committee. The food stamp program issue often dominated debates in the Committee, and each side held the other's priority hostage in order to advance its own priority. Poage eventually concluded that the food stamp program did not help agriculture, tried to weaken it legislatively, and considered it "a give away program." Poage and urban liberals, in general, did not have a good political relationship. He was seen as "trying to help farmers and not giving a damn about urban poor."[79]

---

78. Biggs, *Honor in the House*, 49-50.
79. Fowler West, interview by author, January 19, 2000, telephone tape recording, T. Harry Williams Center for Oral History, Louisiana State University, Baton Rouge, LA.

The food stamp program and many other issues fell under Poage's authority as chairman, and Poage's management of the Committee generated criticism. Fowler West wrote that Cooley had little interest in the details of agriculture and did not possess the patience to run the Committee on a daily basis. Poage, during the sixteen years as vice-chairman to Cooley, exerted great influence, and "He had actually done far more work on the Committee during those years than had Chairman Cooley."[80] West wrote that, "Mr. Cooley was a heavy drinker, with bottles of bourbon seemingly stashed in every conceivable location throughout his Congressional and Committee offices."[81] Poage considered himself a "hard chairman" but thought that he was not as autocratic as Cooley or other chairmen in some ways. Poage admitted that he limited the influence of other members in the Committee's management. He chose subcommittee membership, oversaw witness questioning at hearings, and chaired a few subcommittees. He sometimes attempted to kill bills he opposed but always tried to provide a hearing for them. For several years, he did not allow television cameras to tape committee hearings; he thought that they distracted people.[82]

Fowler West described Poage's management of the Committee in great detail. He believed that Poage managed the Committee as Cooley managed it, and so Poage, as chairman, held most of the authority. West described Poage's management style as: "Autocratic, well, yes, because the rules let chairmen be autocratic." Poage expected his Committee

---

80. Fowler West, *He Ain't No Lawyer! Memories from My Years with Congressman Bob Poage* (Waco, TX: Baylor University, 2009), 72.
81. West, *No Lawyer*, 39-40.
82. Poage, *85 Years*, 130.

members to attend Committee meetings and to be knowledgeable about agriculture. Some younger members served on several committees and divided their attention among them, and as a result, some members had poor attendance records for Agriculture Committee work which frustrated Poage. To work with Poage effectively, members needed to respect the Committee, to work hard, and to act slightly deferential. Then, Poage would award them the work, the responsibility, or the position that they wanted. Some members resented the prospect of having to act deferential. West said, "And he knew in his heart that if anyone halfway tried, they'd get whatever they wanted from the committee." West added, "Poage, in my judgment, was never unfair, at the committee. But he did expect a lot of things."[83]

Fowler West emphasized some admirable traits about Poage. He was honest and spoke his mind without concern that he might anger someone. West explained that ideological differences alone would not prevent Poage from working well with liberals. West considered Tom Foley to be liberal, and Poage and Foley had a good relationship. West said, "And no matter if they were liberal as can be, Poage would never hold that against them at all." Poage and his staff worked hard. They normally left the office at 7:30 p.m. or sometimes even later at approximately 10:00 p.m. They regularly worked on Saturdays. Poage worked harder than any of his staff. West

83. Fowler West, interview by author, January 19, 2000, telephone tape recording, T. Harry Williams Center for Oral History, Louisiana State University, Baton Rouge, LA.

said that he and other people on Poage's staff had a lot of fun working for Poage and pulled pranks on people.[84]

Because of ideology, management style, or both, Poage faced a bloc of critics. West tried to persuade Poage to be more compromising with other members, but Poage refused: "He did not go out of his way to help any of the urban liberals. And he didn't play ball with them, and it cost him." In addition, West said, "But I'd go up and I'd say, 'Mr. Poage, don't. Why can't you do something for this guy?' and he'd turn and say, 'What he wants to do is just not right, you know, we can't do that,' blah, blah blah. It's just the way he was."[85]

The career of Poage paralleled in some ways the career of Lyndon Johnson. Poage and Johnson were close personal friends, and Poage felt he understood Johnson.[86] Poage entered the House in January 1937, and Johnson was elected to the House in a special election in 1937. Poage, Johnson, and Albert Thomas of Houston were all assigned offices close to one another. Poage and his secretary, Thomas and his secretary, and Johnson would stay in the office area past regular working hours at night and talk about politics. Both secretaries were men.[87] Before Johnson enlisted in the military after the start of World War II, he talked over the decision and

---

84. Fowler West, interview by author, January 19, 2000, telephone tape recording, T. Harry Williams Center for Oral History, Louisiana State University, Baton Rouge, LA.

85. Fowler West, interview by author, January 19, 2000, telephone tape recording, T. Harry Williams Center for Oral History, Louisiana State University, Baton Rouge, LA.

86. Poage, *85 Years*, 157-161.

87. Bob Poage, interview by Joe B. Frantz, November 11, 1968, William R. Poage AC74-235, Oral History Collection, Lyndon Baines Johnson Collection, Lyndon Baines Johnson Library, Austin, TX.

his reasons with Poage.[88] Lyndon Johnson's presidency helped define modern notions of liberal and conservative, and Poage faced a dilemma: "I think that I went along with him a great deal. I know that I supported a good many programs that I probably would not have, had it not been for the fact that Lyndon was backing them."[89]

Overall, Poage followed the typical White Southern position on the major civil rights legislation. When the House passed the Civil Rights Act of 1964 in February 1964, Poage voted against it.[90] When the House passed the final version of the Civil Rights Act of 1964, Poage voted against it.[91] Poage voted against the Voting Rights Act when the House passed it in July 1965.[92] Poage voted against the conference report on the Voting Rights Act when the House passed it in August 1965.[93]

Poage explained his reasons for his votes. In his constituent newsletter from February 13, 1964, Poage explained his opposition to the Civil Rights Act by using abstract constitutional arguments and economic issues. He wrote: "Ninety per cent of our people agree that intolerance and prejudice should be removed from the hearts of men. It seems unlikely that this can be achieved by law." He feared the

88. Bob Poage, interview by Joe B. Frantz, November 11, 1968, William R. Poage AC74-235, Oral History Collection, Lyndon Baines Johnson Collection, Lyndon Baines Johnson Library, Austin, TX.
89. "Oral Memoirs Poage," volume 4, p. 1151, Poage Papers.
90. *Congressional Quarterly Weekly Report*, February 14, 1964, 334-335.
91. *Congressional Quarterly Weekly Report*, July 3, 1964, 1414-1415.
92. *Congressional Quarterly Weekly Report*, July 16, 1965, 1402-1403.
93. *Congressional Quarterly Weekly Report*, August 6, 1965, 1588-1589.

consequences of the Civil Rights Act: "We must consider the loss of many individual liberties, the complete change in our judicial system (for instance, the loss of right of trial by jury, etc) and the direct financial loss occasioned to thousands of innocent businessmen and home owners." He argued that economic opportunities were more salient than the civil rights issue: "This bill will not produce one new job."[94] In a later constituent newsletter from June 19, 1964, Poage again explained his opposition to the Civil Rights Act. He wrote that it would "break down such time-honored safeguards of individual liberty as trial by jury." He claimed that it "destroyed more rights than it protected." He also added that: "I pointed out that while I believe in giving every citizen, regardless of race or color, the same treatment at the hands of our government, I do not believe that government has any right to force any citizen to do business with anyone with whom he does not want to deal."[95]

After the changes of the Civil Rights Movement and its significant legislation, Poage discussed his earlier positions and stressed his apathy towards the issue of civil rights in general. He later said, regarding the Civil Rights Act of 1964 and the Voting Rights Act of 1965, that, "I tried to leave them alone. I did leave them alone. I didn't take any particular interest in them." He stated that he felt the Civil Rights Movement moved too swiftly in making social changes. He recognized in the abstract the need to eliminate discrimination and prejudice.[96] He also stated that, "I was not one of those who was urging any action at the time the action was taken. But I was not one who

---

94. Constituent Newsletter, February 13, 1964, File 7, Box 1258, Poage Papers,
95. Constituent newsletter, June 19, 1964, File 7, Box 1258, Poage Papers.

was wanting to stand in the way of—at least the school part—of the civil-rights movement."[97]

Although agriculture was not the most sensational policy subject, the work of the Agriculture Committee influenced the lives of all Americans to varying degrees. Poage believed that the federal government had a legitimate role to play in society and used the federal government to assist many ordinary Americans. Yet, Poage disagreed with many other people on the extent or proper limit to government authority, and the food stamp program symbolized a broader liberal-conservative ideological conflict between Poage and many other people. Despite his earlier progressivism and work for rural America and the agriculture sector, Poage was seen by some people as too conservative, even reactionary, regarding ideology and policy by the 1970s. His management style for the Committee was traditional, but now, that management style faced greater scrutiny and was employed to support policies that much of the Democratic Party considered too extreme. Poage could be seen by some people as an obstacle to progress because of his management style and ideology.

---

96. "Oral Memoirs Poage," volume 4, p. 1164-1173, Poage Papers.
97. "Oral Memoirs Poage," volume 4, p. 1231, Poage Papers.

Chapter 4 - Felix Edward "Eddie" Hebert

Felix Edward "Eddie" Hebert of Louisiana experienced a career with very different aspects. He had a career as a journalist before winning election to the U. S. House of Representatives. To achieve his success, he tried to separate himself from Louisiana's volatile and complicated politics. Hebert was consistently conservative, focused on national security issues, and became chairman of the Armed Services Committee. Hebert displayed an independent streak in politics and government and was uncomfortable with partisanship. Hebert had an abrasive personal demeanor that caused him troubles at times, and Hebert's chairmanship occurred during the last phases of the Vietnam War and the breakdown in the post-World War II Cold War consensus.

Hebert's early life was centered on New Orleans. He was born on October 12, 1901 in New Orleans. His family background was largely Cajun and French, and his family and ancestors arrived in south Louisiana in the early 1800s.[1] He used the French pronunciation of "Hebert" but could not speak French.[2] Hebert's father was Felix Hebert, and he (the future representative) was nicknamed "Eddie".[3] Hebert's family, when he was young, lived at three different houses on Canal Street in New Orleans.[4] Hebert's father was a streetcar conductor. His mother had worked as a teacher. The family took in renters in some of their extra rooms.[5] Dr. Oscar Solomon rented one of these rooms and kept his office at the Hebert's house. Solomon

---

1. Hebert, *Titans*, 4-5.
2. Hebert, *Titans*, 14.
3. Hebert, *Titans*, 7.
4. Hebert, *Titans*, 7-8.

was politically active and was a member of a political machine called the Old Regulars. The Old Regulars controlled New Orleans. Solomon and Hebert's father frequently discussed politics. His father opposed the Old Regulars and was part of the reform bloc led by John P. Sullivan. Hebert's father ran for the state house of representatives on one occasion and lost.[6]

Journalism was a core aspect of Hebert's life and career. Hebert was hired as assistant sports editor for the *Times-Picayune* in 1918 and reported on prep sports. He was still in high school and took this job to promote his high school.[7] While enrolled at Tulane University, Hebert oversaw the sports page of the *Hullabaloo* (the Tulane newspaper), was a co-owner of the *Hullabaloo*, was the assistant sports editor for the *Times-Picayune,* and was the campus correspondent for the *New Orleans States.*[8]

Hebert's academic performance at Tulane was very bad. On one occasion, he appealed to the dean of his college, and the dean changed one of Hebert's grades to passing which enabled him to join his fraternity, Delta Sigma Phi. Hebert failed to pass the required number of subjects at Tulane and entered Tulane law school on probation to avoid being dismissed from Tulane. In law school, he failed to apply himself to his studies and was unprepared for his examinations; therefore, he withdrew from law school. Then, he reentered law school but withdrew again. He finally entered the school of journalism. While at Tulane, Hebert focused on campus politics, socializing, and journalism; he was the manager for the football

---

5. Hebert, *Titans*, 7-9
6. Hebert, *Titans*, 9-10.
7. Hebert, *Titans*, 29-30.
8. Hebert, *Titans*, 32.

team for a while. Hebert wanted to earn a football letter at Tulane and was awarded a letter by serving as manager of the football team. He withdrew from Tulane after the 1923 season ended and never graduated.[9]

Hebert's career in journalism occurred during a volatile era in New Orleans. Hebert described New Orleans in the 1920s and 1930s: "Gambling and prostitution flourished. Police were on the take. Most government jobs were held by patronage. Sports, show business, and misfortune (if not tragedy) occupied the attention of the readers of the city's newspapers."[10] The corruption in Louisiana became terrible: "The magnitude of unmitigated defilement of public trust reached practically all levels of society and is still unique in the history of the United States, Watergate notwithstanding."[11] Regarding the newspaper business in the 1920s and 1930s in New Orleans, he wrote: "There were few college graduates on the staffs, and it was not unusual to find reporters who had not finished high school--not that they were not bright; rather time, place, and circumstance often dictated on-the-job training instead of formal education. This route often produced a newsroom full of 'characters,' individualists who lived by their wits, shunned convention, pampered their hedonistic impulses, and did not give a whit for 'job security.'" He also wrote that: "In New Orleans in those years, reporters with faults and flaws roamed the city rooms, making no pretense at perfection. While they reported wrongdoing, it was with the attitude that it was

---

9. Hebert, *Titans*, 33-35.
10. Hebert, *Titans*, 38.
11. Hebert, *Titans*, 135.

their job, not a holy crusade conducted by morally superior beings."[12]

Hebert described his work during this era. He worked for the *New Orleans States* sports department after withdrawing from Tulane, and his beat included several types of news in addition to sports. At that time, in New Orleans, there was much corruption, and readers were interested in sports, show business, and misfortune.[13] Hebert worked for two years in the *New Orleans States* sports department. Then, he worked for Loyola University of the South managing public relations. He also managed public relations for other groups, too.[14] Hebert returned to journalism after his work in public relations and began working for the *New Orleans States* as a general assignment reporter. He became a columnist and also performed many other tasks for the newspaper while also performing the reporter and columnist work.[15] Eventually, Hebert became city editor for the *States*. When the *Times-Picayune* bought the *States*, Hebert was retained as city editor because the bureau chief of the Associated Press in New Orleans interceded on Hebert's behalf with the publisher.[16]

Hebert's journalism work provided a variety of experiences and opportunities. Hebert wrote that he knew people from many different backgrounds and that his contacts created many opportunities for him as a reporter.[17] Hebert reported on many executions and focused on how people's experiences on death row changed them. He wrote: "Few

---

12. Hebert, *Titans*, 67.
13. Hebert, *Titans*, 38.
14. Hebert, *Titans*, 51.
15. Hebert, *Titans*, 55-56.
16. Hebert, *Titans*, 114-116.
17. Hebert, *Titans*, 78-79.

contemporaries, outside of an executioner, and certainly no other member of Congress, have witnessed as many men drop from the gallows as I have."[18] Hebert met Huey Long and covered him as a reporter. The Long machine seemed to designate him as an opponent in some instances, and Hebert claimed that he did not do anything to precipitate the designation.[19] Hebert ran for the presidency of the Young Men's Business club, a civic organization with strong connections to Louisiana politics. The Old Regulars and the Long political machine (two major factions in Louisiana politics) were connected to and interested in the contest, and they influenced the outcome of the contest. Hebert became the president of the organization in 1932.[20]

The corruption in Louisiana eventually embroiled Hebert. Hebert took serious offense at one of Huey Long's corrupt acts. The Long machine arranged for the expulsion of seven LSU students who printed an anti-Long letter from an LSU student in the LSU campus newspaper; the letter was prompted by Huey Long's corrupt acts. Hebert wrote about the conflict in his column which was published on June 9, 1935.[21]

The *States* began an extensive investigation into corruption in Louisiana government and politics directed by Hebert. In June 1939, the *States* and Hebert discovered evidence of the use of government resources for personal use by a leading member of the Long machine who was close to the governor of Louisiana. This discovery was a catalyst which precipitated more investigations and greater revelations of

18. Hebert, *Titans*, 90.
19. Hebert, *Titans*, 81-83.
20. Hebert, *Titans*, 77-78.
21. Hebert, *Titans*, 87-88.

corruption involving many high-ranking government officials in Louisiana.[22] On June 9, 1939, the *New Orleans States* ran the first article in this discovery process, "Building Materials Taken to N.O. Private Property by L.S.U. Truck."[23]

Hebert parleyed his success in journalism into a political career in 1940, but his candidacy was shaped by the volatile and complicated politics of Louisiana. In the governor's race, James Noe finished third and failed to make the runoff between Earl Long and Sam Jones. A deal was arranged between Jones and Noe. Some of Jones' supporters paid Noe's campaign debts, and Noe supported Jones. Also, there was agreement to divide the patronage between Noe and Jones. Jones won the runoff and was elected governor.[24] Noe tried to persuade Hebert to run for mayor of New Orleans, but Hebert decided to run for the U. S. House of Representatives because service in the House could enhance his journalistic career. He could become established in national politics and gain lifetime floor privilege in the House which would let him interact with members. At this time, he only envisioned serving one term but was impressed with a representative's salary and benefits. Noe was supportive of Hebert's aspirations for the House. Then, Noe and Jones agreed to support each other's choice for the First and Second U. S. House districts. Noe secured the support of the *Times-Picayune* for Hebert, and Hebert received the support of the Old Regulars and the support of two political bosses of two neighboring parishes.[25] He was elected as a Democrat to the Seventy-seventh Congress and served in the

---

22. Hebert, *Titans*, 118-138.
23. "Building Materials Taken to N.O Private Property by L.S.U. Truck," *New Orleans States*, June 9, 1939, Fly Sheet, 4.
24. Hebert, *Titans*, 148-150.

House from 1941 through 1976.[26] By the mid-1970s, Hebert represented the First District of Louisiana which included much of the greater New Orleans metropolitan area.[27]

Hebert began his political career, but political challenges posed by Louisiana's volatile and complicated politics remained. In 1946, the *New Orleans States* publicly opposed and worked against Hebert's reelection. The result was a public rhetorical conflict between the *States* and Hebert.[28] In 1946, Hebert was considered to be an Old Regular, and he worked with them to a limited extent. The other main faction at this time was the anti-Old Regulars or Reformers. New Orleans held an election for mayor in 1946, and the factional divisions were intense.[29] In Hebert's campaign, local politics was significant, and substantive issues had little importance. The political alignments (support/opposition) from the earlier mayor's election helped determine the political alignments in Hebert's campaign (support/opposition).[30] The 1948 Louisiana governor election featured Earl Long and Sam Jones. Hebert actively and publicly supported Long, the winner. Relations between Long and Hebert improved. Then, Hebert was able to extricate himself from Louisiana politics.[31]

Hebert's life and career in Washington, D. C. was much different from his involvement with Louisiana politics. Hebert wrote that Rayburn took an initial interest in him as a protege, but Hebert claimed that he did not want to be a minion of

---

25. Hebert, *Titans*, 150-155.
26. Nystrom, *Biographical Directory*, 1165.
27. Brownson, *1975 Staff Directory*, 45.
28. Hebert, *Titans*, 240-244.
29. Hebert, *Titans*, 228-229.
30. Hebert, *Titans*, 245-253.
31. Hebert, *Titans*, 265-271.

Rayburn and to subordinate his views to the Leadership. Therefore, Hebert never become a true protege of Rayburn and was not selected to advance in the House Democratic Leadership.[32] Hebert was assigned to the District of Columbia Committee as a freshman.[33] At the start of his second term, he was appointed to the Naval Affairs Committee, one of the two committees that were later combined as the Armed Services Committee. An influential Louisiana politician, Paul Maloney, had been reelected to the House after losing an earlier reelection effort. Maloney reacquired his seat on the Ways and Means Committee and arranged for Hebert's appointment to the Naval Affairs Committee. Hebert thought that a strong military deterred aggression and that his investigative abilities could be used on the Committee.[34]

Hebert became a powerful figure on the Armed Services Committee. Hebert claimed that when he was third in seniority on the Armed Services Committee (during the 1960s), he played a significant role in managing the Committee. The chair was L. Mendel Rivers of South Carolina. Hebert sat by Rivers, and when somebody wanted a request or favor, Rivers told them to talk to Hebert. Hebert wrote that "Mendel always leaned on me."[35] He served as chair of that Committee in the Ninety-second Congress (1971 and 1972) and the Ninety-third Congress (1973 and 1974).[36] Hebert interpreted his service as chairman in extreme terms: "As chairman, I was proudest of upholding the defense of the country despite all the efforts to beat down the national defense. They didn't beat it down during

---

32. Hebert, *Titans*, 161-162.
33. Hebert, *Titans*, 163.
34. Hebert, *Titans*, 171.
35. Hebert, *Titans*, 371.

my tenure. I fought them off."[37] As chairman, Hebert used his authority to support Nixon's detente policy and his management of the Vietnam War. He wrote that "Ideologically, Nixon and I agreed." He added that he developed a "personal warmth" towards Nixon.[38] Nixon wrote that during his presidential administration, his greatest support on foreign policy issues was provided by conservatives from both the Republican Party and the Democratic Party. He especially depended on a collection of Southern Democrats which included Hebert.[39]

Hebert wrote that when he became the Armed Services chair, he established a rule requiring that each member, regardless of seniority or party, be permitted five minutes to question witnesses as part of a rotation involving all the members. As chairman, Rivers handled most of the questions, and his friends handled the remainder of the questions. Hebert claimed that he never ended debate on the floor. In contrast, Rivers sometimes arbitrarily ended debate.[40]

Overall, Hebert displayed a non-partisan streak and was ideologically conservative in his Congressional career. Hebert considered himself to have been a "conservative" when he first entered Congress and considered himself a Democrat according to his view of the world and the issues. He opposed "party dictation" which he believed violated the Constitution and the basic right of expression.[41] Hebert stressed his independent streak and explained that, "My relationship with Democrats and

---

36. Nystrom, *Biographical Directory*, 1165.
37. Hebert, *Titans*, 429.
38. Hebert, *Titans*, 430.
39. Richard Nixon, *RN: The Memoirs of Richard Nixon* (New York: Grosset & Dunlap, 1978), 351.
40. Hebert, *Titans*, 427-428.
41. Hebert, *Titans*, 327-328.

Republicans had always depended upon my feelings regarding specific issues. While my registration card reads Democrat my mind thinks Independent." He stressed that, "There's too much of this other stuff--the idea that because a Republican offers a bill it's bad; because a Democrat offers it, it's good; or because a Democrat offers it, it's bad, and a Republican offers it, it's good." His view was clear: "I'm going to vote the way I want to vote. I enjoy the luxury of independence."[42]

Hebert's first national political exposure concerned the House Committee on Un-American Activities and espionage accusations. Hebert requested a seat on the Committee in 1947 because he thought it served a legitimate purpose but wanted to make it fairer and more responsible. After gaining a seat, he convinced the Committee to allow people, whose names had been mentioned in testimony before the Committee, to testify before the Committee, too. Earlier, the Committee denied some individuals the right to testify after their names were mentioned in testimony.[43]

The scandal of Whittaker Chambers and Alger Hiss gave Hebert and the Committee on Un-American Activities a sensational issue. Whittaker Chambers cooperated with the Committee and accused Alger Hiss of being a communist, but Hiss denied the accusation and requested an opportunity to testify before the Committee. Hiss appeared before the Committee on August 5, 1948 and defended himself well; afterwards, Hebert proposed handing over the case to the

---

42. Hebert, *Titans*, 424-425.
43. Hebert, *Titans*, 273-274.

Justice Department.[44] After Chambers testified on August 25, 1948, the Committee met in executive session and debated the next course of action. The mood for the Committee members was angry and argumentative. Hebert wanted to end hearings on the Hiss-Chambers affair, to let the Justice Department resolve the case, and to allow the Committee to proceed to new business. He felt that both the Republicans and the Democrats were allowing partisan politics to interfere and to determine events. The hearings continued.[45] On December 30, 1948, the Committee released a report to the House and new evidence supporting Chamber's charges against Hiss. The report stated that a spy network existed in the 1930s and 1940s and that there was evidence to prove people in the government were involved with Soviet spies.[46] In an official statement, Hebert criticized members of the Committee for being too concerned with publicity. He told reporters that he was referring to Richard Nixon and Karl Mundt of South Dakota, but the official statement did not specifically mention them. Hebert criticized the two for not treating accused people fairly.[47] As for Hiss, on December 15, 1948, a federal grand jury indicted Hiss on two counts of perjury. He was convicted in 1950 and sentenced to five years in prison.[48]

Hebert's role with the Committee on Un-American Activities was limited. In early 1949, Hebert was removed from

---

44. Walter Goodman, *The Committee: The Extraordinary Career of the House Committee on Un-American Activities* (New York: Farrar, Straus and Giroux, 1968), 254-255.

45. Hebert, *Titans*, 312.

46. Marshall Andrews, "Hiss Linked to Spy Paper Typewriter, Probers Say," *Washington Post*, December 31, 1948, 1, 2.

47. "Hebert Brands GOP Probers Publicity Mad," *Washington Post*, December 31, 1948, 2.

48. Goodman, *Un-American*, 265-266.

the Committee because he was not a lawyer. The Democratic House Leadership instituted a new rule requiring that Democrats on the Committee be lawyers in order to establish greater control over the Committee for the Leadership. Another member, John Rankin of Mississippi, was also removed because a new rule prohibited committee chairs from serving on the Committee. He chaired the Veterans' Affairs Committee. Both men were Dixiecrats in 1948 and were replaced by Democratic loyalists.[49]

Hebert's rise on the Armed Services Committee coincided with era of the Vietnam War, and Hebert became embroiled in one of the most controversial events of the Vietnam War, the My Lai Massacre. On March 16, 1968, U. S. Army soldiers assaulted a village known as My Lai seeking to kill or disperse Vietcong. Yet, the people of the village were mostly civilians unprepared for combat. Confusion engulfed the site, and there were many atrocities. Some soldiers broke discipline and refused to continue the assault after realizing the truth about My Lai. Other soldiers only followed orders. Some soldiers went berserk. The soldiers killed between 400 and 500 Vietnamese, and Lieutenant William Calley became the most salient man involved. Calley was the ranking officer at the site and ordered and participated in several executions, believing that he was following the orders of his superior. The military engaged in an initial coverup, and later, Calley was convicted for premeditated murder of twenty-two civilians.[50] The My Lai Massacre became known to the American public when Ronald

49. Goodman, *Un-American*, 272.
50. James S. Olson and Randy Roberts, eds., *My Lai: A Brief History with Documents*, The Bedford Series in History and Culture (Boston: Bedford Books, 1998), 20-25.

Ridenhour, an Army soldier who had fought in Vietnam, wrote letters to his Representative, Morris Udall of Arizona, and other government and military officials in the spring of 1969 detailing the stories that he had learned about My Lai from other men.[51]

After the revelation, the Armed Services Committee was confronted with the My Lai Massacre. The Armed Services Committee began its own investigation into the events at My Lai in November 1969. It was led by Rivers and was conducted by the Investigating Subcommittee of Armed Services, but it was a chaotic and clumsy affair. Then, on December 12, Rivers announced that Hebert would lead a special subcommittee to investigate the events at My Lai.[52] Hebert claimed that he told Rivers that he (Hebert) would take the investigation into the events at My Lai on the understanding that he (Hebert) would have the highest authority for the investigation. Hebert picked the members for the special subcommittee and established rules for the reporters who covered the hearings. Throughout this entire time, the Army tried to impede the investigation into the events at My Lai.[53]

Hebert and the Armed Services Investigating Subcommittee of the Committee on Armed Services faced a controversial and challenging assignment. Hebert stated the scope of his Subcommittee's work. The Subcommittee would not address "criminal responsibility" for civilian deaths at My Lai since the military courts were responsible for that issue. Instead, the Subcommittee would address a set of questions. What were military policies concerning civilians and the inquiry into reports of civilian casualties before 16 March 1968? Did the

---

51. Olson, *My Lai*, 1-2.
52. Hebert, *Titans*, 380-383.
53. Hebert, *Titans*, 384-387.

operations of the troops in the My Lai area on 16 March 1968 produce reports of large civilian casualties? Were any reports of such things reported to the officers with command over the troops at My Lai? If so, what did the officers do? Was what the officers did in line with military policies? Hearings were held on April 15, 16, 17, 23, 24, 27, 28, 29, and 30; May 8, 9, 12, and 13; and June 9, 10, and 22. All hearing were held in 1970.[54] On July 14, 1970, the Subcommittee released its report about the My Lai Massacre.[55] Hebert wrote that he was proud that the report presented the facts to the public and was not a coverup or pro-military apology, but it was also not anti-military.[56]

The report prepared by Hebert's Subcommittee was entitled *Investigation of the My Lai Incident: Report of the Armed Services Investigating Subcommittee of the Committee on Armed Services*. According to the *Report*, on April 4, 1969, Rivers received a letter from Ron Ridenhour describing the events at My Lai on March 16, 1968, and a copy of the letter was forwarded to the Department of the Army on April 7, 1969 with a request for an investigation. On November 24, 1969, Rivers announced that the Armed Services Investigating Subcommittee would begin investigating the events that occurred at My Lai. The Army was slow to investigate My Lai and appeared to impede investigation into My Lai. Rivers announced on December 12 that a special subcommittee would

---

54. U. S. Congress, House, Committee on Armed Services, *Investigation of the My Lai Incident: Hearings of the Armed Services Investigating Subcommittee of the Committee on Armed Services*, 91st Cong., 2nd sess., April 15, 16, 17, 23, 24, 27, 28, 29, 30, May 8, 9, 12, 13, June 9, 10, 22, 1970, 1.

55. William Greider, "Hill Sees Coverup on Mylai," *Washington Post*, July 15, 1970, A1.

56. Hebert, *Titans*, 387.

be created to investigate My Lai fully and deeply. The members of the Subcommittee were Hebert (chair), Samuel S. Stratton (Democrat of New York), Charles S. Gubser (Republican of California), and William L. Dickinson (Republican of Alabama). Former Congressmen Porter Hardy and Charles E. Halleck would serve as special consultants to the Subcommittee. The Subcommittee interviewed 152 witnesses, held 16 days of hearings, compiled 1,812 pages of sworn testimony, and examined hundreds of documents (there were 3,045 pages of statements from witnesses). The Subcommittee conducted a field investigation in Vietnam.[57]

The *Report* included a section entitled "Summary Observations." The village of Son My was composed of a collection of hamlets, and the hamlet identified as My Lai 4 was the site of the Massacre. The "Summary Observations" stated that a lot of unarmed Vietnamese were deliberately killed at My Lai 4 on March 16, 1968 by Task Force Barker, and a relatively few troops committed the deliberate killings. The people of My Lai 4 supported the Viet Cong. They had been warned to leave the area because of the possibility of combat. They had earlier been relocated to a refugee camp but returned. There had been combat in the area in February. Son My was a Viet Cong stronghold, and its hamlets were used as bases for the Viet Cong and North Vietnamese Army units. The U. S. troops had suffered the bad effects of war, and their mission for March 16 was unclear. Yet, they had orders to follow. The events at My

---

57. U. S. Congress, House, Committee on Armed Services, *Investigation of the My Lai Incident: Report of the Armed Services Investigating Subcommittee of the Committee on Armed Services*, 91st Cong., 2nd sess., July 15, 1970, 1-4.

Lai were "wrong" and contrary to U. S. policy and practice. The Army should have done a proper investigation.[58]

The "Recommendations" section contained recommendations. First, the Uniform Code of Military Justice needed reform on two points regarding trial and legal procedures. Second, the United States Code needed reform to allow for trial in the U. S. District Courts of people charged with offenses while on active military duty but who were no longer under military jurisdiction because they were discharged. Third, the Army needed to change procedures on some points regarding training, investigations, photographic evidence, and the award of decorations. Fourth, the Secretary of Defense needed to apply recommendations for the Army to all military departments.[59]

The *Report's* "Findings and Conclusions" section identified twenty-five points, and some points were especially noteworthy. Point number one declared that the events at My Lai were a "tragedy of major proportions." Several points argued that the Army engaged in a massive and intense effort to coverup the events at My Lai and to prevent investigation into the events. Point number ten specifically stated that the events were "'covered up'"; point number eleven stated that direction and organization was necessary for the coverup. Point number twenty stated that before the My Lai 4 events, the

58. U. S. Congress, House, Committee on Armed Services, *Investigation of the My Lai Incident: Report of the Armed Services Investigating Subcommittee of the Committee on Armed Services*, 91st Cong., 2nd sess., July 15, 1970, 52-53.
59. U. S. Congress, House, Committee on Armed Services, *Investigation of the My Lai Incident: Report of the Armed Services Investigating Subcommittee of the Committee on Armed Services*, 91st Cong., 2nd sess., July 15, 1970, 7-8.

troops were told that all civilians were anticipated to be absent from the village when the attack would begin. The troops were told to destroy the village and make it unusable as a base for the Viet Cong. No specific instructions were given regarding civilians in case any civilians were encountered. Point number twenty-one stated that the U. S. troops did not all act alike at My Lai.[60]

Hebert's most important accomplishment was the Uniformed Services University of Health Sciences. Hebert first expressed the idea in 1947 for an institution to train doctors for the military, but the idea never attracted much support. There was opposition from established institutions and special interests.[61] When Hebert became Armed Services chair in 1971, he finally achieved progress on the idea. Yet, some opposition had to still be overcome.[62]

Hebert and the Congress eventually passed legislation for military medical training despite delays. On November 2, 1971, the House began consideration and debate on HR 2 to establish a Uniformed Services University of the Health Sciences.[63] Hebert gave an address to begin general debate and stated that he had worked for this idea for over twenty years. He explained that there was a shortage of medical personnel in the Armed Forces. Currently, there were approximately 14,000 doctors on active duty in the Armed

---

60. U. S. Congress, House, Committee on Armed Services, *Investigation of the My Lai Incident: Report of the Armed Services Investigating Subcommittee of the Committee on Armed Services*, 91st Cong., 2nd sess., July 15, 1970, 4-7.

61. Hebert, *Titans*, 401-404.

62. Hebert, *Titans*, 404-406.

63. *Uniformed Services Health Professions Revitalization Act of 1971*, 92nd Cong., 1st sess., *Congressional Record* 117 (November 2, 1971): 38682-38683.

Forces, and in recent years, the Armed Forces required annually an input of approximately 4,000-5,000 doctors to meet their needs. With the recent changes in the draft and future changes, the shortage would become extremely severe. Retention of doctors in the Armed Forces had been less than 1% since the Korean War. The bill would establish a Uniformed Services University of the Health Sciences.[64] On November 3, 1971, the House passed HR 2 by a vote of 352-31.[65] In 1972, the House considered the conference report on HR 2. Hebert spoke and explained that the Senate earlier in 1972 amended the bill and included "the deletion of the authority for the establishment of a medical school for the Armed Forces." The conference committee chose the House version of the bill and the authorization for the medical school. The conference report version was almost the same as the original House bill passed on November 3, 1971 by the House. Hebert also stated that the Senate had passed the conference report on HR 2.[66] The House voted on the conference report and passed it, 310-13.[67]

The Uniformed Services University of the Health Sciences was established; it eventually occupied 100 acres of land of the National Naval Medical Center in Bethesda, Maryland. The institution's webpage stated that, "Congressman

---

64. *Uniformed Services Health Professions Revitalization Act of 1971,* 92nd Cong., 1st sess., *Congressional Record* 117 (November 2, 1971): 38683-38684.

65. *Uniformed Services Health Professions Revitalization Act of 1971,* 92nd Cong., 1st sess., *Congressional Record* 117 (November 3, 1971): 39063-39064.

66. *Conference Report on H. R. 2, Uniformed Services Health Professions Revitalization Act,* 92nd Cong., 2nd sess., *Congressional Record* 118 (September 7, 1972): 29654.

Hebert lobbied tirelessly for a military medical school and before long, the Uniformed Services University began to receive favorable attention from powerful decision-makers."[68] The institution included the F. Edward Hebert School of Medicine, the Daniel K. Inouye Graduate School of Nursing, and a Postgraduate Dental College.[69] Hebert wrote that, "When my service is ended and I look back over the milestones of my career, I want most of all to be remembered for the military medical school."[70]

Hebert followed the typical White Southern position on civil rights but also made it a high priority during the era of the Dixiecrat movement. Hebert and another member, Rankin, were removed from the Committee on Un-American Activities in January 1949. According to Hebert, the reason for his removal was his Dixiecrat position.[71] Hebert claimed that he believed that the Dixiecrat movement was not a party. It was a rebellion within the Democratic Party. It was an example of a minority expressing its views.[72] Hebert claimed that he consistently opposed excessive government intrusion and that he believed in Jeffersonian democracy. He explained his Dixiecrat experience in this way: "As a Dixiecrat I was not motivated by

---

67. *Conference Report on H. R. 2, Uniformed Services Health Professions Revitalization Act*, 92nd Cong., 2nd sess., *Congressional Record* 118 (September 7, 1972): 29655-29656.

68. "History of USU," Uniformed Services University of the Health Sciences, accessed February 5, 2015, http://www.usuhs.edu/about/usuhistory.html.

69. "Our Schools," Uniformed Services University of the Health Sciences, accessed February 5, 2015, http://www.usuhs.edu/schools.html.

70. Hebert, *Titans*, 412.

71. Hebert, *Titans*, 320-324.

72. Hebert, *Titans*, 326.

the lure of segregation, but by the magnetic appeal of its individualism, and by its insistence on the rights of the states."[73]

Hebert maintained the same position on civil rights during the era of the Civil Rights Movement. Hebert voted against the Civil Rights Act of 1964 in February 1964.[74] Hebert was paired against during the vote on the final version of the Civil Rights Act of 1964 in July 1964.[75] Hebert voted against the Voting Rights Act in July 1965.[76] Hebert voted against the conference report on the Voting Rights Act in August 1965.[77] Afterwards, Hebert maintained his same position on civil rights. He claimed that his opposition to civil rights legislation was based on the idea that it is not possible to legislate personal beliefs. He claimed that his opposition to the 1964 Civil Rights Act was based on "a life-long abhorrence to Big Brotherism."[78]

Hebert became embroiled in a serious controversy concerning women late in his career. Patricia "Pat" Schroeder of Colorado was first elected to the House for the Ninety-third Congress (1973-1974). According to Schroeder, he did not want women to serve on the Armed Services Committee. Ways and Means Committee Chairman Wilbur Mills forced Hebert to accept Schroeder on the Armed Services Committee because of pressure from Mills' own wife. Hebert resented this

73. Hebert, *Titans*, 324.
74. *Congressional Quarterly Weekly Report*, February 14, 1964, 334-335.
75. *Congressional Quarterly Weekly Report*, July 3, 1964, 1414-1415.
76. *Congressional Quarterly Weekly Report*, July 16, 1965, 1402-1403.
77. *Congressional Quarterly Weekly Report*, August 6, 1965, 1588-1589.
78. Hebert, *Titans*, 325.

infringement of his autonomy as a chairman. Typically, he could reject members for the Committee as other chairmen did.[79]

Hebert became embroiled in another serious controversy concerning minorities late in his career. Ronald Dellums, a Black Democrat from California, was first elected to the House for the Ninety-second Congress (1971-1972). He attempted to gain a seat on the Armed Services Committee, and the Congressional Black Caucus (CBC) assisted him. At first, the Committee on Committees rejected his request. Hebert contacted each person on the Committee on Committees to express his opposition to the prospect of Dellums' assignment to the Armed Services Committee. He claimed that Dellums was a radical and a security risk. Dellums learned about Hebert's actions from Jim Corman, California's zone representative who had submitted Dellums' request. A meeting was arranged involving Dellums, Speaker Carl Albert, two other members of the CBC, Tip O'Neill, and Wilbur Mills. Albert agreed to help arrange Dellums' assignment to the Armed Services Committee.[80]

The encounters of Schroeder and Dellums with Hebert were tense. Dellums wrote that when the Committee met to organize in 1973, Hebert arranged the room in order to leave only one chair available to Dellums and Schroeder. They both sat on the single chair during the Committee's organizational meeting as a way to deflect Hebert's insult. They both had their

---

79. Pat Schroeder, *24 Years of House Work...and the Place is Still a Mess: My Life in Politics* (Kansas City: Andrews McMeel Publishing, 1998), 40-41.

80. Ronald V. Dellums and H. Lee Halterman, *Lying Down with the Lions: A Public Life from the Streets of Oakland to the Halls of Power* (Boston: Beacon Press, 2000), 99-103.

own chairs at the next Committee meeting.[81] Schroeder wrote that she and Hebert disagreed often, and he disliked her willingness to oppose him on military issues. She believed that he made the Committee a rubberstamp for the military's requests. In her opinion, "He was an ego run amok. He had long ago lost all sense of the Armed Services Committee as a democratically run body."[82] Schroeder recalled that Hebert controlled all of the Armed Services staff. The staff was loyal to him and worked in cooperation with him, and the Committee members accepted the decisions and direction of Hebert and the staff. Schroeder said that, "No one asked questions or no one ever challenged," and that, "There was exactly no open debate about anything." Other Armed Services members, even those agreeing with Hebert, were intimidated by him and acquiesced in his actions. They were concerned about retaliation if they offended him. Schroeder said that, "Everybody was terrified of him."[83]

Hebert's conflicts with Schroeder received widespread attention through a *Redbook* article in 1973. In the summer of 1973, Albert chose Schroeder to attend the SALT Disarmament Conference in Geneva, Switzerland. Hebert was asked to file a pro forma letter of confirmation but refused because he did not pick her or want her to attend. Hebert admitted that his actions were retaliation against her on account of her voting record on military issues and her criticism of a recent defense bill Hebert supported. He even told her that he would not want her to represent his Committee at a dogfight. Albert arranged for

---

81. Dellums, *Lying Down*, 149-151.
82. Schroeder, *House Work*, 42-43.

Schroeder to attend despite the absence of Hebert's confirmation.[84]

Hebert's ideology and policies, although consistent with many Americans' beliefs, ran contrary to several trends in the Democratic Party and the nation in the 1970s. Hebert was consistently conservative in a Party that showed a growing liberal orientation. The turmoil over the Vietnam War naturally placed great scrutiny on Hebert due to his role in the Armed Service Committee and his focus on national security issues. Hebert's hawkish ideas made him an easily identifiable target for criticism and perhaps even a scapegoat for the frustrations that many people had from the entire experience with Vietnam. Hebert's treatment of women and minorities was offensive to a nation that was trying to correct its past failures and to embrace fairness and equality. Hebert appeared as an inflammatory figure with too much power due to his chairmanship.

83. Pat Schroeder, interview by author, March 27, 2000, telephone tape recording, T. Harry Williams Center for Oral History, Louisiana State University, Baton Rouge, LA.

84. Judith Viorst, "Congresswoman Pat Schroeder: The Woman Who Has a Bear by the Tail," *Redbook*, November 1973, 178.

Chapter 5 - The Stirrings of Reform

While the Bipartisan House System and chairmen such as Patman, Poage, and Hebert dominated, a Congressional reform movement emerged that sought to fundamentally alter the House. From the late 1950s through the middle of the 1970s, the Congressional reform movement implemented gradual and incremental reforms of the House and alternated between directly challenging the House Democratic Leadership and seeking its support for reform. The Democratic Study Group (DSG), a liberal-oriented organization, became the driving force in the Congressional reform movement, and a collection of DSG members were frequently and deeply involved in reform activities throughout the era. Despite the connection, the Congressional reform movement and the DSG were not synonymous. Meanwhile, Richard Bolling articulated the criticisms of many liberals and reformers and proposed plans for reform. In addition, the Congressional reform movement received critical assistance from Carl Albert, a rising member of the House Democratic Leadership.

The DSG's origins lay in the failure of House liberals to implement their goals in the Bipartisan House System of the 1950s. In the Eighty-fifth Congress (1957-1958), liberals drew up a legislative program called the "Liberal Manifesto" and presented it in 1957 with the endorsement of eighty House Democrats.[1] The program was entered into the *Congressional Record*. It was an alternative to the President's State of the Union and budget messages and covered several policy

---

1. "Democratic Study Group Shifts Role in 91st Congress,"
Congressional Quarterly Weekly Report, October 10, 1969, 1940-1945.

issues.[2] Efforts to implement the program failed in 1957 and 1958. In 1958, Democrats gained forty-eight House seats, and many of these freshmen were liberals. Efforts to implement liberal goals still failed in 1959 in the new Eighty-sixth Congress.[3]

The House liberals eventually counterattacked. In the autumn of 1959, a bloc of Democrats from the North, the West, and the Midwest became frustrated with the first session of the Eighty-sixth Congress. Despite a Democratic majority in the House (283 to 153), they believed that a "well-disciplined Dixiecrat-Republican coalition" stymied "progressive legislation."[4] John Blatnik of Minnesota and several others (Chet Bowles of Connecticut, Lee Metcalf of Montana, Henry Reuss, George Rhodes of Pennsylvania, Frank Thompson, and B. F. "Bernie" Sisk of California) issued a letter on September 8, 1959 inviting their Democratic colleagues to a meeting on September 9 at 10:00 a.m. in the House Judiciary Committee Room. The letter stated that this meeting was a successor to earlier meetings of Northern and Western Democrats. The meeting would address "how we can attain the legislative aims of our Democratic Party."[5]

---

2. *Proposed Program for the Democrats in the House of Representatives in the 85th Congress*, 85th Cong., 1st sess., *Congressional Record* 103 (January 30, 1957): 1324-1326.

3. "Democratic Study Group Shifts Role in 91st Congress," *Congressional Quarterly Weekly Report*, October 10, 1969, 1940-1945.

4. Flier entitled "Democratic Study Group," Folder 5, Container 30, Richard W. Bolling Collection, Dr. Kenneth J. LaBudde Department of Special Collections, Miller Nichols Library, University of Missouri-Kansas City, Kansas City, MO.

5. John A. Blatnik, et. al. to "Democratic Colleague," September 8, 1959, Folder: 1959 Congressman VII, Box SRH 3R 479, Rayburn Papers.

The DSG was created. Later, a letter, signed by Lee Metcalf (Temporary Chairman of the DSG), elaborated upon the recent efforts. The letter stated that Democrats had been criticized for failing to better implement the legislative program proposed in the Democratic Platform, and "a breakdown of communication" had been a factor in impeding the implementation of the legislative program. A group of members concluded that an organization for discussion of legislation and issues was necessary. They conducted meetings and created the Democratic Study Group. Over 70 members attended at least one of these meetings. These members (the DSG) set up a whip organization and elected a steering committee. The letter added that more organizational work would be done, and the organizational work would be formalized at a future meeting. Anyone interested in joining was asked to complete the attached form and return it to Lee Metcalf.[6]

The DSG quickly became a powerful bloc and altered the balance of power in the House. By January 1960, over 120 Democrats from thirty-four states had joined, and the DSG claimed success in 1960. In 1959, the liberal bloc in the House had experienced ten losses in eleven efforts on critical roll call votes. In 1960, the DSG defeated the conservative Democrat-Republican coalition on twelve of nineteen critical roll call votes. The DSG helped pass significant pieces of legislation and employed parliamentary maneuvers to avoid the Rules Committee. The DSG defined itself as "a political force to balance the conservative coalition" and described its creation as representing "the first real effort in modern Congressional history by progressive Democratic Members to function as a

---

6. Metcalf to "Fellow Democrat," September 12, 1959, Folder: 1959 Congressman VII, Box SRH 3R 479, Rayburn Papers.

unit on a broad range of issues."[7] Albert described the House Democrats in the late 1950s and early 1960s. The DSG quickly became a major bloc and wanted to support the House Democratic Leadership. In contrast, the Southerners were more status-quo oriented. The House Democratic Leadership stood between these two blocs.[8]

The DSG By-Laws revealed the basic goal and structure of the organization. As amended in March 1965, the By-Laws stated in its preamble that, "A number of Democratic Members of the House of Representatives desires to more effectively support the Leadership efforts to enact the Johnson-Humphrey Administration's legislative proposals, and," then stated, "These Members believe there is a need for a common effort in research and analysis of legislative proposals and a further need for improved communication and coordination of the Democratic Members' activities in support of the Leadership's efforts to enact the Administration's legislative proposals." Regarding structure, the DSG had a Chairman, a Vice-Chairman at large, and a Secretary chosen by secret ballot who served two-year terms in accord with each Congress. A regional Vice-Chairman was elected from each of the six regions by the members of that region. The six regional Vice-Chairmen served two-year terms in accord with each Congress. The Chairman presided at DSG meetings and meetings of the Executive Committee. The Chairman appointed additional ad hoc subcommittees as needed and two standing subcommittees for program responsibility and research direction. The Secretary held responsibility for informing

---

7. Flier entitled "Democratic Study Group," Folder 5, Container 30, Bolling Collection.
8. Albert, *Giant*, 232-235.

members of DSG activities, maintaining the records of the DSG, and operating the DSG whip organization. The Chairman, Vice-Chairman at-large, Regional Vice-Chairmen, Secretary, and Chairmen of the Program and Research Subcommittees constituted the Executive Committee. Former DSG chairmen still serving in the House were also part of the Executive Committee. It held responsibility for "implementing policy decisions of the DSG."[9]

The DSG quickly settled into a stable form and operating procedure. Its membership was generally large but fluctuated from Congress to Congress. The DSG had 180 members in the Eighty-ninth Congress (1965 and 1966) but fell to approximately 120 members in 1969. Most members were from the North or the West. Except for officers, the DSG did not release the names on any of its lists because some DSG members were Southerners who might face electoral problems if their DSG connection became known.[10] Despite a large membership, only a minority of DSG members actively participated in DSG activities. Other members just used the research services of the DSG. The DSG staff usually comprised approximately twelve people and performed the research services. Their salaries were paid from the office payrolls of DSG members who choose to contribute, and approximately eighty DSG members contributed.[11]

The DSG conducted many meetings. A DSG meeting notice, dated June 6, 1963, from John Blatnik (chairman) to

---

9. DSG By-Laws and cover letter, June 1, 1965, Folder 12, Container 40, Bolling Collection.

10. "Democratic Study Group Shifts Role in 91st Congress," *Congressional Quarterly Weekly Report*, October 10, 1969, 1940-1945.

11. "Democratic Study Group: A Winner on House Reforms," *Congressional Quarterly Weekly Report*, June 2, 1973, 1366-1371.

DSG members announced that Attorney General Robert Kennedy was scheduled to meet with the DSG on June 10 at 4:00 p.m. to discuss the civil rights issue. This meeting was a members-only meeting.[12] A meeting notice, dated June 13, 1969, announced that a meeting of the DSG Task Force on Reorganization and Reform was scheduled for 4:00 p.m. on June 18 in the office of Sam Gibbons of Florida, Room 430 Cannon. The members of the Task Force included Bolling, Thompson, and O'Hara.[13]

DSG internal documents revealed much about the organization's regular activities. In 1971, the DSG adopted a new format for its meetings as described in a DSG document. Meetings would be held on the day before the monthly meetings of the Caucus. Meetings would start at 4:30 p.m. and would be followed by a social period from 5:30 to 6:30 with important persons relevant to DSG activities. The monthly membership meetings would be limited to one hour or less. The refreshment bar would open at 4:30.[14] The DSG provided its research services through various publications such as "Fact Sheet," "Special Report," "Staff Bulletin," and "Record Vote Analysis." DSG legislative and research services were funded by DSG members who contributed staff support and paid $100 annual dues and by donations from non-members. A $100-a-plate Tenth Anniversary Dinner in 1969 raised $36,000 and provided much of the money from non-members for DSG legislative and research activities from 1969 to 1971. The DSG

---

12. "DSG Meeting Notice," June 6, 1963, Folder 5, Container 30, Bolling Collection.
13. "DSG Meeting Notice," June 13, 1969, Folder 4, Container 129, Bolling Collection.
14. Burton to DSG members, September 10, 1971, Folder 9, Container 132, Bolling Collection.

campaign services were funded solely through donations from non-members.[15]

An examination of a sample of DSG publications displayed the nature of DSG publications and research services. A DSG "Fact Sheet" from April 18, 1974 was 32 pages long and provided the facts, in an objective manner, on H Res 988, Committee Reform Amendments of 1974.[16] A DSG "Special Report" on the fiscal year 1975 budget examined in detail Nixon's fiscal year 1975 budget proposal and provided analysis of the budget's major points. This "Special Report" was dated May 24, 1974 and was 39 pages long. Typically, the "Special Report" publication addressed a salient issue in great detail.[17] The "DSG Staff Bulletin" was published weekly when Congress was in session in order to foster communication among the staffs of DSG members and to provide information to staff members. A "DSG Staff Bulletin" dated for the week of October 7, 1974 contained a diverse collection of facts and news regarding various issues being addressed by Congress. It had no central theme or topic. It was simply a collection of facts and was 4 pages long.[18] A "DSG Legislative Report" for the week of October 7, 1974 exemplified this publication and was 14 pages long. Its title page stated that this publication was

---

15. "DSG Activity Report," Folder: Mr. Patman's Committee Assignments (1929 to Present Time), Box 486A, Patman Papers.

16. "Fact Sheet," April 18, 1974, Folder: Leg: Special Issues-House Reform (1974-1977-1980) 123:21, Box 123, Gillis W. Long Papers, Hill Memorial Library, Louisiana State University, Baton Rouge, LA.

17. "Special Report," May 24, 1974, Folder: Personal: House Leadership Files-DSG Special Reports (1974) 33:3, Box 33, Long Papers.

18. "DSG Staff Bulletin," October 7, 1974, Folder: Personal: House Leadership Files-DSG Staff Bulletins (1974) 33:11, Box 33, Long Papers.

published weekly for DSG members. It supplied information on each bill scheduled for House action in the week in an objective manner and covered both major and minor bills.[19]

A "Campaign Activity Report" described the DSG's campaign activities in 1968. The DSG provided assistance to all DSG members and to over 150 non-incumbent Democratic House candidates. The DSG possessed a mailing list of almost 10,000 contributors. The DSG raised approximately $150,000 in 1968, its largest amount ever. Over $90,000 was collected by direct mail solicitations, and $60,000 was collected through large block contributions from groups and individuals. The DSG staff prepared various types of campaign materials. The DSG held a campaign workshop for candidates during the national convention and obtained lists of labor union members for direct mailing efforts.[20]

The DSG advanced liberal policies through the legislative process. Bolling wrote that at one time House liberals, overall as a bloc, were less effective at managing legislation's progress and passage than conservatives who were very effective.[21] Eventually, the DSG employed a tactic used by the conservatives in the legislative process: design a plan featuring assigned roles to members for specific actions. The DSG organized its own whip system to supplement the Democratic whip system on selected bills.[22] The DSG experienced success. For example, a "DSG Activity Report"

---

19. "DSG Legislative Report," October 7, 1974, Folder: Personal: House Leadership Files-DSG Legislative Reports (1974) 32:1, Box 32, Long Papers.

20. "Campaign Activity Report" and cover letter from Conlon to DSG Members, Folder 4, Container 129, Bolling Collection.

21. Bolling, *House Out of Order*, 53-54.

22. Bolling, *House Out of Order*, 54-56.

stated that the DSG conducted twenty "special efforts to amend or enact legislation" in the Ninety-first Congress (1969 and 1970). These "special efforts" included supplying research, organizing special briefings, assisting with parliamentary strategy, and establishing whip systems.[23]

Internal DSG documents relating to civil rights legislation in 1966 exemplified the work of the DSG in the legislative process. According to the minutes of the Executive Committee meeting from July 14, 1966, Chairman Thompson called the meeting to order at 4:14 p.m. Discussion was held on the Civil Rights Act of 1966 (HR 14765), and a strategy was crafted to advance the bill's passage that included meetings, packets analyzing the bill, and a whip count on the rule governing the bill. The meeting adjourned at 4:50 p.m.[24] Later, an announcement was distributed stating that Attorney General Nicholas Katzenbach and his staff would describe the Civil Rights Act of 1966 at 3:30 p.m. on July 20, 1966 in the Judiciary Committee hearing room (2141 Rayburn House Office Building). This briefing was open to DSG members only.[25] Another DSG letter, dated July 26, 1966, described DSG efforts on Title IV (housing section) of the Civil Rights Act of 1966 (HR 14765). The DSG would contact members through the DSG whip system on the morning of July 27 about members' position. The contact would be done by telephone between 10:00 a.m. and 11:00 a.m. and would pose two questions. The

---

23. "DSG Activity Report," Folder: Mr. Patman's Committee Assignments (1929 to Present Time), Box 486A, Patman Papers.

24. Udall to Members, DSG Executive Committee, July 15, 1966, Folder 2, Container 42, Bolling Collection.

25. Brademas to Members, July 18, 1966, Folder 2, Container 42, Bolling Collection.

letter also instructed members on strategy for maintaining a quorum when debate occurred on the bill on the floor.[26]

Democrat Richard Bolling of Missouri exercised a critical role in the Congressional reform movement and had connections to the DSG. Richard Walker Bolling was born in New York, New York in 1916 and graduated with a B.A. in 1937 and an M.A. in 1939 from the University of the South in Sewanee, Tennessee. He worked as an educational administrator before serving in the U. S. Army in World War II. He rose to the rank of lieutenant colonel and won a Bronze Star. After the war, he worked as a veterans' advisor at the University of Kansas City. He was elected as a Democrat to the Eighty-first Congress (1949 and 1950).[27] By the mid-1970s, Bolling represented the Fifth District of Missouri which included parts of the Kansas City metropolitan area.[28] Carl Albert wrote that Bolling ranked as one of Rayburn's proteges and regularly attended the Board of Education.[29] Jim Wright wrote that, "Bolling was intellectually gifted, generally respected by the press, ambitious for advancement, but a bit standoffish from rank-and-file members."[30]

Bolling wrote two books in the 1960s that described the House. *House Out of Order* was published in 1965, and *Power in the House* was published in 1968. Overall, they both articulated the criticisms of many liberals and reformers and proposed plans for Congressional reform. These plans advocated a centralized system of management based on

---

26. Thompson to DSG Members, July 26, 1966, Folder 2, Container 42, Bolling Collection.
27. Nystrom, *Biographical Directory*, 639-640.
28. Brownson, *1975 Staff Directory*, 61.
29. Albert, *Giant*, 233-234.
30. Wright, *Balance of Power*, 189.

strong party authority. The DSG and the Congressional reform movement advanced and implemented these reform plans.

In *House Out of Order*, Bolling discussed the House and the need for reform in the context of the larger national interest. He argued that a reform of the House was necessary. The nation faced domestic economic problems, the rise of a stronger presidency, and global conflict. For the U. S. to succeed in the global fight against communism, the Congress needed to present an example to the world of the benefits of representative assemblies for the people's interests. Communists argued that assemblies were oppressive and favored plutocracy. Congress had to become more effective: "It is imperative that our Congress be an example to the world; tyranny cannot flourish where there are responsible and effective parliaments."[31]

Bolling identified specific problems. According to him, the majority of House Democrats were largely "moderate to progressive." Yet, they allowed the seniority system to dominate, and conservative Democrats (a minority of the Party) exercised great power through committee chairmanships: "This minority wing subverts the objectives and defies the spirit of the Democratic party as a whole."[32] He stressed that the committee chairmen were typically Southerners from rural-oriented districts who easily won reelection and served for long periods of time. The Democratic urban machines acted in a similar fashion and also reelected the same people with little or no opposition. Members of both the Southern bloc and the urban

31. Bolling, *House Out of Order*, 12-13.
32. Bolling, *House Out of Order*, 237.

machines sometimes cooperated to stymie progressive legislation.[33]

To remedy these problems, Bolling proposed a plan for Congressional reform that would fundamentally alter the seniority system and the autonomy of the committee chairmen. Leadership elections would be the first action of the Caucus. The nominee for Speaker (or Minority Leader depending on which party had the majority) would possess the power to nominate to the Caucus all Democratic members of the Ways and Means Committee and its chairman (or ranking minority member depending on which party had the majority) and all Democratic members of the Rules Committee and its chairman (or ranking minority member depending on which party had the majority). The Caucus could confirm or reject by majority vote any or all of these nominees. If a nominee was rejected, the Speaker/Minority Leader would make new nominations as required. After the confirmation of the Democratic members of the Ways and Means Committee, the Caucus would order them to serve as the Committee on Committees and make nominations for the Democratic seats for all other standing committees. These nominations would be submitted to the Caucus to be confirmed or rejected by majority vote. If a nomination was rejected, more nominations would be made by the Committee on Committees. The Speaker/Minority Leader would nominate the chairman/ranking minority member of each standing committee. If a nominee was rejected, the Speaker/Minority Leader would make more nominations as needed.[34] He argued that the reform plan would only modify the seniority system because seniority would still be the means of

---

33. Bolling, *House Out of Order*, 37-38.
34. Bolling, *House Out of Order*, 239-240.

selecting most committee members. The nomination/election procedure would act as a deterrent to a member who opposed the Party.[35]

Bolling's *Power in the House* reiterated the themes expressed in the first book. Bolling argued that the House failed in the exercise of its political authority as delegated to it by the American system of government; it was more ineffective than any other branch of the federal government.[36] Reform of Congress depended upon changing the leadership and committee system of the Democratic Party. The majority of House Democrats were "moderate to progressive." The committee chairmen were, at least many of them, conservative. The committee chairmen worked with the Republicans to oppose the more liberal policies of the majority of Democratic members. The conservative Democrats kept control through the Democrats' Committee on Committees which controlled committee assignments. Bolling argued that reforms of the Caucus were necessary to ensure that members of the Democratic majority controlled the committees. In addition, the Caucus needed to award the Speaker greater authority.[37] The rigid adherence to the seniority system helped create the problem: "Intact seniority is usually a product of a safe district-- more bluntly, a politically noncompetitive and politically backwater district. Democratic members representing such districts, mostly in Southern states, are not in sympathy with the majority views of their party."[38]

---

35. Bolling, *House Out of Order*, 241.
36. Bolling, *Power in the House*, 15-16.
37. Bolling, *Power in the House*, 265.
38. Bolling, *Power in the House,* 43.

Bolling again presented a plan for reform. The Speaker/Minority Leader selected by the Caucus would make nominations for the Democratic seats on the Ways and Means Committee and its chairman/ranking minority member and the Democratic seats on the Rules Committee and its chairman/ranking minority member. The Caucus would have to ratify these nominations with a majority vote, and nominations from the floor would not be permitted. If a nomination was rejected by a majority vote, the Speaker/Minority Leader would have to make another nomination, and the Caucus would have to vote again until the position was filled. The Democrats of the Ways and Means Committee would serve as the Committee on Committees. At a later Caucus, they would make nominations for Democratic seats on other committees. A majority vote for confirmation would be required. If the Caucus rejected a nominee, the nomination/election procedure would continue. The Speaker/Minority Leader would nominate members for the chairman/ranking minority member position for each standing committee. If rejected, the Speaker/Minority Leader and the Caucus would continue the nomination/election procedure until all positions were filled.[39]

The reform plan would have great ramifications. Bolling argued that seniority would still act as a determinant in making committee assignments, and the nomination/election procedure would serve as a deterrent to voting against the party majority. The Speaker's nomination power would strengthen his control over legislation and place more responsibility on him, but there would be no changes designed to coerce members on roll call votes. The Democratic majority could have its programs and

---

39. Bolling, *Power in the House*, 267-269.

policies considered by the House without obstruction from opponents.[40]

Tom Foley described DSG strategy. Foley wrote that attempts for Congressional reform in the 1950s failed because they were too ambitious; they were "too much, too fast." The DSG employed a strategy for gradual and incremental reform beginning in the middle of the 1960s, and this strategy was successful. Foley wrote that reformers advanced, in each Congress, "a few, well-chosen, well-organized, well-researched, and well-prepared reforms" which the House would accept. Much of the planning for Congressional reform was "done informally at the DSG office." There was a group of reform activists that included Phillip Burton of California, executive director Dick Conlon, James O'Hara of Michigan, Don Fraser of Minnesota, Abner Mikva of Illinois, and Foley. They discussed reform and strategy for it. There were a lot of senior Democrats, such as Carl Albert and Tip O'Neill, who were very suspicious of Phillip Burton.[41]

Many of the efforts of the Congressional reform movement focused on the seniority system and the autonomy of committee chairmen, and in late 1964, the DSG prepared for an attack on the seniority system and the autonomy of the committee chairmen. On October 2, 1964, John Blatnik addressed the House on behalf of himself and a collection of House Democrats and inserted a statement into the *Congressional Record* entitled "Joint Statement on Democratic Unity--1964 Election." The "Statement" declared that all members and candidates running on the Democratic ticket should support the Johnson-Humphrey ticket and the

---

40. Bolling, *Power in the House*, 267-269.
41. Biggs, *Honor in the House*, 53-54.

Democratic platform. The signatories of the "Statement" would oppose the seating in the Democratic Caucus of any current member or candidate elected to the House on the Democratic ticket who worked for the election of presidential or vice-presidential candidates other than Johnson and Humphrey. This warning also applied to anyone who supported unpledged or independent slates of electors for president and vice-president.[42]

On December 3, the DSG held a meeting on House reform and party dissidents. DSG Secretary Frank Thompson on December 4 sent a letter to DSG members and Democratic representatives-elect identifying proposals supported by members attending the December 3 meeting. The proposals included punishment of two Democratic House members for supporting Republican Barry Goldwater for president, a requirement for Caucus approval for each slate of Democratic committee assignments proposed by the Committee on Committees, creation of a Democratic leadership panel, and creation of a Joint Committee on Congressional Reorganization. The letter also announced that there would be a meeting of the DSG and interested representatives-elect on January 2 prior to the meeting of the Democratic Caucus.[43]

Later, the Democrats took action. The Democratic Caucus voted 157-115 to censure Democrats John Bell Williams of Mississippi and Albert W. Watson of South Carolina for publicly supporting Goldwater. The Caucus stripped them of their seniority, but the proposal to deny them a seat in the

---

42. *Joint Statement on Democratic Party Unity--1964 Election,* 88th Cong., 2nd sess., *Congressional Record* 110 (October 2, 1964): 23759.
43. "DSG Strategy Meeting," *Congressional Quarterly Weekly Report,* December 11, 1964, 2793.

Caucus never actually emerged. Williams had earlier been the second-ranking Democrat on the Interstate and Foreign Commerce Committee and the fifth-ranking Democrat on the District of Columbia Committee. He now became the lowest-ranking Democrat on both Committees. Watson had earlier been a low-ranking member of the Post Office and Civil Service Committee; he now became the lowest-ranking Democrat on his Committee.[44]

The Congressional reform movement struck at the seniority system and the autonomy of the committee chairmen through the case of Adam Clayton Powell of New York, chairman of the Education and Labor Committee, but the issues concerning his case posed complications. He was a Black man, and his case reached its most critical phase during an era of significant racial discord, the 1960s. Powell's case involved scandalous behavior unrelated to the seniority system and the autonomy of the committee chairmen. Therefore, the actions against Powell did not necessarily represent a great victory for Congressional reform but showed that action could be taken against committee chairmen in extreme circumstances.

Powell's case involved scandalous behavior over several years. In 1956, Powell publicly endorsed Republican Dwight Eisenhower for president but ran for reelection as a Democrat. Attempts to deprive him of his seniority were abandoned. In May 1958, a federal grand jury indicted him on three counts of tax evasion. Two of the counts were dismissed, and a trial in 1960 on the third count resulted in a hung jury. The case was dismissed in 1961, but in 1966, Powell and the federal

---

44. "House Mavericks Disciplined; New Rules Approved," *Congressional Quarterly Weekly Report*, January 8, 1965, 33, 35.

authorities agreed to a settlement for back taxes for 1949-1955. He paid a total of $27,833.17, and the federal authorities agreed to withdraw other charges against him. Powell displayed extreme absenteeism from his work in Congress and House roll call votes. His estranged wife was listed on his House office payroll; she lived in Puerto Rico while on the payroll. Powell deposited her checks into his account. A New York state court found him guilty of libel in 1963 and ordered him to make a financial restitution to a woman he called a "bag woman" (graft collector) for the New York City police in a television interview.[45] Eventually, a New York State Supreme Court Justice issued an arrest warrant for Powell based on a thirty-day contempt-of-court sentence. This warrant stemmed from his efforts to avoid paying $164,000 for defamation of character. The new warrant overrode Powell's Congressional immunity because it could be enforced anytime, even on Sundays. Three previous arrest orders had been issued against him in civil contempt cases.[46]

The House eventually took a series of incremental actions against Powell. On September 22, 1966, the House Education and Labor Committee voted 27-1 to establish new rules for the Committee. Frank Thompson played a major role in the action which reduced the authority of the committee chair. Previously, Powell used his authority as chairman to delay progress on an anti-poverty bill, and members of the Committee claimed that he unfairly dismissed Committee staff

---

45. "Controversy Marks Career of Harlem Representative," *Congressional Quarterly Weekly Report*, September 23, 1966, 2222-2224.

46. "Powell Fugitive Status," *Congressional Quarterly Weekly Report*, December 2, 1966, 2928.

members.[47] The House Administration Committee on January 3, 1967 issued a report on Powell stating that he and members of his Committee staff engaged in misuse of travel and payroll money.[48] On January 9, 1967, the Democratic Caucus removed him as chairman of the Education and Labor Committee for the duration of the Ninetieth Congress on a voice vote. Morris Udall offered the resolution for the removal. In addition, the House on January 10 voted 363-65 to deny Powell his seat, pending an investigation.[49] The House on March 1, 1967 passed a resolution to exclude him from the House in the Ninetieth Congress by a vote of 307-116.[50] Time passed, but Powell continued to win reelection. On January 3, 1969, the House swore in Powell but also, on a vote of 254-158, passed a resolution imposing a $25,000 fine on him and stripping him of his seniority. This fine was intended to partially recover approximately $40,000 in Congressional funds misused by Powell.[51]

With the coming of the Ninety-first Congress (1969 and 1970), the Congressional reform movement escalated its efforts. After the election of Republican Richard Nixon as president in 1968, the DSG faced the challenge of advancing liberal policies without the presidential influence of John

---

47. "House Committee Votes to Reduce Powell's Authority," *Congressional Quarterly Weekly Report*, September 23, 1966, 2213-2215.

48. "Few Precedents Guide House in Powell Affair," *Congressional Quarterly Weekly Report*, January 6, 1967, 25-27.

49. "Powell Loses Chairmanship; Seat in Doubt," *Congressional Quarterly Weekly Report*, January 13, 1967, 47-50, 82.

50. "House Refuses to Seat Powell," *Congressional Quarterly Weekly Report*, March 3, 1967, 291-293.

51. "Powell is Seated, Fined $25,000, Stripped of Seniority," *Congressional Quarterly Weekly Report*, January 10, 1969, 58-59.

Kennedy and Lyndon Johnson. A group of DSG activists met in the office of the DSG chairman, James O'Hara, and discussed potential reforms. The group included Richard Conlon (DSG Staff Director), Don Fraser, Phillip Burton, Frank Thompson, John Brademas of Indiana, Morris Udall, Henry Reuss, and Richard Bolling. Fraser suggested attacking the seniority system, but they realized, after gathering intelligence, that it would be difficult to attack the seniority system because it was entrenched. Instead, O'Hara suggested strengthening the Caucus.[52]

DSG activists pursued reform on several fronts in late 1968 and early 1969. John McCormack served as Speaker of the House in the late 1960s and represented the Bipartisan House System, and Morris Udall, a liberal and a reformer, struck at McCormack and the existing System. In a letter to his Democratic colleagues on December 26, 1968, Udall announced that on January 2 he would be nominated in the Democratic Caucus for Speaker but that he was not the candidate of any group of House members. Udall argued that the Democratic Party faced serious challenges. Traditional party identification and loyalties were changing in every region of the U. S., and the Republicans were seeking "traditional Democratic voters" and young voters. He believed that, for the Democratic Party, "there is an overriding need for new directions and new leadership." Udall identified some changes that he would seek if elected, and they included improved communication between the House Democratic Leadership and

---

52. Mary Russell, "Revolt on Capitol Hill," *Washington Post*, February 4, 1975, A3.

rank-and-file members through increased use of the Caucus and additional meetings between the Speaker and members.[53]

In January 1969, Congress convened. On January 2, House Democrats renominated McCormack over Udall for Speaker by a vote of 178-58 and unanimously reelected Carl Albert as Majority Leader. In addition, the Democratic Caucus passed a proposal for monthly Caucus meetings sponsored by liberals and endorsed by McCormack.[54] Previously, the Caucus typically met every two years to confirm committee assignments and leadership positions.[55] The seniority system again received attention. The Democratic Caucus on January 29 voted 101-73 to strip John R. Rarick of Louisiana of his seniority on the Agriculture Committee for supporting the third-party presidential candidacy of George Wallace in 1968. He was the lowest-ranked Democrat on the Committee in the Ninetieth Congress but could have been higher than freshmen Democrats newly appointed to the Committee.[56]

Opposition to McCormack may still have been small but was intense as seen in an incident in December 1969 described by Carl Albert. McCormack met with Democrats who sat on the Education and Labor Committee. These members were upset over McCormack's management of an antipoverty bill. McCormack urged them to be patient. One of the members, age 37, said that he was not interested in what McCormack did prior to his birth. McCormack remained calm and ended the

---

53. Udall to "Democratic Colleague" and cover letter, December 26, 1968, Folder 2, Container 129, Bolling Collection.

54. "91st Congress Convenes," *Congressional Quarterly Weekly Report*, January 3, 1969, 2.

55. Albert, *Giant*, 311.

56. "Rarick Seniority," *Congressional Quarterly Weekly Report*, January 31, 1969, 203.

meeting by stating that some of these members wanted to run the House. Frank Thompson replied that some of them did want to run the House.[57]

Meanwhile, the DSG worked to exploit the emerging opportunities and circumstances. In January 1969, the DSG announced that it embarked on a "two-pronged program to promote reform and modernization in the House of Representatives and to further liberal Democratic ideals and policies." The DSG would work for reform and modernization through the Democratic Caucus. In addition, the DSG would create Task Forces to help craft Democratic alternatives to Republican ideas and policies, protect important programs, maintain focus and effort on critical issues, and provide younger members greater involvement.[58]

The DSG's goal of reform and modernization through the Caucus was expressed in a DSG "Special Report" from February 25, 1970 entitled "The Seniority System in the U. S. House of Representatives." The document examined the background of the seniority system and prospects for reform. The document explained that the Democratic Caucus could not exert influence or oversight over the chair selection process for many years due to the current rules. A single resolution contained all Democratic committee assignments and included the chair nominations by the Committee on Committees, and the Caucus essentially could not judge chairs, "Thus even with caucus review, what exists, for all practical purposes is an automatic system where seniority is sovereign and inviolate in the selection of committee chairmen." Regarding reform

---

57. Albert, *Giant*, 310.
58. DSG Press Release, January 14, 1969, Folder 4, Container 129, Bolling Collection.

possibilities, the document stated that the core intent of all the reform proposals was "not to eliminate the seniority system but to assure that committee chairmen will be responsive to their party caucus and the leadership regardless of how they are selected." One proposal called for creation of a new committee to nominate chairmen and a requirement for majority approval from the Caucus.[59]

The House pursued reform through another means, and this experience revealed the obstacles to and the limits on reform. On February 18, 1970, the Democratic Caucus considered a resolution authorizing a study of the seniority system and the committee system, but Democrats supportive of seniority used obstructionist tactics to delay consideration of the resolution. The caucus postponed consideration of the resolution until the March 18 caucus. The resolution was proposed by members of the DSG.[60] On March 18, the Democratic Caucus passed, by a nearly unanimous voice vote, a resolution offered by Majority Leader Albert calling for a study of the seniority system by a representative committee of eleven members. On a vote of 110 to 46, the Caucus passed an amendment stating that the committee present its report no later than the first Democratic Caucus meeting of 1971. The Albert resolution was drafted on March 17 by Albert and McCormack as a compromise to please senior members.[61] On

59. "The Seniority System in the U.S. House of Representatives," February 25, 1970, Folder 25, Box 55, Henry S. Reuss Papers, 1839-1982, Milwaukee Manuscript Collection 112, Wisconsin Historical Society Milwaukee Area Research Center, Golda Meir Library, University of Wisconsin-Milwaukee, Milwaukee, WI.
60. "House Liberals Plan Strategy for Seniority Challenge," *Congressional Quarterly Weekly Report*, February 27, 1970, 642-643.
61. "House Seniority Study," *Congressional Quarterly Weekly Report*, March 20, 1970, 783.

March 26, eleven House Democrats were appointed to the committee to study the seniority system: Julia Butler Hansen of Washington (chair), Edward Jones of Tennessee, Olin Teague of Texas, Frank Annunzio of Illinois, Phil Burton of California, Shirley Chisholm of New York, Wayne Hays of Ohio, Phil Landrum of Georgia, James O'Hara of Michigan, Neal Smith of Iowa, and Frank Thompson of New Jersey.[62] This committee became known as the Hansen Committee. Albert recalled his role in the Hansen Committee. In the Caucus, Albert spoke for authorizing the Hansen Committee to review the seniority system, and the seniority system was included in the Hansen Committee's jurisdiction despite the opposition of Southern chairs. Albert and Hansen picked the Committee's members.[63]

The Hansen Committee challenged the status quo. A draft of a letter from Patman to Hansen, responding to Hansen's inquiry into opinions on seniority, revealed Patman's opinion regarding the seniority system: "there is no need for any drastic changes in the present system. The alternative suggestions that have come to my attention would create more problems than they solve." Under the seniority system, Patman said Congress "has done a remarkably fine job."[64]

The start of each new Congress brought opportunities for the Congressional reform movement, and the Ninety-second Congress convened in 1971. Henry Reuss and Charles A. Vanik of Ohio issued a statement in June 1970 that stated that candidates for Speaker and Majority Leader needed to express their positions on reform issues, and the issues specifically

---

62. "House Seniority Study," *Congressional Quarterly Weekly Report*, April 3, 1970, 920.
63. Albert, *Giant*, 312.

identified were the selection of committee chairmen, the number of recorded votes, the authority of committee chairmen, and the secret committee sessions.[65] When Congress convened, the Democrats chose Carl Albert for Speaker over John Conyers of Michigan by a vote of 220-20. Conyers ran as a protest against Albert for not supporting an effort to strip Mississippi Democrats of their seniority. Earlier, Conyers challenged the seniority of the Democratic Mississippi members and claimed that they refused to run on the Democratic ticket recognized by the national party but instead ran on an all-White ticket. House Democrats rejected Conyer's challenge, 111-55. In addition, the House Democrats chose Hale Boggs for Majority Leader over four other candidates. On the second ballot, Boggs won 140 votes while Morris Udall won 88 votes and B. F. Sisk won 17 votes. James O'Hara and Wayne Hays withdrew after the first ballot. Liberal reformers were disappointed by the low vote totals for Udall and O'Hara.[66] In addition, Thomas P. "Tip" O'Neill was appointed by Albert and Boggs on January 3 as Majority Whip. O'Neill supported Boggs for Majority Leader.[67]

Carl Albert of Oklahoma rose to power under the Bipartisan House System but greatly advanced the Congressional reform movement which ultimately ended the Bipartisan House System. Carl Bert Albert was born in 1908 in

---

64. Draft of letter from Patman to Hansen, Folder: GD 762, Box 162B, Patman Papers.

65. Reuss and Vanik statement, June 4, 1970, Folder 13, Container 130, Bolling Collection.

66. "The House: New Leaders of Democratic Majority," *Congressional Quarterly Weekly Report*, January 22, 1971, 176, 177, 179.

67. "New House Democratic Whip: Friends in All Factions," *Congressional Quarterly Weekly Report*, January 29, 1971, 259.

North McAlester, Pittsburg County in Oklahoma. He graduated from the University of Oklahoma at Norman in 1931, won a Rhodes Scholarship, and graduated from Oxford in 1934. He practiced law in McAlester, Oklahoma. During World War II, he served in the U. S. Army, rose to the rank of lieutenant colonel, and won a Bronze Star. He returned to the practice of law and won election to the Eightieth Congress (1947 and 1948). He rose in the House and served as Majority Whip and as Majority Leader before becoming Speaker.[68] By the middle of the 1970s, Albert represented the Third District of Oklahoma located in the southern portion of the state.[69] He considered himself a liaison between the House Democratic Leadership and younger reformers in the 1960s.[70] Wright credited Albert with great advancements in House reform: "Speaker Carl Albert has received too little credit for his bold initiatives to democratize House procedure. Under his leadership in the early 1970s, Congress became more open and operationally more democratic."[71]

The House Democrats made incremental reforms regarding the seniority system and the autonomy of the committee chairmen in 1971. On January 20, House Democrats made reforms in the seniority system proposed by the Hansen Committee (formally known as the Committee on Organization, Study, and Review). The Democratic Committee on Committees received the authority to make recommendations for the chairmanship and membership of each committee to the Caucus, and the recommendations

---

68. Nystrom, *Biographical Directory*, 517.
69. Brownson, *1975 Staff Directory*, 88.
70. Albert, *Giant*, 311.
71. Wright, *Balance of Power*, 188.

would not have to follow seniority. The Committee on Committees would make recommendations one committee at a time. With the demand of ten members or more, nominations could be debated and subjected to a vote, and if a nomination was rejected, the Committee on Committees would make another nomination.[72]

The House Democrats also wrestled with a challenge to John L. McMillan of South Carolina, the chairman of the District of Columbia Committee. McMillan was 72 years old and had been the chair for twenty-two years; he was criticized for being unresponsive to D. C.'s needs. On February 3, 1971, House Democrats voted 126-96 to retain McMillan as chairman of the District of Columbia Committee. On February 4, the full House voted 258-32 to defeat an effort by some liberals to remove him as chairman during the full House's confirmation process for committee assignments. One hundred members did not vote, and forty-two members voted present. This vote was a procedural vote preliminary to a vote on committee assignments. House liberals divided on the McMillan issue because of concern that it could inspire conservative Democrat-Republican efforts to remove liberal chairmen.[73]

The Ninety-third Congress, which convened in 1973, brought significant changes. A plane carrying Hale Boggs disappeared over Alaska in 1972; his body was never found. For the House Democratic Leadership, Albert won nomination for Speaker over John Conyers by a vote of 202-25. Tip O'Neill won election as Majority Leader without opposition. The

---

72. "The House: New Leaders of Democratic Majority," *Congressional Quarterly Weekly Report*, January 22, 1971, 176, 177, 179.
73. "House Seniority Vote: 258 to 32 for Status Quo," *Congressional Quarterly Weekly Report*, February 12, 1971, 365.

Democrats debated and voted on whether or not to change the Whip position from appointed to elected. Liberals favored election, but conservatives favored appointment. The vote was 123-114 for appointment.[74]

Meanwhile, the Congressional reform movement achieved reforms regarding the seniority system and the autonomy of the committee chairmen that fundamentally altered the House. The Hansen Committee proposed an automatic vote on each chair but failed to specify a secret ballot. The Democratic Caucus passed a reform, 204-9, for an automatic vote on each chairman position, but the proposal failed to specify a secret ballot. O'Neill proposed that the votes use the secret ballot upon the demand of 20% of the Caucus; this proposal passed, 117-58. The Caucus chose the chairmen in the new manner. Benjamin S. Rosenthal of New York challenged Chet Holifield of California for the Government Operations Committee Chairmanship, but the challenge failed, 172-46. No other chairmen faced organized challenges. All returning chairmen, and all persons in line to become chairmen due to vacancies and seniority, won election to chairman positions. There were no close contests, but the votes revealed varying levels of small opposition as seen in the following examples: Poage, 169-48; Mahon, 190-19; Hebert, 154-41; Patman, 155-40; Wayne Hays (House Administration), 117-39; Teague, 156-9; and Mills, 152-9.[75] Albert recalled these reforms of 1973. The Democrats had intense debate, but Albert

---

74. "An Introspective and Angry Congress Begins Its Work," *Congressional Quarterly Weekly Report*, January 6, 1973, 3-8.
75. "Seniority Rule: Change in Procedure, Not in Practice," *Congressional Quarterly Weekly Report*, January 27, 1973, 136-138.

endorsed the change and believed his speech of endorsement helped foil an attempt for repeal.[76]

In addition, the House Democrats instituted a significant reform that increased the power of the House Democratic Leadership and reduced the autonomy of the committee chairmen. On February 22, 1973, the Caucus voted to create a new Democratic Steering and Policy Committee (DSPC). The DSPC would include the Democratic House Leadership, twelve members elected by regional divisions of the Caucus, and members appointed at-large by the Speaker. Albert would chair the DSPC; he also supported its creation.[77] The DSPC conducted its first meeting on April 5, 1973. The DSPC voted to conduct regular meetings on the first and third Thursdays of each month when the House was in session.[78] Albert saw the creation of the DSPC as a fundamental change in the House: "For the first time since Joe Cannon's one-man rule, it gave the majority party a means to recommend legislation and coordinate its passage."[79]

The DSG exercised an active role in the major events and achievements of the Congressional reform movement. A "DSG Activity Report" discussed the reform efforts in the Ninety-first Congress and in the first half of 1971. The report stated that: "Other DSG reform activities included a campaign to modify the seniority system and a continuing effort to reinvigorate the long-dormant Democratic Caucus, source of Democratic power in the House but overshadowed in recent

---

76. Albert, *Giant*, 343.
77. "House Reforms: More Moves Toward Modernization," *Congressional Quarterly Weekly Report*, February 24, 1973, 419.
78. Press Release from Office of the Speaker, April 5, 1973, Folder: Democratic Steering Committee, Box 381 A, Patman Papers.
79. Albert, *Giant*, 347.

years by Dixiecrat-dominated committee fiefdoms. At the start of the 91st Congress DSG won approval of a new rule requiring monthly meetings of the Caucus and permitting individual Members to initiate action in the Caucus--previously a prerogative of the leadership alone."[80] The DSG received recognition as a driving force in implementing the reforms in 1973. Richard Conlon drafted the reform proposals to ensure that they were acceptable to the majority of House Democrats, and Phil Burton acted as a major proponent and strategist for the reforms. The DSG worked with the House Democratic Leadership to pass the reforms.[81]

Meanwhile, another reform effort began; it also revealed the obstacles to and the limits on reform. On January 31, the House passed a resolution, 282-91, to create a select committee to study the House's committee system. The committee would be chaired by Bolling and would include five Democrats and five Republicans. The Democratic members were, in addition to Bolling, Robert Stephens of Georgia, John Culver of Iowa, Lloyd Meeds of Washington, and Paul Sarbanes of Maryland. The Republican members were Dave Martin of Nebraska, Peter Frelinghuysen of New Jersey, Charles Wiggins of California, William Steiger of Wisconsin, and C. W. Bill Young of Florida.[82] The Bolling Committee would operate for 1.5 years with $1.5 million. Albert and Gerald Ford

---

80. "DSG Activity Report," Folder: Mr. Patman's Committee Assignments (1929 to Present Time), Box 486A, Patman Papers.
    81. "Democratic Study Group: A Winner on House Reforms," *Congressional Quarterly Weekly Report*, June 2, 1973, 1366-1371.
    82. "House Committee System," *Congressional Quarterly Weekly Report*, February 3, 1973, 254.

formulated the idea of the committee study.[83] The Bolling Committee on March 13, 1974 unanimously approved its plan proposing major changes in committee jurisdictions, the elimination of two committees, the division of one committee into two committees, and the limitation of members to one major committee.[84] Bolling described the work of his Committee in a letter to other members on September 26, 1974. Officially called the Select Committee on Committees, the Bolling Committee worked for one and a half years and unanimously issued H Res 988, the Committee Reform Amendments of 1974, in March 1974. It was decided to let H Res 988 be debated before the full House along with the Hansen Committee plan as an alternative.[85]

In the fall of 1974, the House considered the Bolling Committee plan and the Hansen Committee plan, H Res 1248. In addition, Bolling's vice-chair, Dave Martin, introduced a compromise plan. The Bolling Committee plan proposed greater change than the Hansen Committee plan.[86] On October 8, the House passed the Hansen Committee plan, 203-165, and then passed H Res 988 which included the Hansen Committee plan as an alternate, 359-7. The House also rejected Martin's compromise plan, H Res 1321, by a vote of

---

83. Richard L. Lyons, "House Will Study Committee Reform," *Washington Post*, February 1, 1973, A2.

84. "House Committee Jurisdiction Overhaul Approved," *Congressional Quarterly Weekly Report*, March 16, 1974, 688.

85. "Highlights of H. Res. 988: Committee Reform Amendments of 1974" from Bolling, September 26, 1974, Folder: House Reform, Box 604C, Patman Papers.

86. "Restructuring of Committees Stalled In House," *Congressional Quarterly Weekly Report*, October 5, 1974, 2655-2657.

41-319.[87] Albert wrote that the Bolling Committee plan was defeated because it threatened the power of too many people, and they banded together to keep their power safe from changes that could decrease it.[88]

As passed by the House, the Hansen Committee plan contained the following major provisions. It increased each committee's staff and gave the minority party control of one-third of the staff and one-third of the investigative funds. It banned proxy voting in committee and mandated that committees with more than fifteen members set up at least four subcommittees. It required Congress starting in 1974 to return between December 1 and December 20 in election years to prepare for the next Congress. It empowered the Speaker to refer bills to more than one committee at a time or to multiple committees in sequence. It empowered the Speaker to divide a bill into different parts and to send the parts to different committees. It required the Speaker to complete the compilation of House precedents by January 1, 1977 and to update them every two years afterwards. It allowed resident commissioners and delegates to be on conference committees and required that a majority of House conferees support the House position on the bill in question. It changed the jurisdiction of several committees and changed a few committees' names. The Committee on Banking and Currency was renamed the Committee on Banking, Currency and Housing. The House rejected some parts of the Hansen Committee plan, and in addition, some parts of the Bolling Committee plan were added to the final version of the Hansen Committee plan such as the

---

87. "Hansen Reorganization Plan Adopted," *Congressional Quarterly Weekly Report*, October 12, 1974, 2896-2898.
88. Albert, *Giant*, 346.

ban on proxy voting and the guarantee of minority party staffing. The House added eight amendments to the Hansen Committee plan before it was passed. Also, the House rejected a proposal to limit the terms of committee chairs to three terms beginning in the Ninety-fourth Congress.[89]

While the Congressional reform movement won incremental reforms, the changes experienced by the nation found expression in the House. Albert observed that the composition of the House changed significantly during his six years as Speaker. Because of Black migration to the North, the number of Black members from the urban North increased while the number of urban machine members (who were White) declined. In some cases, these Black members replaced these White members. Republicans became more competitive in the South and elected more Southern Republicans to Congress. In many instances, Southern Republicans replaced traditional Southern Democrats. In other instances, traditional Southern Democrats were replaced by younger Democrats with the support of Black voters. Meanwhile, the number of women and persons of other minority groups increased in Congress. In addition, federal court orders required that House districts have roughly equal populations, and many House districts were redrawn. Large metropolitan areas gained representation at the expense of rural and small-town areas. Generational change occurred. By 1973, half of the members of Congress began their service after 1966, and the younger generation of members reached political maturity under different circumstances than the people of Albert's generation.[90]

---

89. "Hansen Reorganization Plan Adopted," *Congressional Quarterly Weekly Report*, October 12, 1974, 2896-2898.
90. Albert, *Giant*, 315-317.

Jim Wright also observed the changes that appeared by the middle of the 1970s. Conservative Democrats lost influence in the South, and racial minorities began voting regularly. Cities gained seats in Congress at the expense of rural areas. Many middle-class Whites left their traditional urban neighborhoods and moved to the suburbs, and Republican support was strong in the suburbs. Urban machines lost influence as the number of Black residents increased in cities and as Whites declined as a percentage of the urban population.[91]

The party affiliation of Southern Congressmen reflected the trends noted by Albert and Wright. In 1951 (the Eighty-second Congress), the South had 122 representatives in the House. There were 116 Democrats and 6 Republicans. In 1973 (the Ninety-third Congress), Southern Congressmen included 84 Democrats and 37 Republicans.[92]

Even while the Bipartisan House System reigned, a Congressional reform movement emerged that sought to fundamentally alter the House. The Democratic Study Group became the driving force in the Congressional reform movement, and Richard Bolling articulated the criticisms of many liberals and reformers and proposed plans for Congressional reform. The House Democrats implemented these plans in large measure through incremental reforms from the late 1950s through the mid-1970s, and Carl Albert used his position within the House Democratic Leadership to advance these reforms. The Congressional reform movement weakened the seniority system and the autonomy of the committee chairmen and thereby fundamentally altered the House. The

---

91. Wright, *Balance of Power*, 241.
92. "The New Congress: Its Members and Its Mood," *Congressional Quarterly Weekly Report*, January 6, 1973, 13-14.

power of the Speaker increased, and the Caucus was revived. The Democrats established a procedure to nominate and elect chairmen, and the means now existed to remove chairmen. Yet, actual use of this new procedure was needed to complete the overthrow of the seniority system and the autonomous committee chairmen. The Bolling Committee plan and the Hansen Committee plan were the objects of great effort and attention, but despite all of the effort and attention, the final result yielded only modest changes and revealed the obstacles to and the limits on reform.

Chapter 6 - The Demand for Accountability

Although the Congressional reform movement had accomplished much, the Watergate Crisis acted as a catalyst for the complete reform of the seniority system. The Watergate Crisis greatly changed the nation, and the post-Watergate political environment featured a demand for accountability. The elections of 1974 produced a freshmen bloc interested in Congressional reform. Meanwhile, the Bipartisan House System received greater scrutiny through a scandal involving one of the autonomous committee chairmen from the South, Ways and Means Committee Chairman Wilbur Mills of Arkansas.

The U. S. experienced a tumultuous period of years that culminated in 1974, and the year 1974 provided the circumstances to implement the removal of the chairmen. Americans were divided and exhausted by the Civil Rights Movement, racial conflict, the Vietnam War, the anti-war movement, the Women's Liberation Movement, the Black Power movement, the rise of minority activism, the New Left, conflicts over social mores, White backlash, and finally, the Watergate Crisis. The Watergate Crisis was a constitutional crisis that exposed the negative consequences of the long-term growth of federal authority and presidential authority and generated a general distrust and suspicion of public officials and institutions previously unknown in U. S. history.

The events and issues from these tumultuous years had profound ramifications for politics and government. Both parties had to contend with the cynicism and disillusionment that followed the Watergate Crisis and the Vietnam War. It became more difficult to rally the public for a cause or issue, and criticism of the status quo became frequent. National issues and the ideas of the parties' national organizations gained attention at the expense of local issues. People increasingly tried to define issues, public policy, the parties, and themselves using a liberal-conservative paradigm. The Republican Party gradually gained support in the South, and the Democratic Party's dominance was in decline in the South. Gradually, the South was developing a competitive two-party system. The Northern and Midwestern states also experienced political shifts. The Democratic Party became more competitive, overall, in states that had traditionally been Republican, and some of them became Democratic strongholds. White backlash was often directed against Liberalism and was found in all regions. In the Northeast and the Midwest, there was a loss of support for the Democratic Party and Liberalism among some traditional Democratic constituencies; the Republicans gained support among these people. The Democratic Party gained support from Black Americans and other minorities because of its support for civil rights.

The Watergate Crisis precipitated the fall of the Nixon administration. Faced with growing opposition, Richard Nixon fired Watergate Special Prosecutor Archibald Cox in October 1973 in the "Saturday Night Massacre," but this act did not save Nixon. Texan Leon Jaworski became the new Special Prosecutor and completed the investigation. Meanwhile, Vice-President Spiro Agnew resigned and pleaded no-contest to charges of corruption. Needing a respectable person whom Congress would confirm, Nixon appointed House Minority Leader Gerald Ford of Michigan as vice-president in 1973. On July 24, 1974, the Supreme Court ruled in *United States v. Richard M. Nixon* that the President had to release taped conversations to Judge Sirica. Nixon's claim of "executive privilege" failed to save him. Meanwhile, the House Judiciary Committee recommended three carefully-drawn articles of impeachment against the President, making him and Andrew Johnson the only presidents, at that point in time, that seriously contended with the issue of impeachment and removal from office. Realizing the inevitability of defeat, Nixon, on August 8, 1974, became the first president ever to resign from office. Ford succeeded to the presidency; he pardoned Nixon on September 8, 1974. With the appointment of Nelson Rockefeller as vice-president, the nation had an unelected president and an unelected vice-president for the first time in its history.

Gerald Ford faced cynicism, suspicion, and a demand for accountability as President, and these factors affected the whole nation. He wrote: "But in August 1974, tranquility was in short supply. The years of suspicion and scandal that had culminated in Nixon's resignation had demoralized our people. They had lost faith in their elected leaders and in their institutions. I knew that unless I did something to restore their trust, I couldn't win their consent to do anything else."[1] By the fall of 1974, Ford wrote that, "Overriding almost everything else was the precipitous decline in the faith that Americans traditionally placed in their nation, their institutions and their leaders."[2]

The Watergate Crisis generated cynicism, suspicion, and a demand for accountability expressed in many forms. O'Neill wrote that although Watergate concerned the

---

1. Gerald R. Ford, *A Time to Heal: The Autobiography of Gerald R. Ford* (New York: Harper & Row, 1979), 124-125.
2. Ford, *Heal*, 181.

presidency instead of Congress, "the fallout from that period was so widespread that aspersions were cast on all elected officials in Washington."[3] In a *New Republic* article in November 1973, Morris Udall discussed the many problems facing the nation and the need for America to retool itself. He worried about the electorate's growing cynicism towards politics as well as the legacy of protest from the late 1960s and the early 1970s. Udall warned that this cynicism could result in the breakdown of the two-party system, ideological conflicts, and the splintering of the two major parties.[4] A Gallup Poll conducted among college students in the winter and spring of 1974 found that 42% of respondents rated distrust in government/Watergate as the most salient problem. Next, 33% of respondents rated the energy crisis as the most salient problem, and 16% of respondents rated Nixon's leadership as the most salient problem.[5]

The American people held great anger towards Nixon. Three Gallup polls conducted in August 1974 revealed great anger. The first poll, conducted before the resignation, found that 66% of respondents disapproved of Nixon's handling of his job as president while only 24% of respondents approved. Democrats and Republicans naturally displayed their respective partisan biases against and for Nixon to a degree, but 69% of the Independents, holding the swing votes needed to win elections, disapproved of Nixon's handling of his job as president.[6] In another pre-resignation poll, 57% of respondents

---

3. O'Neill, *Man of the House*, 274.
4. Morris K. Udall, "Where Do We Go from Here? The Democratic Party," *New Republic*, November 24, 1973, 16.
5. George H. Gallup, ed., *The Gallup Poll: Public Opinion 1972-1977*, vol. 1, *1972-1975* (Wilmington, DE: Scholarly Resources, 1978), 257.
6. Gallup, *Gallup Poll 1*, 325-327.

wanted Nixon removed from office; only 31% felt that his actions did not justify removal. A majority of Independents, 55%, considered removal justifiable.[7] Following the resignation, 56% of respondents in another poll felt that Nixon should face trial for Watergate-related offenses, and only 37% of respondents believed that he should not face trial. Once again, the Independents tended to oppose Nixon: 55% favored a criminal trial while only 36% opposed a trial.[8] Ford believed that had Nixon remained in office, probably the House would have impeached him and the Senate would have convicted him.[9]

The demand for accountability was not a mere fad or mood swing. Jimmy Carter recognized the strength of the demand for accountability and its connection to his election as President in 1976: "I realized that my own election had been aided by a deep desire among the people for open government, based on a new and fresh commitment to changing some of the Washington habits which had made it possible for the American people to be misled. Because of President Ford's pardon of Nixon, Watergate had been a largely unspoken though ever-present campaign issue, and the bitter divisions and personal tragedies of those recent events could not quickly be forgotten."[10]

The Watergate Crisis served as a catalyst for the Congress to reassert its constitutional authority against excessive presidential power. The presidency had increased its power in the government in the previous decades, and the excessive presidential power had been a core feature in

---

7. Gallup, *Gallup Poll 1*, 308-310.
8. Gallup, *Gallup Poll 1*, 349-351.
9. Ford, *Heal*, 4.

several of the crises of the late 1960s and early 1970s. Richard Bolling had expressed concerns about Congress' constitutional authority in the 1960s and linked it to the need for Congressional reform. Congress passed three acts designed to restrain presidential power and to reassert Congress' constitutional authority: the War Powers Act, the Federal Elections Campaign Amendments of 1974, and the Budget and Impoundment Control Act. Jim Wright recognized the meaning of the first and third of these statutes: "The resulting legislation amounted to a legislative counterrevolution, the resolute reassertion of congressional powers threatened by presidential usurpation."[11]

In 1973, the Congress passed, over Nixon's veto, the War Powers Act, the first successful veto override of the Ninety-third Congress. The House voted 284-135; the Senate voted 75-18. The Act required the president to notify Congress within forty-eight hours of the commitment of U. S. forces abroad. The commitment could face termination after sixty days unless Congress provided authorization, and Congress could force the president to end the commitment through a concurrent resolution unless authorization had already occurred.[12]

Congress addressed campaign finance. Nixon had greatly outspent the Democratic nominee George McGovern to win reelection in the 1972 presidential election. The exposure of campaign finance abuses in the 1972 presidential campaign generated momentum to restrict the influence of money in

---

10. Jimmy Carter, *Keeping Faith: Memoirs of a President* (Fayetteville: The University of Arkansas Press, 1995), 29.
11. Wright, *Balance of Power*, 202.

politics. In response, Congress passed the Federal Elections Campaign Amendments of 1974 as an addition to the Federal Election Campaign Act of 1971. The Amendments established limits on individual contributions; limits on spending by candidates for presidential, House, and Senate elections; a system of public financing for presidential elections; rules for disclosure of campaign finances; and a board, the Federal Elections Commission, to enforce the new provisions.[13]

Congress and Nixon battled over his impoundment of funds already appropriated by the Congress, and in response, Congress sought to increase its control over the budget process through the Budget and Impoundment Control Act in 1974. The Act created separate House and Senate Budget Committees and the Congressional Budget Office to assist the legislative branch with the budget. A schedule was designed for the creation of the budget in order to make the whole process more orderly. The Act established procedures to protect the budget plans of Congress from obstruction by a president refusing to spend appropriated money.[14]

The elections for the Ninety-fourth Congress were held on November 5, 1974 in the post-Watergate political environment, and the demand for accountability was strong. The Democrats achieved great victories. Ford identified the reasons for the Democrats' success: "Watergate, the Nixon resignation and my pardon of the former President all combined with the deteriorating economy to make our chances of scoring any gains remote. The only thing we could do was fight a

---

12. *Congressional Quarterly Almanac, 93rd Congress 1st Session 1973* (Washington, D.C.: Congressional Quarterly, 1974), 905-907.
    13. *Congressional Quarterly Almanac, 93rd Congress 2nd Session 1974* (Washington, D.C.: Congressional Quarterly, 1975), 611-615.

holding action and try to cut our losses as much as possible."[15] John Rhodes, the House Republican Leader after Ford, stressed the challenges for the Republicans in 1974: "But by pardoning Nixon *before*, rather than *after*, the elections, Ford created a furor that swamped many Republican candidates at the polls." He wrote that he was campaigning for his twelfth term. He was the Republican House Leader, and his opponent was a little-known Democrat. Yet, this race was close.[16]

The Democrats' victories in 1974 greatly altered the party division in the House. The Democrats gained forty-three seats to increase their majority to 291, leaving the Republicans only 144 seats. The ninety-two freshmen representatives-elect included seventy-five Democrats but only seventeen Republicans. Thirty-six incumbent Republicans lost reelection as opposed to only four incumbent Democrats. Four Republicans who supported Nixon during the impeachment inquiry lost; the Republicans of the Judiciary Committee who regularly worked for impeachment won reelection. Some general patterns emerged. Retiring liberal Democrats typically were replaced by liberal Democrats; losing conservative Republicans typically were replaced by new liberal Democrats.[17] Individually, Patman, Poage, and Hebert all won reelection. Patman won reelection against a Republican, James W. Farris, with 43,569 votes (66.6%) to 21,862 votes (33.4%). Poage defeated his Republican opponent, Don Clements,

---

14. *Congressional Quarterly Almanac 1974*, 146, 150-153.

15. Ford, *Heal*, 200.

16. John Rhodes with Dean Smith, *I Was There* (Northwest Publishing, Incorporated, 1995), 178-179.

17. "The House: More Than Two-Thirds Democratic," *Congressional Quarterly Weekly Report*, November 9, 1974, 3065-3066.

46,329 votes (82.7%) to 9,674 votes (17.3%). Meanwhile, Hebert ran unopposed.[18]

Several measures of public opinion revealed strong support for the Democrats. Five national opinion polls conducted between September 1973 and January 1974 asked people whether they identified themselves as a Republican, a Democrat, or an Independent. The results, compiled by the Gallup Poll, revealed Republicans with 24%, Democrats with 42%, and Independents with 34%. This number for the Independents marked a new high for Independents, breaking the old high of 29% from the 1972 campaign period.[19] The Gallup Poll computed the national vote total percentages for House races based on official state figures. Democrats captured 58.9% of the vote; Republicans garnered only 41.1% of the total vote.[20] The Democrats also had success in state government elections. The Democrats increased their number of governorships from thirty-two to thirty-seven. There were elections for thirty-five governorships, and Democrats won twenty-eight of them. Republicans won six, and one Independent won a governorship. Therefore, the new totals for governors were set to be thirty-seven Democrats, twelve Republicans, and one Independent. The only times any party held more governorships occurred in 1936 (when the Democrats held thirty-eight) and in 1937 (when the Democrats held thirty-nine).[21]

---

18. "State Returns for Senate, Governor and House," *Congressional Quarterly Weekly Report*, November 9, 1974, 3084-3091.

19. Gallup, *Gallup Poll 1*, 233.

20. Gallup, *Gallup Poll 1*, 370.

21. "Governors: Net Gain of 5 for the Democrats," *Congressional Quarterly Weekly Report*, November 9, 1974, 3071-3072.

On the eve of the Ninety-fourth Congress, the House had achieved small but significant progress in reflecting the American people in terms of demographics. With the election of six women freshmen in 1974, the new House would have a record eighteen women. The average age of House members would decline from 51.3 years to 49.8 years, the first time since World War II that the average age of House members fell below fifty years. Furthermore, 157 representatives, more than one-third of the House, had won election since 1972. With the election of another Black representative, there would be sixteen Black representatives in the House.[22] These sixteen representatives would be the largest number of Black members in the House since Reconstruction.[23]

The Watergate Crisis and the demand for accountability significantly influenced the freshmen bloc of seventy-five Democrats and their election. Several individuals from different perspectives characterized the freshmen bloc in the same general terms. Oren Teicher worked as an assistant to one of the leaders of the freshmen Democrats, Richard Ottinger of New York. Teicher recalled that the freshmen were "an extraordinary group of individuals." They were smart, independent-minded, and eager for action. Many of them won election through their own merit or personal standing without the support of established political powers. Unlike some members of Congress, the freshmen had no previous ties to the committee chairmen and were not intimidated by them.

22. "New Congress Is Youngest Since World War II," *Congressional Quarterly Weekly Report*, November 9, 1974, 3106-3107.
23. Richard D. Lyons, "House Reform Faces Action Today in Party Caucuses; Major Struggles Expected," *New York Times*, December 2, 1974, 34.

Many of the freshmen "were really there to shake things up a lot."[24]

Tip O'Neill noted the characteristics of the freshmen. He recalled that many of these freshmen qualified as genuine Washington outsiders lacking political experience in the traditional fashion of holding local or state offices to gain advancement. Many of them drew inspiration from Robert Kennedy's 1968 campaign or were social activists motivated by the Vietnam War, the Watergate Crisis, or environmental issues. He also wrote this description of the freshmen, "Party discipline went out the window. These people were impatient, and they wanted to be part of the action right away."[25] O'Neill also credited the Watergate Crisis as helping to elect the freshmen Democrats of 1976. Together, 118 freshmen Democrats were elected in 1974 and 1976.[26]

The Texans noted the significance of the freshmen, too. Jim Wright wrote that, "Most of the big batch of new Democratic members had been elected as self-styled reformers. Appealing to public outrage over Watergate, they had promised change. The class of 1974 was like a combustible pile of dry timber awaiting a spark."[27] Fowler West observed that the freshmen displayed an anti-authoritarian streak and had opposed the Vietnam War and Richard Nixon. They were elected with less help from the Party than candidates had received in previous

---

24. Oren Teicher, interview by author, November 23, 1999, telephone tape recording, T. Harry Williams Center for Oral History, Louisiana State University, Baton Rouge, LA.
25. O'Neill, *Man of the House*, 283.
26. O'Neill, *Man of the House*, 282.
27. Wright, *Balance of Power*, 236.

years.[28] Wright Patman apparently formulated a positive opinion of the freshmen bloc. An anonymous Banking and Currency Committee memo, surely authored by Patman, stated that, "Have talked with a number of freshman Members and I am encouraged that they will be activist....many of them ran on platforms similar to positions I have been pushing for years. Looks like a strong Democratic-populist trend among many of the new Members. This has been one of the most encouraging groups of new Democrats since I arrived here."[29]

Tom Foley observed the freshmen. He wrote that House reformers saw the freshmen Democrats of 1974 as increasing the possibilities for reform because of their size. House reformers focused on reforming procedures and imposing limits on committee chairs' authority, but the freshmen had their own opinions and wanted bolder action and change. Foley wrote, concerning the freshmen of 1974, that, "Changing the process was fine, but they wanted some trophies on the hunting lodge wall in the form of some chairmen's heads."[30] Also, he noted a general characteristic that applied to large groups of freshmen: "The risk is that they will gum it up because every change in the structure of the institution of Congress creates other changes and usually unintended consequences."[31]

As the freshmen rose to prominence, a scandal involving Wilbur Mills captured the public's attention. Wilbur Daigh Mills was born in Kensett, White County, Arkansas on May 24, 1909.

---

28. Fowler West, interview by author, January 19, 2000, telephone tape recording, T. Harry Williams Center for Oral History, Louisiana State University, Baton Rouge, LA.

29. B&C Priority, December 12, 1974, Folder: 94th Congress (1975-1976 Programs) B&C, Box 931A, Patman Papers.

30. Biggs, *Honor in the House*, 54-55.

31. Biggs, *Honor in the House*, 187.

He attended Hendrix College in Conway, Arkansas and the Law Department at Harvard University. From 1934 to 1938, Mills practiced law and held local judicial offices in White County before winning election to the House of Representatives. He became chairman of the Ways and Means Committee in 1958.[32] By the middle of the 1970s, Mills' Second District was located in central Arkansas and included Little Rock.[33] Mills' legacy concerning tax policy was described by his biographer, Julian E. Zelizer, as "forging new ties between Congress and technocratic expertise, by transforming taxation into a central component of economic and social policy."[34]

Mills' career featured contrasts. Albert wrote that Mills had a deep knowledge of the U. S. tax code. Before he took a bill to the floor, Mills wanted the support of Ways and Means Committee members (both Democrats and Republicans) and wanted confidence that he had sufficient votes to win on the floor. The Ways and Means Committee did not have subcommittees. The Committee members worked on all the Committee bills together. The Rules Committee generally gave the Committee's bills closed rules, and the full House could only approve or reject the bills.[35] Richard Ottinger of New York, one of the prominent members of the freshmen bloc, recalled that although Mills was a "thorough scoundrel," he worked with his Committee. He managed his Committee effectively and granted or withheld legislative favors as a means to win the

---

32. Nystrom, *Biographical Directory*, 1508.
33. Brownson, *1975 Staff Directory*, 8.
34. Julian E. Zelizer, *Taxing America: Wilbur D. Mills, Congress, and the State, 1945-1975* (New York: Cambridge University, 1998), 27.
35. Albert, *Giant*, 266-267.

support of his Committee.[36] For many years, Mills avoided the socialite scene and instead focused on his work. In the early 1970s, his Arkansas associates believed he changed or became sick when he developed back problems, started drinking heavily, and ran for the 1972 Democratic presidential nomination.[37] The long-time House Doorkeeper, William "Fishbait" Miller, noted the changes and problems of Wilbur Mills. Mills worked very hard. When Miller worked in the House Post Office, Mills' wife Polly came to Mills' office and brought their children in order to keep Mills company while he worked. Miller sometimes babysat the kids on these occasions. Mills was serious for many years but changed. He lost interest in his House work and partied. Mills had a bad back and was also a heavy drinker in general. According to Miller, when the Mills scandal became public, the members of the House felt sorry for him.[38]

The Mills scandal became public in the early morning hours of October 7, 1974. A Park Police vehicle stopped a car registered to Mills near the Tidal Basin in Washington, D. C. The officers found a struggle inside the car containing Mills, another man, and three women. One of the women promptly leaped into the Tidal Basin, requiring one of the officers to rescue her despite her attempt to fight him. Another officer was injured by the people in the car. Mills identified himself to the

---

36. Richard Ottinger, interview by author, November 18, 1999, telephone tape recording, T. Harry Williams Center for Oral History, Louisiana State University, Baton Rouge, LA.

37. Roy Reed, "Mills Puzzles the Folks Back Home," *New York Times*, December 5, 1974, 32.

38. Miller, *Fishbait*, 178-180.

officers that night, but his aides claimed he denied the incident afterwards.[39]

Annabel Battistella was Mills' partner in the scandal and the infamous Tidal Basin jumper. Battistella worked as a stripper and had met Mills in June 1973 at a Washington, D. C. burlesque club called the Silver Slipper.[40] Battistella wrote that she and Mills began a romantic relationship within about three weeks after first meeting.[41] A native of Argentina, Battistella, 38 years old, was a divorced mother of four whose stage name was Fanne Foxe the "Argentine Firecracker." She chose her profession on account of the financial rewards, but Mills wanted her to retire and lead a more normal life for the sake of her children.[42] Mills and Battistella wanted to marry one another, but the chairman's wife, Polly, who knew of the affair, would not agree to a divorce.[43]

Mills' circumstances deteriorated. On the night of November 30, 1974, Mills joined Battistella on stage at the conclusion of her performance at the Pilgrim Theater in Boston. He appeared sick and gave a series of strange comments to the press afterwards. The press quoted him as saying, "'This won't ruin me'" and "'Nothing can ruin me.'"[44] Battistella believed the years of stress and work had weakened Mills, and

39. Alfred E. Lewis and Martin Weil, "Riders in Mills' Car Involved in a Scuffle," *Washington Post*, October 9, 1974, A1, A4.

40. Annabel "Fanne Foxe" Battistella and Yvonne Dunleary, *Fanne Foxe* (New York: Pinnacle Books, 1975), 109-110.

41. Battistella, *Fanne Foxe*, 120-122.

42. Sally Quinn, "'A Little Talent...A Little Personality,'" *Washington Post*, December 6, 1974, B1, B3.

43. Battistella, *Fanne Foxe*, 122-124.

44. "Mills Does a Walk-On With Stripper," *New York Times*, December 2, 1974, 42.

now he wanted to relinquish the responsibilities he held.[45] The Mills scandal received a mixed reaction in the Congress. Some members thought the events were humorous, but other members talked seriously about reducing Mills' power or even removing him from the chairmanship.[46] Meanwhile, Battistella hired a new producer who used the scandal to publicize her. It was announced that she was hired for $17,500 for a one-week stint performing in Orlando, Florida.[47]

The Mills scandal was connected to the removal of Patman, Poage, and Hebert in 1975. Admittedly, the circumstances of Wilbur Mills were very different than the circumstances of Patman, Poage, or Hebert. Nonetheless, the scandal focused attention on the power of committee chairmen and the appearance of a lack of accountability among politicians. Discussion about removing one chairman, even if for extreme reasons, made the general idea of removing chairmen seem more possible and acceptable.

In late 1974, the demand for accountability had swept the nation in reaction to the Watergate Crisis. The bloc of freshmen Democrats could provide the votes that reformers had long lacked. With Mills as an embarrassment to the House, an atmosphere favorable to challenges of authority developed. The battle lines were drawn: the critics, the reformers, and the freshmen versus the traditional chairmen, Wright Patman, Bob Poage, and Felix Edward Hebert.

---

45. Battistella, *Fanne Foxe*, 168-169.

46. "Mills Derided in Congress Over Link to Stripper," *New York Times*, December 3, 1974, 1, 32.

47. Albin Krebs, "Notes on People," *New York Times*, December 6, 1974, 34.

Chapter 7 - The Coalition Assembled

As the Ninety-fourth Congress began its work in late 1974 and early 1975, the participants in and the circumstances for the removal of the chairmen began to converge. The demand for accountability drove the general direction and momentum of events, and Phillip Burton and Richard Ottinger played critical roles in organizing the coalition for removal. The House Democrats made critical rules changes for the Ninety-fourth Congress, and the freshmen Democrats were active and held hearings at which the committee chairmen testified. Finally, the coalition for removal targeted Patman, Poage, and Hebert because of their management of their committees and their political ideology.

The coalition for removal was based on the specific circumstances of the moment. The members of the House of Representatives are elected every two years, and each Congress is a unique entity. Each Congress features the selection of committee chairs. The selection of committee chairs for the Ninety-fourth Congress was a single event, and the supporters or opponents of any potential chair were a collection of individuals linked by the circumstances of the moment. A coalition for removal, in this context, does not refer to any perennial or permanent bloc or viewpoint that would reappear in an identical or similar form on later occasions. A coalition for removal, in this context, is simply the people for or against a potential chair, and the cooperation among them might only be informal or limited to just some individuals. For Patman, Poage, and Hebert, their opponents, particularly the DSG and the freshmen, employed some organization and strategy, but these efforts did not constitute a perennial or permanent bloc. The votes against the three chairmen were not the same; not every member voted the same way on all three chairmen. Even if a member did not cooperate with anyone else, that member still had the opportunity to vote on the chairmen. Some members probably did not directly cooperate with the coalition regarding organization and strategy but still voted for removal because that choice reflected their viewpoint. The votes were conducted by secret ballot, and no certain identification of support or opposition could be made for each member. Once these three men were removed, the coalition against them ceased to exist because the issues that motivated the coalition ceased to exist. Other issues such as the economic problems of the era, the legislative goals of the House Democratic Leadership, or the agenda of the Ford administration were separate issues not directly related to the three chairmen and the coalition that removed them.

Phillip Burton played a critical role in the removal of the chairmen. He was born in Cincinnati, Ohio in 1926 but graduated with a B.A. from U.S.C. in 1947 and an LL.B. from Golden Gate Law School in San Francisco in 1952. He served in both World War II and the Korean War in the U. S. Air Force and was discharged as a first lieutenant. He served in the California State Assembly from 1956 to 1964. He won election to the U. S. House of Representatives in a special election in February 1964.[1] By the mid-1970s, Burton represented the Sixth District of California which included a part of the city and the county of San Francisco.[2] Burton's biographer, John Jacobs, wrote that Burton "worked like a Tammany ward heeler and rose to be a political boss in a media state famous for its

---

1. Nystrom, *Biographical Directory*, 714.
2. Brownson, *1975 Staff Directory*, 10.

blow-dried celebrity politicians" and that "His was a politics centered on people's needs, often desperate needs, for government help without regard to cost." He was an advocate for welfare and labor issues, an early critic of the Vietnam War, a strong supporter of Congressional reform, an expert at reapportionment or gerrymandering for election districts, and an environmental activist.[3] Jim Wright wrote that Burton "was as clever a political strategist as Congress had in either house."[4]

Burton's place and role in the House Leadership was critically influenced by his personal actions as revealed in an incident described by his biographer, John Jacobs. On one occasion in the fall of 1972, Tip O'Neill, Burton and his wife, and another couple socialized together in a cocktail lounge. The other couple were wealthy contributors. Burton was drunk and became rude and vulgar. O'Neill advised him to act more appropriately, but Burton became worse. O'Neill then became angry with him, and Burton challenged him to a fight. Burton reached for O'Neill but the other woman present intercepted Burton before any violence happened. As a result of the incident, O'Neill decided that he could not and would not support Burton for a leadership position. O'Neill later thwarted Burton's scheme to make the Majority Whip elected in order to run for the post himself.[5]

Richard Lawrence Ottinger played a critical role in the removal of the chairmen. He was born in New York City in 1929 and graduated with a B.A. from Cornell University in 1950 and an LL.B. from Harvard Law School in 1953. He served in the U.

---

3. John Jacobs, *A Rage for Justice: The Passion and Politics of Phillip Burton* (Berkeley, CA: University of California Press, 1995), xxiii-xxvi.

4. Wright, *Balance of Power*, 236.

5. Jacobs, *Rage for Justice*, 237-241.

S. Air Force from 1953 to 1955 and was discharged as a captain. He later practiced international and corporate law and served as a Peace Corps administrator. His political career was not continuous. He served in the U. S. House of Representatives from 1965 to 1971 and failed in a bid for the U. S. Senate in 1970. He failed to win a race for the House in 1972 but won election to the House in 1974.[6] By the mid-1970s, Ottinger's residence was Pleasantville, and he represented the Twenty-fourth District of New York.[7]

Burton's role in the removal of the chairmen started with his efforts to assist Democratic House challengers in the 1974 elections, and these efforts involved cooperation between him and Wayne Hays. Burton arranged for contributions to be collected from frequent contributors and distributed the money to selected Democratic challengers.[8] Hays served as chair of the Democratic Congressional Campaign Committee (DCCC) and possessed the authority to distribute over $200,000 in campaign money. Burton advised Hays on the distribution of the money, and Democratic challengers received much of it. These challengers received $87,000 (an average of $1,260 for each) from the DCCC. Burton contacted many of these challengers and campaigned in forty House districts. He consulted regularly with Hays, labor union leaders and activists, and DNC chair Robert Strauss.[9] Jim Wright wrote about the operation and the implications of the Burton-Hays cooperation. Burton announced his candidacy for Caucus Chairman in the middle of 1974. Hays told Burton about the campaign money

6. Nystrom, *Biographical Directory*, 1598.
7. Brownson, *1975 Staff Directory*, 75.
8. Jacobs, *Rage for Justice*, 234.
9. Jacobs, *Rage for Justice*, 252-254.

that he was sending to candidates. Burton called the candidates to discuss the elections and then said that he would recommend that they receive campaign money. Burton talked to candidates, regardless of whether or not they were chosen to receive money, to offer advice and encouragement. Therefore, Burton received credit for arranging money for them and developed ties to them.[10]

Following the elections, Burton and Ottinger organized the freshmen Democrats and directed them to support Congressional reform. Jim Wright wrote that after being elected, the freshmen Democrats looked to Burton as a leader and a helper. Burton recommended that the freshmen meet, choose leaders, and make plans to achieve an objective.[11] Ottinger also helped organize the freshmen. He contacted the DSG. In November of 1974, he, aided by fellow freshmen James H. Scheuer of New York, Andrew Jacobs of Indiana, and Abner Mikva of Illinois, sent telegrams to the freshmen Democrats. Scheuer, Jacobs, and Mikva all had previous Congressional service, and Ottinger and Scheuer met for planning sessions.[12] Oren Teicher worked on Ottinger's staff and recalled the organizational efforts. Ottinger knew from his previous House experience that it could be difficult to achieve results in the House because most times there was not a bloc of members united on goals and ideas. The seventy-five freshmen Democrats won election on the idea of reform and as a reaction to Watergate, and their background influenced Ottinger to organize the freshmen for action. The freshmen met

---

10. Wright, *Balance of Power*, 237.
11. Wright, *Balance of Power*, 237.
12. Martin Tolchin, "New Yorkers Played Key Role in House Rebellion," *New York Times*, January 24, 1975, 33, 61.

several times. When the freshmen met, they soon discovered that they were united in support of Congressional reform as part of the national demand for accountability. The freshmen discussed reform of the seniority system and agreed to support reform, and reform of the seniority system was one of the few topics on which consensus emerged.[13] Ottinger recalled that the freshmen did not understand the seniority system or know the senior members of the House very well. Reform of the seniority system was a major concern to Ottinger after the election, and it was important to establish a new precedent showing that the House would actually remove chairmen deemed ineffective.[14]

The National Committee for an Effective Congress (NCEC) provided support to the freshmen. The NCEC provided consultants to forty-nine Democratic challengers, and thirty-five won. There was a post-election meeting in the office of Don Fraser attended by several NCEC-supported freshmen. The idea of an office for the freshmen emerged at this meeting, and the NCEC found financial support for the office used by the freshmen. J. Irwin Miller, a Republican industrialist from Columbus, Indiana, and Clementine Tangeman, his sister from New York, provided $6,000 of the $8,500 for the freshmen office.[15] Finally, the freshmen set up an office on New Jersey

---

13. Oren Teicher, interview by author, November 23, 1999, telephone tape recording, T. Harry Williams Center for Oral History, Louisiana State University, Baton Rouge, LA.

14. Richard Ottinger, interview by author, November 18, 1999, telephone tape recording, T. Harry Williams Center for Oral History, Louisiana State University, Baton Rouge, LA.

15. David S. Broder, "House 'Revolt' Had Backing," *Washington Post*, January 26, 1975, A14.

Avenue two blocks from the Capitol and hired a staff consisting of two people.[16]

The House Democrats held organizational caucuses for the upcoming Ninety-fourth Congress in the last weeks of 1974. The House Democratic Caucus convened on Monday, December 2, 1974, in the House of Representatives Chamber. Caucus Chairman Olin Teague brought the Caucus to order. Leonor Sullivan of Missouri read the Notice of Caucus which officially announced that the Democratic Caucus was to meet at 12:00 noon on Monday, December 2, 1974 in the Hall of the House of Representatives. The Notice was issued on November 12, 1974 by the Majority Leader. The Clerk called the roll by states, and 268 members were present.[17] The Caucus elected on a voice vote Patsy Mink of Hawaii and Shirley Chisholm of New York as Secretary and Assistant Secretary of the Caucus, respectively. There were no other nominations. Sullivan of Missouri offered the resolution to elect them.[18] Carl Albert was renominated for Speaker on a voice vote without opposition and delivered a victory speech.[19] Tip O'Neill won election as Democratic Majority Leader without opposition on a voice vote.[20] In the contest for Chairman of the House Democratic Caucus, Burton defeated B. F. Sisk of

---

16. Richard D. Lyons, "House Reform Faces Action Today in Party Caucuses; Major Struggles Expected," *New York Times*, December 2, 1974, 34.

17. Caucus minutes, December 2, 1974, p. 1, Folder 46, Box 219, Legislative Series, Carl Albert Collection, The Carl Albert Congressional Research & Studies Center, University of Oklahoma, Norman, OK.

18. Caucus minutes, December 2, 1974, p. 24-26, Folder 46, Box 219, Legislative Series, Albert Collection.

19. Caucus minutes, December 2, 1974, p. 36, Folder 46, Box 219, Legislative Series, Albert Collection.

California, 162-111.[21] Jim Wright wrote that Burton was elected Caucus chairman with strong support from the freshmen.[22]

There were also elections for the officers of the House. The Caucus elected on a voice vote, without opposition, W. Pat Jennings, Kenneth R. Harding, Robert V. Rota, and Rev. Edward G. Latch as Clerk, Sergeant at Arms, Postmaster, and Chaplain, respectively, for the House in the Ninety-fourth Congress. The election was conducted through a vote on a resolution offered by Thomas Morgan of Pennsylvania. These positions were the officers of the House.[23]

The House also considered the position of Doorkeeper, and this contest was more salient due to the person who held the position, William "Fishbait" Miller. Miller was from Pascagoula, Mississippi. He survived several diseases as a child and was very scrawny as a teenager; other people nicknamed him "Fishbait". A local baseball team would not let him join the team because he was considered too small. His father left him, his siblings, and their mother when he was 12 years old. Fishbait worked several jobs when he was a teenager.[24] Miller came to Washington, D. C. and the Capitol to work in 1933. He received a job in the House of Representatives post office through the influence of Representative William Colmer. Earlier, Miller worked on Colmer's campaign in his race for the House in 1932.[25] Miller

---

20. Caucus minutes, December 2, 1974, p. 50-51, Folder 46, Box 219, Legislative Series, Albert Collection.
21. Caucus minutes, December 2, 1974, p. 21, Folder 46, Box 219, Legislative Series, Albert Collection.
22. Wright, *Balance of Power*, 237.
23. Caucus minutes, December 2, 1974, p. 54, Folder 46, Box 219, Legislative Series, Albert Collection.
24. Miller, *Fishbait*, 23-28.
25. Miller, *Fishbait*, 31-33.

then held other jobs at the Capitol building including messenger to the Doorkeeper, special assistant to the Sergeant at Arms, and Minority Doorkeeper.[26]

Miller recalled his ascent to the Doorkeeper position. After the Democrats won control of the House in the 1948 elections, he had an opportunity for advancement. He spoke with John McCormack and showed him a list of House members to formally advance his candidacy for Doorkeeper. McCormack found great fault with the list and gave him some advice. McCormack identified a collection of House members whose support he should seek to formally advance his candidacy. The original list prepared by Fishbait contained too many Dixiecrats, but the names McCormack suggested reflected greater regional diversity.[27]

The Doorkeeper was an important figure for the Capitol, and Miller described the position in the 1970s. He had jurisdiction over much of the Capitol building such as the House press galleries, the House cloakrooms, the House restrooms, the House Prayer Room, and the House floor. He oversaw more than 300 permanent employees, and there were twenty-six Assistant Doorkeepers. The persons/staff under the Doorkeeper included messengers, pages, cloakroom employees, barbers of the barbershops, attendants of the ladies' restrooms and men's lounges, janitors, House Document Room employees, and Publication Distribution Service employees. He and his staff managed twenty-eight special telephones that conveyed messages to and from members of Congress when the House was in session. He became famous for introducing the President when the

---

26. Miller, *Fishbait*, 36-40.
27. Miller, *Fishbait*, 42-43.

President addressed a joint session of Congress. Typically, the door opened, and Miller said, "'Mistah Speakah, the President of the United States.'" He performed many routine functions and informal duties to make the House work effectively and to assist the members of Congress.[28] Miller explained that as Doorkeeper, "Not only was I all things to all congressmen--supervisor of their patronage workers, guardian of the doors, babysitter and escorter of dignitaries--but I even was there to help in important moments of their private lives."[29] Miller knew members of the House, including leaders such as Rayburn and McCormack, very well.[30]

The contest for Doorkeeper was contested. Jamie Whitten of Mississippi nominated William M. "Fishbait" Miller for Doorkeeper.[31] Four members spoke in support of Miller: Richard Ottinger, Andrew Jacobs of Indiana, John Dingell of Michigan, and F. E. Hebert.[32] While delivering a seconding speech for Miller for Doorkeeper, Hebert made a reference to the freshmen and reform: "Mr. Chairman and Members of the Caucus, particularly to the new Members who are here attending the Caucus for the first time: I welcome you here. I welcome you as the oldest man present in the room. I have been here thirty-four years and I am one of the seniors you perhaps want to disrupt. But after you have been here so long as I have you will appreciate seniority."[33] McFall of California

---

28. Miller, *Fishbait*, 4-7.
29. Miller, *Fishbait*, 46.
30. Miller, *Fishbait*, 219.
31. Caucus minutes, December 2, 1974, p. 56-59, Folder 46, Box 219, Legislative Series, Albert Collection.
32. Caucus minutes, December 2, 1974, p. 59-61, 61-62, 63-65, 65-66, Folder 46, Box 219, Legislative Series, Albert Collection.
33. Caucus minutes, December 2, 1974, p. 65-66, Folder 46, Box 219, Legislative Series, Albert Collection.

nominated John L. Monahan for Doorkeeper.[34] Moorhead of Pennsylvania nominated Frank M. Clark for Doorkeeper.[35] Stanton of Ohio nominated J. T. Molloy for Doorkeeper. Stanton stated that Molloy was 38 years old. Molloy was then the Chief Disbursing Officer of the House.[36]

The balloting for the Doorkeeper began. On the first ballot, the results were: Molloy 100, Miller 77, Monahan 42, and Clark 34. Clark was eliminated from the contest, and balloting continued.[37] The next ballot results were Molloy 150, Miller 77, and Monahan 34. Molloy won the nomination for Doorkeeper.[38] On December 3, 1974, the *New York Times* ran an article on Miller and his removal, and the article offered reasons for Miller's defeat. The article reported that it was said that some liberals thought he favored conservative Democrats. Some people did not like his practice of kissing women on the cheek and whispering Bible verses to them. It was reported that Albert and O'Neill disliked Miller's demeanor.[39]

Miller credited Morris Udall and James Stanton for his removal. Miller wrote that Stanton targeted him and acted antagonistically towards him. Gossip in the House indicated that Stanton wanted to remove Miller and to replace him with someone he preferred, James Molloy. In preparation for the

---

34. Caucus minutes, December 2, 1974, p. 66-68, Folder 46, Box 219, Legislative Series, Albert Collection.

35. Caucus minutes, December 2, 1974, p. 70-72, Folder 46, Box 219, Legislative Series, Albert Collection.

36. Caucus minutes, December 2, 1974, p. 75-77, Folder 46, Box 219, Legislative Series, Albert Collection.

37. Caucus minutes, December 2, 1974, p. 84, Folder 46, Box 219, Legislative Series, Albert Collection.

38. Caucus minutes, December 2, 1974, p. 87, Folder 46, Box 219, Legislative Series, Albert Collection.

Ninety-fourth Congress, Miller asked Udall to second his nomination for reelection as Doorkeeper. Udall said that he did not want to be connected or associated with him because he (Udall) was preparing for a presidential candidacy.[40] Miller admitted that he kissed women on the cheek, and the women came from all age groups, young and old.[41]

Gerald Ford actually was an issue in Miller's removal. He had known Ford as "Jerry" when Ford served in the House and continued addressing him as "Jerry" when Ford became Vice-President and President. Miller wrote that Ford was not the type of person to be offended by the use of his name by friends. Other people, such as Wayne Hays and James Stanton, were offended by Miller's use of "Jerry". Miller wrote that Hays and Stanton claimed that the use of "Jerry" was the reason Miller lost his reelection. Miller claimed that the issue was distorted by his enemies and that incoming freshmen were told that he offended the President. His enemies also claimed that Miller "'manhandled'" President Ford. Miller wrote that he grabbed President Ford on one occasion to prevent him from falling over Speaker Albert because Ford was unaware of Albert's location; Albert was short.[42]

In addition to the elections and nominations, the Caucus also considered rules changes. Tom Foley offered a resolution (a substitute resolution) that fundamentally altered the structure of power in the House. This resolution provided that the Democratic Steering and Policy Committee (DSPC) act as the Democratic Committee on Committees in the Ninety-fourth

39. Anthony Ripley, "House Doorkeeper Out After 24 Years in Post," *New York Times*, December 3, 1974, 30.

40. Miller, *Fishbait*, 223-224.

41. Miller, *Fishbait*, 303.

Congress. The DSPC, as the Committee on Committees, would make committee assignments for Democrats for all standing committees except the Budget Committee. The Budget Committee had special procedures/rules.[43] Foley explained the change. The DSPC had twelve members elected yearly with limits on their time of service on the DSPC. In contrast, the members of the Ways and Means Committee were elected to their seats and remained in those seats for years. The DSPC was the preeminent committee of the Caucus and included all of the Leadership positions. The Speaker could appoint members to the DSPC and ensure that all groups of the Caucus had representation. The committee appointment power would strengthen the DSPC.[44] Foley's substitute resolution for the Committee on Committees won approval, 146-122.[45]

The Caucus addressed other rules changes. The Caucus adopted the rules from the Ninety-third Congress to be the rules for the Ninety-fourth Congress with two minor changes.[46] Next, Charles Vanik introduced a resolution to expand the Ways and Means Committee from twenty-five to thirty-seven members for the Ninety-fourth Congress. The resolution passed on a voice vote.[47] O'Neill offered an amendment regarding party ratios on committees. The

---

42. Miller, *Fishbait*, 293-294.

43. Caucus minutes, December 2, 1974, p. 94, Folder 46, Box 219, Legislative Series, Albert Collection.

44. Caucus minutes, December 2, 1974, p. 96-97, Folder 46, Box 219, Legislative Series, Albert Collection.

45. Caucus minutes, December 2, 1974, p. 116, Folder 46, Box 219, Legislative Series, Albert Collection.

46. Caucus minutes, December 3, 1974, p. 127-128, Folder 46, Box 219, Legislative Series, Albert Collection.

47. Caucus minutes, December 3, 1974, p. 128-130, Folder 46, Box 219, Legislative Series, Albert Collection.

amendment would require that the ratio of Democrats on each committee, except the Committee on Standards of Official Conduct, be not less than the ratio of Democratic members and delegates in the House or one more than two Democrats for each Republican on each committee.[48] The Caucus passed O'Neill's amendment on party ratios on a voice vote.[49] Fraser offered an amendment regarding the selection of Democratic members of the Ways and Means Committee. A change was needed, according to Fraser, because the DSPC would now serve as the Committee on Committees. For vacant seats, the DSPC would make nominations, and nominations could be made by members, also. Then, the Caucus would vote on the nominations. Nominations for members who served on the Ways and Means Committee in the previous Congress would be treated in the same manner nominations were treated for other standing committees.[50] The Caucus passed Fraser's amendment on the Ways and Means Committee member selection process by a vote of 115-31.[51] Later, Robert Giaimo of Connecticut offered an amendment to the Caucus rules to allow the Democratic Caucus to select chairmen of the Appropriations Committee subcommittees using the same procedure used for chairmen of standing committees.[52] The

---

48. Caucus minutes, December 3, 1974, p. 130, Folder 46, Box 219, Legislative Series, Albert Collection.

49. Caucus minutes, December 3, 1974, p. 137, Folder 46, Box 219, Legislative Series, Albert Collection.

50. Caucus minutes, December 3, 1974, p. 138-140, Folder 46, Box 219, Legislative Series, Albert Collection.

51. Caucus minutes, December 3, 1974, p. 149, Folder 46, Box 219, Legislative Series, Albert Collection.

52. Caucus minutes, December 3, 1974, p. 157-158, Folder 46, Box 219, Legislative Series, Albert Collection.

Giaimo amendment passed, 147-116.[53] Richard Bolling offered an amendment to grant the Speaker, rather than the DSPC, the authority to nominate the chair and the Democratic members of the Rules Committee; they would require Caucus confirmation.[54] The Caucus passed the amendment to the House Democratic Caucus Rules offered by Bolling, 106-65.[55] James O'Hara offered an amendment to the Caucus rules to allow nominations to be made from the floor if a nominee for a committee chairmanship was rejected by the Caucus. The nominations would be made when the next nominee was offered to the Caucus. It passed on a voice vote.[56]

Albert noted the great changes that occurred during his Speakership. Under him, the Democratic Caucus operated regularly for the first time since the 1920s, and the elected House leadership controlled committee assignments and the progress of bills through the Rules Committee for the first time since 1911. Albert wrote that: "In less than four years, I had seen the Speaker's institutional authority grow to transcend even Sam Rayburn's personal influence." He added that, "For the first time since Joe Cannon's one-man rule, it gave the majority party a means to recommend legislation and coordinate its passage."[57]

Meanwhile, the House Democrats addressed the scandal of Wilbur Mills, Annabel Battistella, and their unusual

---

53. Caucus minutes, December 3, 1974, p. 198-199, Folder 46, Box 219, Legislative Series, Albert Collection.

54. Caucus minutes, December 3, 1974, p. 199-201, Folder 46, Box 219, Legislative Series, Albert Collection.

55. Caucus minutes, December 3, 1974, p. 223, Folder 46, Box 219, Legislative Series, Albert Collection.

56. Caucus minutes, December 3, 1974, p. 226-230, Folder 46, Box 219, Legislative Series, Albert Collection.

57. Albert, *Giant*, 347.

appearances. Mills entered Bethesda Naval Hospital on December 3, and among House Democrats in early December, there was widespread belief that he would be removed as chair.[58] On December 11, Albert stated that Mills chose not to continue as chair of the Ways and Means Committee in the Ninety-fourth Congress.[59] On January 27, 1975, Mills left Bethesda Naval Hospital.[60]

The scandal greatly altered the lives of Mills and Battistella. As reported in September 1975, she began a tour to publicize her book, *Fanne Foxe: The Stripper and the Congressman*, started an acting career, and performed nightclub shows. Battistella claimed that she had not talked to Mills in two months since she moved from Virginia to Westport, Connecticut.[61] Battistella wrote that she had been pregnant and aborted the child fathered by Mills. She was in her late thirties and feared health risks to herself. She feared that Mills' heavy drinking might have hurt the unborn child.[62]

Meanwhile, the general direction and momentum of events indicated change for the Ninety-fourth Congress, and Henry Reuss was both a participant in and a beneficiary of the removal. Henry Schoellkopf Reuss was born in Milwaukee, Wisconsin in 1912. He graduated from Cornell University with an A.B. in 1933 and from Harvard Law School with an LL.B. in 1936. He practiced law in Milwaukee, worked for the Office of

---

58. "New Congress Organizes; No Role for Mills," *Congressional Quarterly Weekly Report*, December 7, 1974, 3247-3253.

59. "House Committees," *Congressional Quarterly Weekly Report*, December 14, 1974, 3355.

60. "Rep. Mills Leaves Hospital," *Washington Post*, January 30, 1975, A6.

61. William Gildea, "Splash! Fanne Foxe Surfaces Again," *Washington Post*, September 9, 1975, B1.

62. Battistella, *Fanne Foxe*, 141.

Price Administration in 1941 and 1942, and served in the U. S. Army from 1943 to 1945. He won a Bronze Star and rose from private to second lieutenant. He then practiced law and did private business before being elected to the U. S. House of Representatives in 1954.[63] By the middle of the 1970s, he represented the Fifth District of Wisconsin which included part of the Milwaukee metropolitan area.[64]

Reuss openly challenged Patman. Reuss wrote that when he ranked fourth in seniority on the Banking and Currency Committee, in the 1970s before the removal, he feared that by the time he became chair, he would be too old to work effectively.[65] On December 6, 1974, Reuss stated that he was deliberating a challenge to Patman for the chairmanship and had been encouraged by other members to challenge.[66] On January 2, 1975, Reuss confirmed that he had sought support for a challenge to Patman for the chairmanship. In addition, rumors circulated that Hebert and Poage would also be challenged.[67]

In contrast to traditional House customs, the freshmen Democrats displayed boldness and assertiveness. They held private hearings and invited the chairmen to testify and answer questions as Congress began its work. Jim Wright wrote that Burton suggested the idea for this event to the freshmen and that, "Some crusty old chairmen regarded it as an impertinence, but most tolerantly accepted the invitation and spoke to the

---

63. Nystrom, *Biographical Directory*, 1707.
64. Brownson, *1975 Staff Directory*, 115-116.
65. Reuss, *When Government Was Good*, 102-103.
66. David S. Broder, "Rep. Reuss Eyes Race For Patman's Post," *Washington Post*, December 7, 1974, A4.
67. Edward Cowan, "Reuss Weighs Bid To Oust Patman," *New York Times*, January 3, 1975, 5.

freshmen group, answering their questions."[68] The committee chairmen accepted invitations to testify before the freshmen Democrats on January 9, 10, 11, and 13.[69]

Reports about the hearings indicated great significance rather than grandstanding. The freshmen questioned the committee chairs for about five hours behind closed doors on January 9. After the hearings on January 9, Timothy Wirth of Colorado stated that he and about twelve freshmen conspired "'to make sure that bothersome questions were asked that had to be asked.'" Wirth added that, "'We want to make this new House much more accountable to the country.'" Patman's speech to the freshmen impressed some of them while boring others, and some freshmen considered removing Patman.[70] The freshmen held hearings with the committee chairs for four days. Afterwards, Ottinger stated that Hebert was condescending to the freshmen in contrast to the other chairs. He also announced that he would vote against Patman, Poage, and Hebert.[71] Ottinger recalled that some chairs made good impressions, but other chairs made bad impressions. Patman and Hebert made bad impressions. In addition, the chairs gave arguments for the seniority system and warned that minorities and members with unpopular ideas would face disadvantages without it. Ottinger viewed the hearings with the chairmen as

---

68. Wright, *Balance of Power*, 237-238.

69. "New Committee Chairmen," *Congressional Quarterly Weekly Report*, January 11, 1975, 64.

70. "New Democrats in House Raise Tough Questions With Leaders," *New York Times*, January 10, 1975, 27.

71. Richard L. Lyons, "Freshmen Assess House Chairmen," *Washington Post*, January 14, 1975, A2.

highly significant: "It was the first time they were ever held accountable to anybody."[72]

Patman's speech to the freshmen expressed his ideology and proposed plans for the Ninety-fourth Congress. He stated that the Democrats' large majority in the Ninety-fourth Congress provided them an opportunity to produce a strong legislative record and to accomplish important objectives that earlier faced obstruction. He conceded that he was controversial and was associated with controversial issues, but the Banking and Currency Committee addressed issues that often raised controversy and attracted the special interests. At one point in the speech he stated that: "There are some people who believe we can get things done in a nice quiet tea-house atmosphere, but I have found you have to be willing to fight--to do battle with the special interests--if you really want to get something accomplished. And I trust we have a fair number of fighters in this new class--people who don't mind taking on controversy." Patman claimed that the Committee Democrats should be responsive to the basic policies of the Democratic Party, the House Democratic Leadership, and the Democratic Caucus. In addition, Patman reminded the freshmen that his efforts on the Committee earned him a place "on the first of President Nixon's famous 'enemies list.'" Patman wanted the Committee to address the most salient issues, in his opinion, facing the nation: "First, I fell very strongly that we must straighten out our monetary policies and make the Federal Reserve responsible to the will of the people and their elected representatives." Also, he wanted the Committee, and perhaps

---

72. Richard Ottinger, interview by author, November 18, 1999, telephone tape recording, T. Harry Williams Center for Oral History, Louisiana State University, Baton Rouge, LA.

other committees, to "launch a full-scale study of economic concentration and the effects of this concentration on our current economic ills. I am very distrustful of this growing corporate power--power which not only cuts across all jurisdictions in the United States but also across foreign boundaries--and I don't think the Congress has done enough in this area." Patman made a special offer to the freshmen: "I'll be very honest with you...I'm hopeful that you people--the new Members--are going to provide the majorities to push through legislation which some of us have been fighting for and which has lacked just a handful of votes for success." Patman stated that the freshmen added to his Committee could expect him to be open-minded to new ideas that they might have. They could fully participate in the Committee's work.[73]

Poage's encounter with the freshmen revealed ideological differences. Poage wrote that he believed that the hearings were intended to show that he was autocratic in his management of the Committee and that he disagreed with them on spending for social programs. Poage told the freshmen that these points were true; he felt that a chairman needed to act autocratically in order for a committee to work effectively.[74] Fowler West recalled that, "And I know Poage flatly told them-- these were all closed, it didn't go--but Poage told them that he didn't like the food stamp program and he was sorry if they didn't like it."[75]

---

73. "Remarks of Chairman Wright Patman House Banking, Currency and Housing Committee to the Democratic Class of the 94th Congress" January 9, 1975, Folder: GD-412, Box 144B, Papers of Wright Patman.

74. Poage, *85 Years*, 147-148.

75. Fowler West, interview by author, January 19, 2000, telephone tape recording, T. Harry Williams Center for Oral History, Louisiana State University, Baton Rouge, LA.

Hebert's hearing with the freshmen featured hostility. Some opinions of Hebert's appearance before the freshmen were reported. George Miller of California said, "'I think he's out of touch with the thinking of the rest of the country on the use of the military.'" Anthony T. Moffett of Connecticut said, concerning Hebert's ideas on the military, "'In one word-- frightening!'"[76] Tip O'Neill wrote that during the hearings, Hebert recommended that the freshmen remain passive, learn about the House, and wait before taking an active part in affairs.[77] Jim Wright wrote that he was told by a freshman afterwards that Hebert had angered them with a patronizing demeanor.[78] It was reported that Hebert supposedly addressed the freshmen as "'boys and girls'" at the hearings.[79] Hebert denied that he called the freshmen "boys and girls," compared the hearings to "inquisition sessions," and believed that some freshmen thought he was subservient to the Pentagon and arrogant. He defended the bombing of North Vietnam (after the U. S. had left the war and after U. S. POWs had been released) and his endorsement of Republican Marjorie Holt of Maryland of the Armed Services Committee. He wrote that one freshman said that the freshmen were targeting him regardless of his statements at the hearings.[80]

The House officially convened at noon on Tuesday, January 14, 1975. The members-elect were called to order by the Clerk of the House of Representatives, W. Pat Jennings.

---

76. "Newcomers Give Hebert Sharp Quiz," *Washington Post*, January 12, 1975, A3.

77. O'Neill, *Man of the House*, 284.

78. Wright, *Balance of Power*, 238.

79. James M. Naughton, "Upheaval in the House," *New York Times*, January 17, 1975, 29.

80. Hebert, *Titans*, 441-442.

The chaplain, the Rev. Edward G. Latch, D. D., read from the Bible and delivered a prayer. The roll of the representatives-elect was called by states in alphabetical order (roll by states). Members-elect who were present responded. The Clerk announced that 432 representatives-elect responded, and therefore, a quorum was present.[81] The clerk announced the election of the Resident Commissioner from Puerto Rico and the Delegates from the District of Columbia, Guam, and the Virgin Islands.[82]

Next, the House conducted elections and administered oaths. Albert was elected Speaker over Republican John Rhodes of Arizona, 287-143. Two members-elect voted present. Rhodes and Albert both gave speeches.[83] Wright Patman was the Dean of the House and administered the oath to Albert for the Speaker position. The members also took the oath of office and officially became representatives, not representatives-elect, of Congress. Phillip Burton reported that the House Democratic Caucus chose Thomas P. O'Neill to serve as Majority Leader. John Anderson of Illinois, chairman of the Republican Conference, announced that Rhodes would serve as Minority Leader and that Robert H. Michel of Illinois would serve as Minority Whip.[84] Phillip Burton offered a resolution, H Res 1, to elect W. Pat Jennings as Clerk, Kenneth R. Harding as Sergeant at Arms, James T. Molloy as

---

81. No Subject Heading, 94th Cong., 1st sess., *Congressional Record* 121 (January 14, 1975): 15-17.

82. *Announcement by the Clerk*, 94th Cong., 1st sess., *Congressional Record* 121 (January 14, 1975): 17.

83. *Election of Speaker*, 94th Cong., 1st sess., *Congressional Record* 121 (January 14, 1975): 17-19.

84. *Majority Leader and Minority Leader and Minority Whip*, 94th Cong., 1st sess., *Congressional Record* 121 (January 14, 1975): 19.

Doorkeeper, Robert V. Rota as Postmaster, and Rev. Edward G. Latch, D.D. as Chaplain. Anderson of Illinois offered a substitute resolution to elect Joe Bartlett as Clerk, Walter P. Kennedy as Sergeant at Arms, William R. Bonsell as Doorkeeper, and Tommy Lee Winebrenner as Postmaster. There were no other nominations for Chaplain. The substitute by Anderson was rejected by the House; Burton's resolution was passed by the House. The officers who were elected took their oaths of office.[85]

The House then addressed some bureaucratic matters. O'Neill offered a resolution to send a message to the Senate informing them that the House had convened. The resolution was passed.[86] O'Neill offered a resolution for a committee of two members chosen by the Speaker to join with a Senate committee to inform the President that a quorum of each chamber had been assembled and that Congress was ready to receive any messages from the President. The resolution passed. Albert chose O'Neill and Rhodes for this committee.[87] Mahon offered a resolution for the Clerk to be instructed to inform the President that the House elected Albert as Speaker and chose Jennings as Clerk. The resolution passed.[88]

---

85. *Election of Clerk of the House, Sergeant at Arms, Doorkeeper, Postmaster, and Chaplain*, 94th Cong., 1st sess., *Congressional Record* 121 (January 14, 1975): 19-20.

86. *Notification to Senate of Organization of the House*, 94th Cong., 1st sess., *Congressional Record* 121 (January 14, 1975): 20.

87. *Committee to Notify the President of the United States of the Assembly of the Congress*, 94th Cong., 1st sess., *Congressional Record* 121 (January 14, 1975): 20.

88. *Authorizing the Clerk to Inform the President of the Election of the Speaker and the Clerk of the House of Representatives*, 94th Cong., 1st sess., *Congressional Record* 121 (January 14, 1975): 20.

The House rules were addressed. O'Neill offered a resolution, H Res 5, to adopt the previous rules of the House in the Ninety-third Congress as the rules in the Ninety-fourth Congress with some modifications. These rules also included relevant portions of some earlier pieces of legislation. The changes were listed.[89] Debate on the rules began. The House voted on the rules and passed them, 259-150.[90]

After years of effort by the Congressional reform movement, a new demand for accountability from the public, and a new bloc of pro-reform freshmen, the strategy for executing the removal had to be formulated. Ottinger credited the DSG as the driving force in the removal of the chairmen. Ottinger recalled that, "There was a group of those guys from the DSG who put this whole thing together." He also said, "It's the Study Group people that put this together." Burton was the "real strategist" in the removal, and Ottinger and Burton met to discuss strategy. Ottinger explained that he did not serve as one of the chief strategists. He kept the freshmen organized and only helped a little with strategy: "I was the person who met the troops to get it done." Ottinger stated that O'Neill and Albert were members of the House Democratic Leadership and favored the status quo. They would not have participated in the removal.[91] Henry Reuss stated that the removal was not an

---

89. *Rules of the House*, 94th Cong., 1st sess., *Congressional Record* 121 (January 14, 1975): 20-22.

90. *Rules of the House*, 94th Cong., 1st sess., *Congressional Record* 121 (January 14, 1975): 22-33.

91. Richard Ottinger, interview by author, November 18, 1999, telephone tape recording, T. Harry Williams Center for Oral History, Louisiana State University, Baton Rouge, LA.

official DSG activity. Rather, the removal was executed by members of the DSG.[92]

Ottinger discussed the selection of Patman, Poage, and Hebert for removal. Ottinger stated that: "Well, the guys that put this together wanted to take three people, three chairmen, who it was obvious that they'd abused their positions, and where we'd win." He explained that, "So we wanted to pick people who really had misused their position as chair in a pretty obvious, sustained way." He added that, "No, you wanted to pick people whose problems as chairmen were pretty well defined and notorious." Concerning the selection of Patman, Poage, and Hebert, Ottinger said, "That they'd been running things in a pretty high handed way, and not allowing the views of people to disagree with them, to be heard fairly. We didn't want to do it on an ideological basis. We wanted to do it on a basis of effectiveness of a person as a chairman, respect for members of a committee. Giving them the opportunity to have their views considered." He stated that, "We didn't go after people who sold out to lobbyists or whose views we disagreed. We just went after people who abused their power as chair." Poage and Hebert were conservative compared to the freshmen who, overall, were liberal, but Patman's ideology had some points of overlap with the generally liberal ideology of the freshmen. Ottinger explained that, "And they picked Wright Patman because they didn't want to just go against conservatives. Patman was a liberal guy. Because we didn't want to make this appear to be an ideological war." Patman ignored the majority of his Committee and abused his authority

92. Henry Reuss, interview by author, January 27, 2000, telephone tape recording, T. Harry Williams Center for Oral History, Louisiana State University, Baton Rouge, LA.

as chair in extreme ways. Ottinger explained that there was no anti-Southern bias in the removal. Many of the chairs were Southerners because Southern representatives typically won reelection easier and accumulated greater seniority than representatives from other regions such as the Northeast.[93]

In later sessions of the Democratic Caucus, two opinions of the freshmen's decision-making process were revealed. Stephen Neal of North Carolina stated, on January 22, 1975, that, "Now, in our four class meetings we have used three criterians to judge committee chairmen, we asked the question, is this committee effective? Is this committee responsive to other committee members and is the committee responsive to the will of the Caucus?"[94] John LaFalce of New York stated on January 22, 1975, that: "We were united on a single theme, and that theme was reform." He said: "We wanted to change some of the chairmanships to make this House operate better. And certain names were mentioned. And it was said we ought to evaluate seriously the credentials of this individual and that individual and another individual if we want reform."[95]

With the completion of these events, the coalition of critics, reformers, and freshmen were prepared to implement the removal of the chairmen. Experienced members such as Burton and Ottinger organized the coalition, and the House Democrats set new rules that reflected the rising demand for accountability. The galvanized freshmen were critical in the

---

93. Richard Ottinger, interview by author, November 18, 1999, telephone tape recording, T. Harry Williams Center for Oral History, Louisiana State University, Baton Rouge, LA.

94. Caucus minutes, January 22, 1975, p. 703-704, Folder 48, Box 219, Legislative Series, Albert Collection.

95. Caucus minutes, January 22, 1975, p. 717-718, Folder 48, Box 219, Legislative Series, Albert Collection.

events of these weeks, and the hearings with the chairmen were a bold and unprecedented event. The Bipartisan House System had been slowly dismantled, and its full demise would be solidified through the removal of three of its exemplars: Patman, Poage, and Hebert.

Chapter 8 - The Removal

After much time and effort, the coalition for removal composed of the critics, the reformers, and the freshmen took action against Patman, Poage, and Hebert. The coalition worked through the chairmen selection process which featured critical roles for the DSPC and the Caucus. The removal fundamentally altered the House forever.

The Democrats, as the majority party, prepared to select the committee chairmen in accord with the chairmen selection process. The DSPC would nominate members for the chairmen positions, and the Caucus could then confirm or reject the nominees. If the Caucus rejected a nominee, then the DSPC would nominate another member for that position, and additional members could be nominated from the floor when the Caucus met. The Caucus would then vote again on the nominees.

Due to the Congressional reform movement, the DSPC began playing a critical role in Party and House affairs. The DSPC for the Ninety-fourth Congress was composed of twenty-four members. The members elected by the Caucus were Speaker Carl Albert, Majority Leader Tip O'Neill, and Caucus Chairman Phillip Burton. The members elected from the regional groupings of the Caucus were John Moss of California, Morris Udall of Arizona, Henry Reuss of Wisconsin, Melvin Price of Illinois, Richard Bolling of Missouri, Wright Patman of Texas, Tom Bevill of Alabama, Robert Stephens of Georgia, Frank Thompson of New Jersey, John Dent of Pennsylvania, Jonathan Bingham of New York, and Robert Giaimo of Connecticut. The members appointed by the Speaker were John McFall of California (Majority Whip), John Brademas of

Indiana (Chief Deputy Whip), Jim Wright of Texas (deputy whip), Richard Fulton of Tennessee (deputy whip), Spark Matsunaga of Hawaii (deputy whip), Mendel Davis of South Carolina (for second and third term members), Ralph Metcalfe of Illinois (for the Black Caucus), Barbara Jordan of Texas (for women), and William Brodhead of Michigan (for first-term members).[1]

The DSPC met in January to nominate members for the chairmen positions, and the results marked the start of the removal. Albert described a critical event that occurred when the DSPC met. O'Neill made a motion to recommend for chairmanships all the chairs who held chairmanships of standing committees at the conclusion of the Ninety-third Congress who were reelected to the Ninety-fourth Congress with the exception of Wilbur Mills and the Ways and Means Committee chair. Bingham offered a substitute that would require the DSPC to conduct separate votes by secret ballot on each returning chair except the Ways and Means Committee chairman. The DSPC debated the options and voted. The substitute from Bingham won, and the DSPC abided by it.[2] The DSPC meeting featured more surprises. Patman was rejected by a vote of 11-13 for the chairmanship of the Banking and Currency Committee, and then, William Barrett of Pennsylvania and Leonor Sullivan of Missouri were also voted on as nominees for the Committee chair and rejected. Instead, Henry Reuss was nominated by a vote of 15-9 for the Banking and

---

1. "New Steering Committee," *Congressional Quarterly Weekly Report*, December 7, 1974, 3250.

2. Caucus minutes, January 16, 1975, p. 515-516, Folder: Caucus Minutes Jan. 13, 16, 22, 1975, Box 185, Congressional Papers of Thomas S. Foley, Manuscripts, Archives, and Special Collections, Holland/New Library, Washington State University, Pullman, WA.

Currency Committee chair. Poage and Hebert were nominated on votes of 14-10 for their respective positions. The DSPC conducted four votes on Wayne Hays, chairman of the House Administration Committee. The first three votes tied at 12-12. The fourth vote was 11-13, and Hays was rejected. The DSPC then nominated Frank Thompson by a vote of 20-4. All other chairs won nomination without serious contention.[3]

Wayne Hays' background differed from the backgrounds of Patman, Poage, and Hebert, but his management of his Committee and his personal characteristics generated opposition. Hays' reputation among House members was partially revealed in a statement from Carl Albert about the selection of Hale Boggs as the Majority Leader in 1971. He wrote: "Though I could have worked with any of those men as my majority leader (except maybe Hays, whom no one could work with in any capacity), Hale was my own favorite."[4] Tip O'Neill wrote this description of Hays: "The man had a mean streak and was often abusive to people he didn't agree with."[5] Phillip Burton's biographer, John Jacobs, explained a critical aspect about Hays. Hays' House Administration Committee had jurisdiction over internal operations of the House often viewed as minor issues or details. Hays used his power over these operations to reward friends and harass enemies. For example, he might revoke good parking spots or assign small offices in poor locations. Frank Thompson, Tip O'Neill, and Richard Bolling all disliked Hays.[6]

---

3. "Democrats Oust Hebert, Poage; Adopt Reforms," *Congressional Quarterly Weekly Report*, January 18, 1975, 111-116, 118-119, 165-166.

4. Albert, *Giant*, 326.

5. O'Neill, *Man of the House*, 216.

6. Jacobs, *Rage for Justice*, 252.

William "Fishbait" Miller gave a relatively significant amount of attention to Hays and his personal characteristics in his autobiography. Miller wrote that, "He seemed to love to terrorize people. He did things that were downright mean." He also wrote, "He would be too mean, insulting anyone in front of an audience, sometimes when the person was there and sometimes behind his back." The House Administration Committee had the responsibility of processing pay vouchers for House employees. Miller wrote that Hays sometimes impeded the processing of some people's paychecks. Hays tried, unsuccessfully, on one occasion to remove an aide to Don Fraser from his job by impeding the processing of the aide's pay voucher. Fraser resorted to obstructionist techniques to stop House work as a means to pressure Hays to sign the voucher. Hays, on one occasion, refused to pay a man that Speaker Albert had appointed to a position in the House press and television galleries. Albert had to pressure Hays to process the pay voucher for the man.[7] Miller noted Hays' frequent rude behavior: "He had fiendish names for everyone. He called Congressman Don Fraser, who dared stand up to him in the matter of signing a voucher, a 'mush head.' And almost everyone suffered the name of 'potato head' at one time or another, including me." Miller added that, "Ethnic slurs came easily from the bully of the House."[8] Hays had other problems, too: "Wayne Hays was another acknowledged girl-chaser, always talking about his great goal--to be shot at, but missed, at age ninety, by a jealous husband. He would greet pretty young things around the Hill with a big hello and a handshake.

---

7. Miller, *Fishbait*, 238-240.
8. Miller, *Fishbait*, 164-165.

He would say, 'Hi, I'm Dr. Wayne Hays, D.D.--Doctor of the Divan.'"[9]

The Caucus considered the nominees for the chairmanships in a relatively brief and uneventful manner. The Caucus convened on January 16 at 10:05 a.m. The rules of the Caucus required that no one, except Democratic House members, a Caucus Journal Clerk, and other necessary persons, be admitted to Caucus meetings unless they received the permission of the Caucus Chairman.[10] The only persons present were Democratic House members and other persons granted permission because they were selected to perform necessary tasks for the Caucus. These other persons included members of the Teller's Office, members of the Journal Clerk's office, and members of the staff of the Leadership. The staffers would help conduct the balloting.[11]

It was apparent to keen observers that a momentous event was unfolding. As the proceedings began, James O'Hara spoke about the recent reforms which now were truly revolutionizing the House. His statement seemed contrary to the goals of the DSG and the Congressional reform movement but may have revealed the actual view of the practical impact of the reforms: "I think that it is only fair to state at the outset that none of us on the Hansen Committee, I do not believe--and we are the ones that wrote these rules--really anticipated that the Committee on Committees would exercise the power we gave it, to choose to nominate a chairman without regard to seniority. I think when we put that in the rule, we thought it was probably

---

9. Miller, *Fishbait*, 106.

10. Caucus minutes, January 16, 1975, p. 509, Folder: Caucus Minutes Jan. 13, 16, 22, 1975, Box 185, Foley Papers.

just a gesture."[12] Jim Wright wrote that he learned shortly before the first votes of the Caucus that some of the freshmen had made a pact to show their support for reform by removing at least three chairmen. Some older members did not know about this pact.[13] Foley wrote that he and a small group tried to lobby for Poage before the votes occurred. They did not think that Poage would be targeted for removal by the freshmen. There was a general opinion among Poage's friends that it would be best not to stimulate an intense debate over Poage's nomination and the chairmanship. It was thought that Poage would be spared if only a little lobbying was done and Poage avoided attention. Foley spoke for Poage to the freshmen.[14]

The Caucus proceeded to the Agriculture Committee. Albert placed the nomination of Poage for Agriculture Committee Chairman before the Caucus, and the vote would employ the secret ballot. Members would vote in the affirmative with an "aye" to support the recommendation of the DSPC. Members would vote in the negative with a "nay" to oppose the recommendation of the DSPC. The Caucus voted. Also, the Caucus approved without a recorded vote the nominees from the DSPC for the Democratic seats on the Agriculture Committee.[15] Later, Burton announced the result of the vote on

---

11. Caucus minutes, January 16, 1975, p. 509-510, Folder: Caucus Minutes Jan. 13, 16, 22, 1975, Box 185, Foley Papers.

12. Caucus minutes, January 16, 1975, p. 601-603, Folder: Caucus Minutes Jan. 13, 16, 22, 1975, Box 185, Foley Papers.

13. Wright, *Balance of Power*, 238.

14. Biggs, *Honor in the House*, 56.

15. Caucus minutes, January 16, 1975, p. 517-519, Folder: Caucus Minutes Jan. 13, 16, 22, 1975, Box 185, Foley Papers.

Poage, 141-144. The DSPC's recommendation for the Agriculture Committee chair was rejected.[16]

Next, the Caucus considered the Armed Services Committee. Albert announced the nomination by the DSPC of Hebert for the Armed Services Committee chair. The vote was conducted in the same manner as Poage's vote; "aye" or "nay" on Hebert. The Caucus approved the DSPC's nominees for the Democratic seats of the Armed Services Committee; there was no recorded vote.[17] Burton announced the result of the vote on Hebert, 133-152. The DSPC's recommendation was rejected.[18] Later, the vote on the Armed Services chair had to be corrected. The vote was 133-152, with one voting present.[19]

The Caucus' consideration of the Banking and Currency Committee chairmanship featured contention. Albert announced that the DSPC nominated for chairman Henry Reuss, and Burton announced that debate was requested for this nomination. Discussion began on the rules, and consideration of the Banking and Currency Committee chairmanship was postponed until later in the day.[20]

Later, the Caucus resumed consideration of the Banking and Currency Committee chairmanship. Debate would be

---

16. Caucus minutes, January 16, 1975, p. 529, Folder: Caucus Minutes Jan. 13, 16, 22, 1975, Box 185, Foley Papers.

17. Caucus minutes, January 16, 1975, p. 524-526, Folder: Caucus Minutes Jan. 13, 16, 22, 1975, Box 185, Foley Papers.

18. Caucus minutes, January 16, 1975, p. 533, Folder: Caucus Minutes Jan. 13, 16, 22, 1975, Box 185, Foley Papers.

19. Caucus minutes, January 16, 1975, p. 572, Folder: Caucus Minutes Jan. 13, 16, 22, 1975, Box 185, Foley Papers.

20. Caucus minutes, January 16, 1975, p. 527-529, Folder: Caucus Minutes Jan. 13, 16, 22, 1975, Box 185, Foley Papers.

controlled equally by two members.[21] Several members spoke in either support of or opposition to the Reuss nomination, and the issue of whether Patman had received fair treatment under the rules received considerable attention. One general opinion argued that because the rules for nomination were followed, he had received fair treatment. The other general opinion argued that because the DSPC nominated someone else first, he had not received fair treatment. Patman was denied a chance to have his record evaluated by the Caucus, and the Caucus was denied the opportunity to evaluate Patman's record. There was very little direct criticism of Patman, overall, and there was very little discussion of Reuss' record and abilities, overall. There was a significant amount of praise for the great service of Patman and his accomplishments. During debate, several people spoke for Patman; they were Thomas Ashley of Ohio, Barbara Jordan of Texas, Gillis Long of Louisiana, Leonor Sullivan, and Jim Wright. During debate, several people spoke for Reuss; they were William Moorhead of Pennsylvania, Frank Evans of Colorado, Edwin Lloyd Meeds of Washington, Gladys Spellman of Maryland, Thomas Rees of California, Bolling of Missouri, and James Scheuer of New York.[22]

The supporters of Patman stressed fairness and Patman's record of achievements and credentials as a reformer. Thomas Ashley of Ohio was the first to speak during debate. He criticized the DSPC for failing to nominate Patman for the chairmanship and thereby depriving the Caucus of its opportunity to evaluate Patman. Instead, a small group of

---

21. Caucus minutes, January 16, 1975, p. 547-548, Folder: Caucus Minutes Jan. 13, 16, 22, 1975, Box 185, Foley Papers.

22. Caucus minutes, January 16, 1975, p. 547-571, Folder: Caucus Minutes Jan. 13, 16, 22, 1975, Box 185, Foley Papers.

individuals, the DSPC, evaluated Patman. Ashley believed that the DSPC misused the rule allowing it to nominate members for chairmanships without following seniority. He believed the rule was not intended to remove returning chairs. Ashley stated that Patman "is being denied the least and the most to which he is entitled--the opportunity to stand on his record before this Caucus and to be judged accordingly." He also decried the fact that Reuss, a member of the DSPC, ultimately benefited from the DSPC's decision.[23] Barbara Jordan of Texas spoke next and made the same argument made by Ashley. Patman deserved an opportunity to defend himself, and the Caucus deserved the opportunity to evaluate him. A small group on the DSPC should not override the will of the entire Caucus.[24] Jim Wright rhetorically asked why Patman was chosen for removal and how the Democrats would appear to the nation if they removed a man with Patman's record and credentials. Wright said, "I know some of you won't feel fulfilled unless you make an example of some committees here. Why in the name of sweet reason do you single out Wright Patman for this kind of treatment--...?" Patman fought against the economic special interests. He displayed great loyalty to the Democratic Party. He became the first member in the Congress to publicly call for an investigation into the matters that became known as the Watergate Crisis. Over the years, Patman consistently sold more tickets for Democratic dinners and raised more money for Democratic candidates than any other Democrat in Congress.[25]

---

23. Caucus minutes, January 16, 1975, p. 548-551, Folder: Caucus Minutes Jan. 13, 16, 22, 1975, Box 185, Foley Papers.

24. Caucus minutes, January 16, 1975, p. 553-554, Folder: Caucus Minutes Jan. 13, 16, 22, 1975, Box 185, Foley Papers.

25. Caucus minutes, January 16, 1975, p. 567-569, Folder: Caucus Minutes Jan. 13, 16, 22, 1975, Box 185, Foley Papers.

The supporters of Reuss stressed the idea of reform and the need for change. William Moorhead of Pennsylvania identified Reuss with reform and the end of strict adherence to the seniority system. He believed that the Caucus rules should be followed and respected. Since the Reuss nomination proceeded in accord with the rules, it was fully proper and fair. He rejected the idea that Patman was being denied an opportunity to defend himself. Poage and Hebert were removed without any debate. Members could vote "aye" or "nay" on Reuss, and this choice provided them an opportunity to evaluate Patman's record.[26] Thomas M. Rees of California argued that Patman and the Caucus both received fair treatment in accord with the established rules. He recognized that Patman had many achievements in his long career but felt that the Committee had been a "very ineffective committee" in recent years. The Committee needed leadership, and he urged the Caucus to vote for Reuss.[27] Bolling defended the chairmen selection process as fair and reminded members that the Democratic Caucus created the process. He stressed that the Democrats had the opportunity to implement their reforms into practice and to truly attack excessive adherence to the seniority system. He stated that, "The issue that is here is whether this Party of Democrats, after many, many years of allowing system without mind to choose its subleaders, will decide to implement the proposals that it has incepted for a method of selecting its subleaders as well as its leaders."[28]

---

26. Caucus minutes, January 16, 1975, p. 551-553, Folder: Caucus Minutes Jan. 13, 16, 22, 1975, Box 185, Foley Papers.

27. Caucus minutes, January 16, 1975, p. 558-559, Folder: Caucus Minutes Jan. 13, 16, 22, 1975, Box 185, Foley Papers.

28. Caucus minutes, January 16, 1975, p. 562-563, Folder: Caucus Minutes Jan. 13, 16, 22, 1975, Box 185, Foley Papers.

Finally, the Caucus voted. The Caucus considered nominees for Democratic seats on the Committee, and the nominees were approved with no recorded vote.[29] The results of the vote on Reuss were announced, 141-146. The DSPC's recommendation was rejected.[30]

In addition, contention surrounded only one other committee chairmanship, House Administration. Albert announced the nominee for the chairmanship of the House Administration Committee, Frank Thompson of New Jersey.[31] The following people spoke for either Thompson or Hays because discussion was requested. Thompson's advocates included Udall of Arizona, Abner Mikva from Illinois, Gene Maguire of New Jersey, James Oberstar of Minnesota, Fraser of Minnesota, Bolling of Missouri, and O'Hara of Michigan. Hays' advocates included James Stanton of Ohio, Louis Stokes of Ohio, Elliott Levitas of Georgia, Edward Koch of New York, Thomas Morgan of Pennsylvania, John Burton of California, and John Murtha of Pennsylvania.[32]

The debate on Hays and Thompson was substantive. Fraser spoke and explained that he did not know of any organized movement to remove Hays from the chairmanship. He described a conflict with Hays. In 1972, a problem surrounded a staff member on his subcommittee who was appointed by him, and the committee chair approved the

29. Caucus minutes, January 16, 1975, p. 571-574, Folder: Caucus Minutes Jan. 13, 16, 22, 1975, Box 185, Foley Papers.

30. Caucus minutes, January 16, 1975, p. 578-579, Folder: Caucus Minutes Jan. 13, 16, 22, 1975, Box 185, Foley Papers.

31. Caucus minutes, January 16, 1975, p. 581, Folder: Caucus Minutes Jan. 13, 16, 22, 1975, Box 185, Foley Papers.

32. Caucus minutes, January 16, 1975, p. 582-605, Folder: Caucus Minutes Jan. 13, 16, 22, 1975, Box 185, Foley Papers.

appointment. Hays told the staff member that he was fired. Hays had not talked with the chair. Hays refused to sign the voucher. This problem continued for six weeks. He sent a letter to House members warning them about his plans. He kept the House at a standstill one day with quorum calls until Hays agreed to sign the voucher. He received the sympathy and support of many House members.[33] Levitas spoke for Hays and offered a freshmen perspective. He claimed that he developed his own standards for the committee chairs: "Did he do a good job as chairman? Did he treat his members and the Members of Congress fairly? Is he a loyal Democrat?" He stated that Hays met these standards and stressed one issue in particular: "Wayne Hays was the Chairman of the Democratic Congressional Committee to which many of us owe our presence here today, and in an unprecedented way getting over half of the funds available, not to incumbent members, my fellows of the class of 94, but to the new members."[34] The Caucus voted on Thompson.[35] The vote on Thompson was 109-176. The recommendation of the Committee on Committees was rejected.[36]

There were many other nominations for many other posts, and overall, the results showed support for the status quo. There were no other removals and no close contests. The Caucus approved on voice vote the Democratic nominees for

---

33. Caucus minutes, January 16, 1975, p. 594-596, Folder: Caucus Minutes Jan. 13, 16, 22, 1975, Box 185, Foley Papers.
34. Caucus minutes, January 16, 1975, p. 590-591, Folder: Caucus Minutes Jan. 13, 16, 22, 1975, Box 185, Foley Papers.
35. Caucus minutes, January 16, 1975, p. 605-607, Folder: Caucus Minutes Jan. 13, 16, 22, 1975, Box 185, Foley Papers.
36. Caucus minutes, January 16, 1975, p. 610, Folder: Caucus Minutes Jan. 13, 16, 22, 1975, Box 185, Foley Papers.

the Ways and Means Committee in a single vote. There were ten nominees.[37] Speaker Albert nominated Ray J. Madden of Indiana for chair of the Rules Committee.[38] Albert nominated, for seats on the Rules Committee, the following people: James J. Delaney of New York, Richard Bolling of Missouri, B. F. Sisk of California, John Young of Texas, Claude Pepper of Florida, Spark M. Matsunaga of Hawaii, Morgan F. Murphy of Illinois, Gillis Long of Louisiana, Joseph Moakley of Massachusetts, and Andrew Young of Georgia.[39] The Caucus approved these nominees for seats on the Rules Committee.[40] The following nominations were made for the other committee chairmanships:

George H. Mahon of Texas, Appropriations

Charles C. Diggs of Michigan, District of Columbia

Carl D. Perkins of Kentucky, Education and Labor

Thomas E. Morgan of Pennsylvania, International Relations

Jack Brooks of Texas, Government Operations

James A. Haley of Florida, Interior and Insular Affairs

Harley O. Staggers of West Virginia, Interstate and Foreign Commerce

Peter W. Rodino of New Jersey, Judiciary

Leonor K. Sullivan of Missouri, Merchant Marine and Fisheries

---

37. Caucus minutes, January 16, 1975, p. 511, Folder: Caucus Minutes Jan. 13, 16, 22, 1975, Box 185, Foley Papers.

38. Caucus minutes, January 16, 1975, p. 512, Folder: Caucus Minutes Jan. 13, 16, 22, 1975, Box 185, Foley Papers.

39. Caucus minutes, January 16, 1975, p. 514, Folder: Caucus Minutes Jan. 13, 16, 22, 1975, Box 185, Foley Papers.

40. Caucus minutes, January 16, 1975, p. 515, Folder: Caucus Minutes Jan. 13, 16, 22, 1975, Box 185, Foley Papers.

David N. Henderson of North Carolina, Post Office and Civil Service

Robert E. Jones of Alabama, Public Works and Transportation

Olin E. Teague of Texas, Science and Technology

Joe L. Evins of Tennessee, Small Business

Melvin Price of Illinois, Standards of Official Conduct

Ray Roberts of Texas, Veterans' Affairs

Al Ullman of Oregon, Ways and Means.[41]

These nominees were elected with little opposition:

Madden, Rules, 236-48

Diggs, District of Columbia, 259-18

Mahon, Appropriations, 193-94

Perkins, Education and Labor, 258-27

Morgan, International Relations, 260-13

Brooks, Government Operations, 261-9

Haley, Interior and Insular Affairs, 205-48

Staggers, Interstate Commerce, 194-54

Rodino, Judiciary, 240-6

Sullivan, Merchant Marine, 219-16

Henderson, Post Office and Civil Service, 206-7

Jones, Public Works, 208-10

Teague, Science and Technology, 182-26

Evins, Small Business, 188-12

Price, Standards of Official Conduct, 193-3

Roberts, Veterans' Affairs, 184-8

Ullman, Ways and Means, 185-19.[42]

---

41. Caucus minutes, January 16, 1975, p. 520, 530, 532, 576, 578, 609, 613, 616, 619, 623, 626, 629, 634, 638, 643, 648, Folder: Caucus Minutes Jan. 13, 16, 22, 1975, Box 185, Foley Papers.

Due to the coalition of critics, reformers, and freshmen, the chairmanships of four committees required resolution. Two chairmen, Poage and Hebert, had been removed, and two other chairmen faced major challenges to their positions. No other nominations from the DSPC for chairmanships were rejected. The DSPC met on January 17 and unanimously nominated Patman, Tom Foley, Melvin Price, and Hays for the chairmanships of Banking and Currency, Agriculture, Armed Services, and House Administration, respectively.[43]

Despite the votes of the Caucus, Poage and Hebert could possibly retain their positions. Technically, Foley and Price, if confirmed by the Caucus, would only be the Democratic nominees for the chairmanships, and ultimately, the full House, including both Democrats and Republicans, would vote on these and other chairmanships. The votes by the House were typically pro forma votes. If a bipartisan coalition could assemble a majority on the floor of the House, then this bipartisan coalition could reject the nominees in the votes and instead elect Poage and Hebert. This type of endeavor was rarely attempted, and members abandoning the party line in a pro forma vote faced serious consequences.

Poage wrote about the possibility of regaining his chairmanship and his rejection of this possibility. He wrote that some people encouraged him to fight on the House floor, and perhaps the Republicans would support him against the

---

42. Caucus minutes, January 16, 1975, p. 520-521, 540, 543, 574-575, 605-606, 606, 617-618, 620, 623, 627, 630, 634, 638, 647, 649, 656, 659, Folder: Caucus Minutes Jan. 13, 16, 22, 1975, Box 185, Foley Papers.

43. "Democrats Oust Hebert, Poage; Adopt Reforms," *Congressional Quarterly Weekly Report*, January 18, 1975, 111-116, 118-119, 165-166.

Caucus. Poage thought the Republicans would have supported him. Nonetheless, Poage rejected this possibility: "I admit I spent an unhappy and lonely night, but I never seriously considered any challenge to my party. I am a Democrat and I have always felt that party loyalty was essential to the perpetuity of our form of government, and I still think so."[44]

Hebert considered the possibility of regaining his chairmanship but ultimately rejected the possibility. After the Caucus rejected him, Hebert went to the press gallery and stated that he would fight on the House floor and thereby empower both Democrats and Republicans to resolve the controversy over the chairmanship. Hebert wrote that David Treen, a Republican from Louisiana, said that he intended to organize a pro-Hebert Republican movement for a floor fight. Other influential Democrats and Republicans also said they supported Hebert. Hebert even claimed that he had a plan to regain the chairmanship. The DSPC would nominate Melvin Price for the chair. When the Caucus met, Price would say that he did not want the job, and Hebert would be nominated. If he lost again, he would take the fight to the floor, and the entire House would vote.[45]

The House Democratic Leadership acted to forestall any efforts to support former chairs on the House floor. On January 17, Speaker Albert stated that he would use his power to force the Caucus selection to bind all Democrats in order to prevent any challenges on the House floor to the Caucus' selection for chairmen. Any Democrat who voted against the Caucus

---

44. Poage, *85 Years*, 148.
45. Hebert, *Titans*, 445-446.

selection would be excluded from majority party privileges.[46] On January 21, Hebert announced that he would end all his efforts to keep his chair. He reached his decision based on the threat of punishment against Democrats and Republicans who supported him if he tried to regain the chairmanship.[47] Hebert wrote that he learned from Democrat G. V. "Sonny" Montgomery of Mississippi that the House Democratic Leadership was serious about punishing dissidents and that Hebert's supporters could not keep their members in line for Hebert on future votes.[48]

With new nominations from the DSPC, the Caucus considered the four unresolved chairmanships. The House Democratic Caucus convened at 9:05 a.m. on Wednesday, January 22 in the House of Representatives Chamber.[49] Albert announced that Foley was the nominee for the chairmanship of the Agriculture Committee.[50] Poage delivered a speech endorsing Foley's nomination for the Agriculture Committee chairmanship and received a standing ovation from the Caucus. Poage explained that he opposed any attempt to reinstall him as chair and that he would not want secret deals and surprise tactics used against Foley as they were used against him. Regarding ideology, Poage said, "I have no intention of changing my position on issues even when it cost me a coveted position unless someone shows me I am wrong,

---

46. "Democrats Oust Hebert, Poage; Adopt Reforms," *Congressional Quarterly Weekly Report*, January 18, 1975, 111-119, 165-166.

47. "Hebert Gives Up Fight to Keep Chairman Post," *New York Times*, January 22, 1975, 21.

48. Hebert, *Titans*, 447.

49. Caucus minutes, January 22, 1975, p. 661-662, Folder 48, Box 219, Legislative Series, Albert Collection.

50. Caucus minutes, January 22, 1975, p. 662, Folder 48, Box 219, Legislative Series, Albert Collection.

and right now nobody has done that." Regarding Foley, Poage said, "His views are doubtless much closer to the views of the majority of the Members of this Caucus than are mine. He believes that government can and should do far more for our people and far more for our Members than seems possible to me. I hope he is correct."[51] The Caucus voted on the Foley nomination.[52] The vote was 257-9; he was confirmed.[53] In his acceptance speech, Foley praised Poage's abilities and character and said he would try to emulate Poage's great service.[54] Price's nomination for the Armed Services Committee chairmanship was announced.[55] Hebert addressed the Caucus. He complimented Price on his work on the Committee and asked that the members unanimously elect Price as chairman. He received a standing ovation. Hebert said, "I shall ask him, when he does become Chairman and elected by the House, to tell me what to do, and what you want me to do I will do."[56] The Caucus voted on Price's nomination.[57] Price won confirmation, 215-7.[58] In a short speech to the Caucus, Price complimented Hebert for his work on the

---

51. Caucus minutes, January 22, 1975, p. 662-665, Folder 48, Box 219, Legislative Series, Albert Collection.

52. Caucus minutes, January 22, 1975, p. 665-666, Folder 48, Box 219, Legislative Series, Albert Collection.

53. Caucus minutes, January 22, 1975, p. 669, Folder 48, Box 219, Legislative Series, Albert Collection.

54. Caucus minutes, January 22, 1975, p. 670-671, Folder 48, Box 219, Legislative Series, Albert Collection.

55. Caucus minutes, January 22, 1975, p. 666, Folder 48, Box 219, Legislative Series, Albert Collection.

56. Caucus minutes, January 22, 1975, p. 667-668, Folder 48, Box 219, Legislative Series, Albert Collection.

57. Caucus minutes, January 22, 1975, p. 669, Folder 48, Box 219, Legislative Series, Albert Collection.

Committee and added that, "I hope to be the committee chairman that Mr. Hebert has been during his term in the chair."[59]

The Caucus proceeded to the contested Banking and Currency chairmanship. Albert announced the recommendation of the DSPC for this chairmanship, Wright Patman.[60] The Committee had been renamed, in preparation for the Ninety-fourth Congress, the Committee on Banking, Currency and Housing.[61] The proposed procedure for the contest was based on the Caucus' standard rules and on consultation with the nominees for the chairmanship. The nominations would be announced, and the DSPC nominee's name would appear first. Each nominee's supporters would receive ten minutes of speeches controlled by the nominee's designee. The winner needed a majority of the votes cast. Blank ballots would not be counted. If there were more than three nominees and no nominee received a majority on the first ballot, then the nominee that finished last would be eliminated, and another vote would occur. The nominees were Patman, Robert Stephens of Georgia, and Reuss. The Stephens supporters would begin debate as a result of a "draw of the lot."[62]

Most of the speeches expressed a lot of vagueness about the nominees. Several speakers cited the current

---

58. Caucus minutes, January 22, 1975, p. 696, Folder 48, Box 219, Legislative Series, Albert Collection.

59. Caucus minutes, January 22, 1975, p. 696-697, Folder 48, Box 219, Legislative Series, Albert Collection.

60. Caucus minutes, January 22, 1975, p. 670, Folder 48, Box 219, Legislative Series, Albert Collection.

61. Caucus minutes, January 22, 1975, p. 671, Folder 48, Box 219, Legislative Series, Albert Collection.

62. Caucus minutes, January 22, 1975, p. 671-673, Folder 48, Box 219, Legislative Series, Albert Collection.

economic problems as making the Committee chair decision a very critical one, with the notion that their candidate could best confront the problems. Pro-Reuss and pro-Stephens speakers typically expressed vague statements of support for their candidate. Some of the speeches from supporters of Reuss and Stephens actually praised Patman. There was very little direct criticism of Patman and his management of the Committee. Some of the speeches for Reuss and Stephens hinted at problems on the Committee but were not specific or clear. Patman's supporters stressed his record of achievements and credentials as a reformer.[63]

The supporters of Stephens began debate. Phil M. Landrum of Georgia spoke first for Stephens and described him as talented, qualified for the chairmanship, and capable of working well with other members.[64] Ronald "Bo" Ginn of Georgia described the Committee as being in a state of "disarray" and in need of being pieced "back together again." He believed that Stephens could accomplish this task. Yet, he recognized that Patman had a great record and that Reuss had great potential.[65]

The supporters of Reuss advocated for their candidate. William Moorhead was the first to speak in support of Reuss and argued that the nation faced grave economic challenges. Because the Committee helped oversee the economy, a person of Reuss' talents was needed to chair the Committee and to help reinvigorate the economy. In his opinion, Reuss

---

63. Caucus minutes, January 22, 1975, p. 673-695, Folder 48, Box 219, Legislative Series, Albert Collection.
64. Caucus minutes, January 22, 1975, p. 673-674, Folder 48, Box 219, Legislative Series, Albert Collection.
65. Caucus minutes, January 22, 1975, p. 690-691, Folder 48, Box 219, Legislative Series, Albert Collection.

was "the ablest person for the next few years to lead this Congress and this country back to economic health."[66] Floyd V. Hicks of Washington spoke of the need to establish unanimity on the Committee and wanted either Stephens or Reuss to become chairman. He preferred Reuss and stated that: "He is knowledgeable. He is hard-working. He is patient. He has all the qualities that any of you people would want. He is progressive looking. He is vigorous."[67] Robert Bergland of Minnesota spoke for Reuss and praised Reuss as an innovator willing to consider other viewpoints and as a good legislator capable of achieving results.[68]

The supporters of Patman defended their man. Robert Krueger of Texas spoke first for Patman. He stressed that Patman possessed a record of fighting for the interests of the common American and refused to serve or be controlled by the "special interests." He described Patman as "A man that 50 years of special interests have not been able to buy. A man that the Morgans and Rockefellers and others have not been able to conquer." Krueger raised the issue of fairness and Patman's age: "We are a party that has consistently spoken out against discrimination. Are we now to discriminate against someone because of his age? That would not be a fit approach for our Party."[69] Jim Wright again spoke in support of Patman. Wright made a vague reference to the regional aspect of the

---

66. Caucus minutes, January 22, 1975, p. 674-675, Folder 48, Box 219, Legislative Series, Albert Collection.
67. Caucus minutes, January 22, 1975, p. 677-678, Folder 48, Box 219, Legislative Series, Albert Collection.
68. Caucus minutes, January 22, 1975, p. 685-686, Folder 48, Box 219, Legislative Series, Albert Collection.
69. Caucus minutes, January 22, 1975, p. 675-677, Folder 48, Box 219, Legislative Series, Albert Collection.

chairmen's removal when he stated that, "God knows this Party and this country needs the south." More specifically, Wright hailed Patman for his courage; he opposed the Ku Klux Klan in the 1920s, supported civil rights, and supported George McGovern loyally. Patman caused Andrew Mellon to be removed from office and initiated the investigation into the matters that became the Watergate Crisis.[70] Leonor Sullivan spoke in support of Patman. The nation faced serious economic challenges, and Patman had the wisdom and abilities to serve effectively as chairman and to fight these economic challenges.[71]

With the conclusion of the speeches, the moment of decision had arrived, and the Caucus voted on the chairmanship.[72] On the first vote, the results were Reuss 130, Patman 90, and Stephens 58. The rules required that the candidate with the least number of votes be eliminated. Therefore, Stephens was eliminated.[73] On the final vote, Reuss defeated Patman, 152-117.[74] In his victory speech, Reuss praised Patman for his integrity and service in the House.[75]

The Caucus still had to dispose of the House Administration Committee chairmanship. The Caucus voted on and approved the membership for the House Administration

---

70. Caucus minutes, January 22, 1975, p. 694, Folder 48, Box 219, Legislative Series, Albert Collection.

71. Caucus minutes, January 22, 1975, p. 678-680, Folder 48, Box 219, Legislative Series, Albert Collection.

72. Caucus minutes, January 22, 1975, p. 695-696, Folder 48, Box 219, Legislative Series, Albert Collection.

73. Caucus minutes, January 22, 1975, p. 705, Folder 48, Box 219, Legislative Series, Albert Collection.

74. Caucus minutes, January 22, 1975, p. 722, Folder 48, Box 219, Legislative Series, Albert Collection.

Committee. There was no recorded vote.[76] Albert submitted the nomination of Hays for the House Administration Committee chairmanship.[77] Speeches on the Hays-Thompson contest stressed fairness (by both men's supporters) and generally avoided direct criticism of Hays. The following people made speeches either in support of Hays or Thompson. The advocates of Hays included Charles Rangel of New York, Stephen Neal of North Carolina, Flowers (not fully identified in the Caucus minutes), Charles Wilson of Texas, Edward Koch of New York, John LaFalce of New York, and James Stanton of Ohio. The advocates of Thompson included Meeds (not fully identified in the Caucus minutes), Edward Patten of New Jersey, McClory (not fully identified in the Caucus minutes), Edward Pattison of New York, and Bolling of Missouri.[78]

Hays' supporters spoke on his behalf. Rangel of New York endorsed Hays and spoke in reference to a *New York Times* editorial about Hays which seemed to have been critical of Hays. He identified some of the accusations made about Hays but did not refute them. Rangel said: "After reading all these comments about Chairman Hays, I did not know he was doing that many things for the House and after considering everything that was involved, I for one, will not hold these things against him."[79] Wilson of Texas spoke for Hays but used

---

75. Caucus minutes, January 22, 1975, p. 722-724, Folder 48, Box 219, Legislative Series, Albert Collection.

76. Caucus minutes, January 22, 1975, p. 607-608, Folder 48, Box 219, Legislative Series, Albert Collection.

77. Caucus minutes, January 22, 1975, p. 699, Folder 48, Box 219, Legislative Series, Albert Collection.

78. Caucus minutes, January 22, 1975, p. 699-721, Folder 48, Box 219, Legislative Series, Albert Collection.

79. Caucus minutes, January 22, 1975, p. 702-703, Folder 48, Box 219, Legislative Series, Albert Collection.

a joke which did not seem helpful to Hays: "I like Frank Thompson. I am not sure whether Wayne Hays likes me or not. I don't think he ever told me. He has shown some interest in my wife." Wilson said that the previous freshmen class, which included him, on several occasions requested meetings with Hays and received the meetings. They submitted a list of requests, and Hays granted the requests.[80] James Stanton of Ohio claimed that Hays was fair. Regarding Hays' performance, he said: "And when you test whether your House has been in order for the last four years I believe that you have to arrive at the conclusion that (1) it is in order, (2) that the charges that have been made by the editorial writers have been unsubstantiated." Stanton also said, "Mr. Chairman, Wayne Hays is a sone of a bitch but he is our son of a bitch."[81]

The supporters of Thompson presented their argument. Lloyd Meeds of Washington nominated Thompson and stressed the issue of fairness. He thought that it was not good, and could be bad, for one to hold both the chair of the DCCC and the House Administration Committee. Both positions dispensed benefits, and potential existed for someone to misuse these powers for personal gain. Thompson was by nature fair. Meeds did not directly criticize Hays but implied that Hays was unfair as chairman. He said: "It is my sincere feeling that if we elect Frank Thompson as Chairman of the House Administration Committee, we will have procedural fairness. I am compelled to say unfortunately, I do not believe that is the

---

80. Caucus minutes, January 22, 1975, p. 712-713, Folder 48, Box 219, Legislative Series, Albert Collection.
81. Caucus minutes, January 22, 1975, p. 718-719, Folder 48, Box 219, Legislative Series, Albert Collection.

case if we elect Wayne Hays as Chairman."[82] Bolling praised Thompson for his past record and his credentials. He said: "His record of effective fighting in controversial causes has left him a noncontroversial figure because he has always conducted himself in whatever he did with absolute fairness, with absolute fairness."[83]

Ultimately, the Caucus decided not to change the leadership of the House Administration Committee. On the critical vote, Hays received 161 votes to Thompson's 111. In his victory speech, Hays said, "I will try to be a nicer S.O.B."[84] Yet, there was talk of corruption behind the vote. It was reported that Hays, after the first DSPC vote, lobbied many of the freshmen. Hays received strong support from Burton. According to *Congressional Quarterly Weekly Report*, "Sources in the freshmen delegation" stated that Hays reached an agreement with Burton to provide the Democratic Caucus with money and office space for the first time.[85]

The Caucus used secret votes for the removal, but people theorized about members' votes. Henry Reuss claimed that most of the freshmen voted for him. The Texas delegation, even the liberals in the Texas delegation such as Bob Krueger, supported Patman. Southern Democrats supported Patman as well as Poage and Hebert because of regional loyalty and a desire to maintain Southern power through the chairmanships;

---

82. Caucus minutes, January 22, 1975, p. 699-701, Folder 48, Box 219, Legislative Series, Albert Collection.

83. Caucus minutes, January 22, 1975, p. 720-721, Folder 48, Box 219, Legislative Series, Albert Collection.

84. Caucus minutes, January 22, 1975, p. 730, Folder 48, Box 219, Legislative Series, Albert Collection.

85. "Democrats Oust Hebert, Poage; Adopt Reforms," *Congressional Quarterly Weekly Report*, January 18, 1975, 111-116, 118-119, 165-166.

yet, many of them did not like Patman. Most other Democrats voted for Reuss.[86] Jim Wright wrote that the freshmen seemed to see Patman only as a very old man and failed to realize his record of achievements and credentials as a reformer. Reuss was viewed as more liberal than Patman.[87]

Although he became Poage's successor, the evidence indicates that Tom Foley, a leading member of the DSG, promoted Poage's reelection to the chairmanship. Foley wrote that he spoke on Poage's behalf to the freshmen caucus. Foley did not think that Poage would be a prime target of the freshmen.[88] Fowler West explained that Foley and Poage were "very good friends" and that Foley supported Poage's reelection as Agriculture Committee chairman. Based on information he was told, West claimed that Foley actually sat next to Poage as a sign of support during the Democratic Caucus session.[89] In his book, West also wrote that Foley openly declared his support for Poage's reelection as Agriculture Committee chairman. West wrote that he (West) was informed afterwards that Foley talked with Poage, before the vote on Poage, and offered to speak on Poage's behalf. They rejected the idea of a pro-Poage speech by Foley because it might incite some members to specifically speak for Poage's removal. In his book, West again stressed that Foley and Poage sat side by side on the front row in the House Chamber during the Caucus.[90] Jim

---

86. Henry Reuss, interview by author, January 27, 2000, telephone tape recording, T. Harry Williams Center for Oral History, Louisiana State University, Baton Rouge, LA.

87. Wright, *Balance of Power*, 238-239.

88. Biggs, *Honor in the House*, 56.

89. Fowler West, interview by author, January 19, 2000, telephone tape recording, T. Harry Williams Center for Oral History, Louisiana State University, Baton Rouge, LA.

90. West, *No Lawyer*, 70-72.

Wright also wrote that Foley did not campaign for the chairmanship before the vote on Poage. Foley did not expect Poage to be removed.[91]

West theorized about Poage's opposition and support. West thought that the Agriculture Committee members were almost unanimous in support of Poage. Any votes against Poage from Committee members would probably have been cast by one or two urban liberals. West believed that the non-freshmen who voted against Poage were probably urban, liberal, and had served one, two, or three terms in the House. Probably most of the freshmen did not vote for Patman, Poage, and Hebert. Most likely, some of the freshmen from rural districts supported Poage.[92]

Hebert's past conflicts with other members undoubtedly contributed to his removal. Pat Schroeder claimed that her feud with Hebert in the early 1970s exposed his autocratic nature and helped build support among non-freshmen Democrats to remove him.[93] Schroeder recalled that Hebert tried to act cordial towards other members before the vote, but he could not remember the names of some senior representatives who had served on the Committee for several terms. Schroeder did not think there were many votes against Hebert from Committee members. Schroeder thought that younger

---

91. Wright, *Balance of Power*, 238.

92. Fowler West, interview by author, January 19, 2000, telephone tape recording, T. Harry Williams Center for Oral History, Louisiana State University, Baton Rouge, LA.

93. Schroeder, *House Work*, 57.

members, overall, were "appalled" at Hebert's treatment of Schroeder and Dellums.[94]

Yet, despite his management of the Committee and his personal characteristics, Hays retained his chairmanship. Ottinger thought Wayne Hays was not removed because he was too popular for opponents to build a majority coalition, and the evidence against Hays was too weak to clearly identify him as being as autocratic as Patman, Poage, and Hebert. Ottinger said, "And my recollection is that Hays just had too many friends."[95] Hays' work as chair of the Democratic Congressional Campaign Committee (DCCC) was significant. It provided $202,814 to 143 members of the Ninety-fourth Congress during the 1974 election campaigns. The DCCC provided $102,980 to seventy-four incumbents reelected in 1974, and $87,000 was provided to sixty-nine of the seventy-five freshmen Democrats elected in 1974. Phillip Burton received $3,250, and the average freshman received $1,260. It was alleged by some people that the contributions helped persuade the freshmen to support Hays for the chairmanship. Several freshmen denied the allegation.[96]

The Caucus addressed the Appropriations Committee's subcommittees, too, and the results showed the limits of reform. Anthony T. Moffett, freshman Democrat of Connecticut, declared that he would push for the Caucus, on January 22, to

94. Pat Schroeder, interview by author, March 27, 2000, telephone tape recording, T. Harry Williams Center for Oral History, Louisiana State University, Baton Rouge, LA.

95. Richard Ottinger, interview by author, November 18, 1999, telephone tape recording, T. Harry Williams Center for Oral History, Louisiana State University, Baton Rouge, LA.

96. "House Democratic Revolt Claims 3 Chairmen," *Congressional Quarterly Weekly Report*, January 25, 1975, 210-215.

deprive Jamie Whitten of his Appropriations Subcommittee chair that oversaw agriculture and environmental and consumer protection programs. Three other Appropriations subcommittee chairs were also being considered for removal by the freshmen. The additional three were Otto Passman of Louisiana (Foreign Operations), Robert Sikes of Florida (Military Construction), and Joe Evins of Tennessee (Public Works). All four were Southern conservatives.[97]

George Mahon addressed the Caucus about the thirteen subcommittee chairmanships of the Appropriations Committee. He stated that the Democratic Caucus of the Appropriations Committee unanimously selected the nominees for the positions.[98] The following people were nominated for the Appropriations Committee's subcommittee chairmanships:

George H. Mahon of Texas, Defense
Jamie L. Whitten of Mississippi, Agriculture
William H. Natcher of Kentucky, District of Columbia
Otto Passman of Louisiana, Foreign Operations
Edward P. Boland of Massachusetts, HUD, Space, Science, EPA and Related Agencies
Sidney Yates of Illinois, Interior
Daniel J. Flood of Pennsylvania, Labor, Health, Education and Welfare
Bob Casey of Texas, Legislative
Robert Sikes of Florida, Military Construction
Joe Evins of Tennessee, Public Works

97. James M. Naughton, "Four More House Leaders Reportedly Facing Ouster," *New York Times*, January 19, 1975, 1, 40.
98. Caucus minutes, January 22, 1975, p. 726-727, Folder 48, Box 219, Legislative Series, Albert Collection.

John Slack of West Virginia, State, Justice, Commerce and Judiciary

John McFall of California, Transportation

Tom Steed of Oklahoma, Treasury, Postal Service, General Government.[99]

The results for the subcommittee chairmanship votes were as follows:

Mahon, Defense, 188-47

Whitten, Agriculture, 187-56

Natcher, District of Columbia, 205-16

Yates, Interior, 185-4

Passman, Foreign Operations, 159-72

Boland, HUD, Space, Science, EPA and Related Agencies, 174-8

Flood, Labor, Health, Education and Welfare, 174-26

Casey, Legislative, 172-7

Sikes, Military Construction, 148-49

Steed, Treasury, Postal Service, General Government, 177-8

Slack, State, Justice, Commerce and Judiciary, 177-10

McFall, Transportation, 180-8

Evins, Public Works, 178-12.[100]

The contention regarding the chairmanships disrupted normal work, but with the actions of January 22, normal work

---

99. Caucus minutes, January 22, 1975, p. 728, 732, 743, 746, 755, 756, 758, 759, 760, 761-763, 761-763, 761-763, 761-763, Folder 48, Box 219, Legislative Series, Albert Collection.

100. Caucus minutes, January 22, 1975, p. 744, 746, 754, 759, 756-757, 758, 760, 766-767, 766-767, 766-767, 766-767, 766-767, 766-767, Folder 48, Box 219, Legislative Series, Albert Collection.

resumed in the House. Earlier on January 20, on the House floor, O'Neill offered a privileged resolution designating the membership and chairs for certain standing committees of the House. Yet, O'Neill stated that the Committees on Agriculture, Armed Services, Banking, Currency and Housing, and House Administration were not included in the resolution. This resolution only concerned Democratic committee members. O'Neill asked for unanimous consent that the resolution be considered as read and printed in the *Record*. The resolution was agreed to.[101] On January 23, in the House, O'Neill offered a privileged resolution concerning the members and chairs for the Committees on Agriculture, Armed Services, Banking, Currency and Housing, and House Administration. The resolution named Foley, Price, Reuss, and Hays as chairmen, respectively. This resolution only concerned Democratic committee members. He asked unanimous consent that the resolution be considered as read and printed in the *Record*. The resolution was agreed to.[102] On January 23, 1975, Rhodes offered a resolution to elect Republican members of the Ways and Means Committee. The resolution was agreed to.[103] On January 28, 1975, Michel introduced a privileged resolution for electing the Republican members of standing committees in the

---

101. *Election to Certain Standing Committees of the House*, 94th Cong., 1st sess., *Congressional Record* 121 (January 20, 1975): 803-804.

102. *Designating Membership on Certain Standing Committees of the House*, 94th Cong., 1st sess., *Congressional Record* 121 (January 23, 1975): 1159-1160.

103. *Election as Members of Committee on Ways and Means*, 94th Cong., 1st sess., *Congressional Record* 121 (January 23, 1975): 1164.

House except for the Ways and Means Committee. The resolution was agreed to.[104]

The removal marked a significant shift regarding seniority and ideology. Patman, Poage, and Hebert ranked first, third, and fifth, respectively, in seniority among House Democrats. In contrast, Reuss, Foley, and Price ranked tied for twentieth, tied for forty-third, and tied for ninth, respectively.[105] An examination of voting habits revealed a sharp ideological difference among Patman, Poage, and Hebert and their successors. The Conservative Coalition appeared on 235 votes in the Ninety-third Congress. Poage voted with and against the Conservative Coalition on 82% of the votes and on 8% of the votes, respectively. Patman voted with and against the Conservative Coalition on 32% of the votes and on 33% of the votes, respectively. Hebert voted with and against the Conservative Coalition on 43% of the votes and on 8% of the votes, respectively. In contrast, Foley voted with and against the Conservative Coalition on 18% of the votes and on 72% of the votes, respectively. Reuss voted with and against the Conservative Coalition on 6% of the votes and on 91% of the votes, respectively. Price voted with and against the Conservative Coalition on 24% of the votes and on 76% of the votes, respectively.[106] There were 384 House Party Unity votes in the Ninety-third Congress. Poage voted with and against the majority of his Party on 34% of the votes and on 58% of the votes, respectively. Patman voted with and against his Party on

---

104. *Election of Members to Standing Committees*, 94th Cong., 1st sess., *Congressional Record* 121 (January 28, 1975): 1611-1612.

105. "Characteristics of Members of 94th Congress," *Congressional Quarterly Weekly Report*, January 18, 1975, 120-130.

106. "Conservative Coalition: Influence Holds Firm," *Congressional Quarterly Weekly Report*, January 25, 1975, 189-194.

51% of the votes and on 16% of the votes, respectively. Hebert voted with and against his Party on 19% of the votes and on 33% of the votes, respectively. In contrast, Foley voted with and against his Party on 80% of the votes and on 11% of the votes, respectively. Price voted with and against his Party on 91% of the votes and on 8% of the votes, respectively. Reuss voted with and against his Party 86% and 11%, respectively. [107]

The general direction and momentum of the removal acted as a catalyst for some other immediate changes and conflicts. The Commerce Committee felt the effects of the removal. The Commerce Committee adopted significant rules changes on January 21, and the addition of eleven freshmen to the Committee aided the adoption of the changes. The chairman's authority to control budgets was limited. Ratios on subcommittees were fixed. The Committee became the first committee in the House to choose to elect its subcommittee chairs by secret ballot by Committee Democrats. Each subcommittee chair was empowered to craft his or her own budget, and all the subcommittee budgets would be confirmed by Committee Democrats. [108] The Commerce Committee removed its chair, Harley O. Staggers of West Virginia, from the chairmanship of the Commerce Subcommittee on Investigations and elected John E. Moss of California to this position. The Committee required seven ballots to make this change in leadership. [109]

---

107. "Party Unity Voting: Slight Drop in 1974," *Congressional Quarterly Weekly Report*, January 25, 1975, 199-203.

108. "Freshman Pressures," *Congressional Quarterly Weekly Report*, January 25, 1975, 211.

109. "Subcommittee Challenges," *Congressional Quarterly Weekly Report*, February 1, 1975, 225.

One member used the removal as a justification for his change in party affiliation. John Jarman was a twelve-term House member from Oklahoma. He announced on January 23 that he was leaving the Democratic Party and joining the Republican Party. As the reasons for his action, he cited, in his opinion, the liberal takeover of the House Democratic Caucus and the overthrow of the seniority system.[110]

Patman's removal may have contributed to the removal of Leonor K. Sullivan from a Banking, Currency and Housing subcommittee position. She defended Patman on Friday, January 17, 1975 in an extension of remarks in the House. Sullivan argued that Patman fought for consumer interests and small businesses and described Patman as fair and honest.[111] On January 28, Sullivan was removed from the chair of the Subcommittee on Consumer Affairs by a vote of 15-13. She claimed that her support of Patman made her a target of Patman's opponents. Frank Annunzio of Illinois took over this chairmanship.[112]

Although Poage was removed, the challenges facing the Agriculture Committee did not change. Foley explained that the work of the Agriculture Committee during his chairmanship also showcased the urban-rural split and the salience of food stamps as seen earlier during Poage's chairmanship. Demographic changes in the nation were affecting the House and the Agriculture Committee. There were fewer House

---

110. "Jarman's Party Switch," *Congressional Quarterly Weekly Report*, January 25, 1975, 211.

111. *The Irony of Making Wright Patman a Target of "Congressional Reform,"* 94th Cong., 1st sess., *Congressional Record* 121 (January 17, 1975): 792-793.

112. "Rules Committee Given New Hampshire Dispute," *Congressional Quarterly Weekly Report*, February 1, 1975, 224-225.

members from rural districts. The older Democratic coalition that included urban political machines, rural/farm areas, labor unions, and minorities was splintering. Urban members voiced concerns over the importance of agriculture issues and bills, and reasons for their importance needed to be provided to urban members. Foley explained the rationale that guided some of the Agriculture Committee's work and attracted urban interest in agriculture bills and issues. Poor people needed assistance with food costs and nutrition, and some programs such as food stamps and WIC were under the Agriculture Committee's jurisdiction. In order to maintain low food prices for the people, the agriculture sector had to be both profitable and sustainable. Therefore, farmers needed assistance in an unstable and competitive global market.[113]

The management of the Armed Services Committee changed. Ron Dellums wrote that after Price became chair, Price invited him to his office. Price told him that he was aware of the poor treatment that he had received from Hebert and that he would receive fair treatment.[114]

The removal was totally unconnected to President Gerald Ford and his work. Ford's only public reference to the removal of Patman, Poage, and Hebert immediately after it occurred came in the President's news conference of January 21, 1975. Ford was asked a general question that was connected to the removal. He replied with a general statement about willingness to work with members of Congress. His response lacked substance or specificity about the removal. He said, "We will have to be very pragmatic as we try to get our

---

113. Biggs, *Honor in the House*, 57-58.
114. Dellums, *Lying Down*, 151-152.

legislation through, and that means working with the majority from the top to the most junior Member."[115]

Interpretations of the removal differed greatly, and Carl Albert had an ambiguous connection to the removal of the chairmen. He served as Majority Leader and then Speaker during the era when the Congressional reform movement implemented reforms that fundamentally altered the House. He actively promoted some of these reforms. Yet, Albert personally opposed the removal of the chairmen. Regarding the freshmen bloc elected in 1974 and the removal in 1975, he wrote, "Sometimes they had more muscle than heart or brains. They showed the strength of the first (and, in my view, the absence of the second and third) at our organizational caucus." In addition, he wrote, "As Speaker, I tried to be the leader of this group that refused to be led." Regarding Patman, he wrote, "Patman's loss of Banking and Currency's chairmanship pained me most. For twenty-three terms, Wright Patman had been a fighting congressman, fighting for farmers and poor people and black people. His only sin was his age, eighty-one when the Ninety-fourth Congress convened." Regarding Poage, whose name was misprinted in Albert's book, he wrote, "Pogue was a fine chairman of Agriculture, but he had goaded the professional liberals too often." Concerning Hebert, Albert wrote: "Hebert could be a pain in the neck, but I thought he deserved another term leading Armed Services."[116] In a letter from 1976, Albert expressed a similar interpretation about Poage's removal, "In my opinion, his removal was due to the

---

115. Gerald R. Ford, *Public Papers of the Presidents of the United States: Gerald R. Ford, 1974-1977*, 1975, book 1, 60-72.
116. Albert, *Giant*, 368.

fact that he was not a 'yes-man' for the majority of the Members of the House."[117]

Patman interpreted his removal in terms of his ideology, and his separation from mainstream thought can again be gauged by this interpretation. Patman discussed the removal in a constituent newsletter from January 30, 1975. He stated that he accepted the decision of the Caucus, would work with his successor, and wanted the Committee to focus on economic problems. Patman saw the removal as part of the ongoing fight against "the big money interests." He thanked his supporters in the Caucus and the DSPC and relished the fact that they supported him against "the blandishment of the Big Bank lobby and the lure of personal power politics." He believed that his supporters' strength meant that "we have a good chance for ultimate victory against the big money interests."[118] Later in a personal letter, Patman called the removal the "Revolution in the House of Representatives." He stressed the regional aspect of the removal: "Undoubtedly, one of the motives of the reformers was the desire to weaken the power of the Southern Delegations in the House, delegations which contributed an unusually large number of committee chairman."[119]

Poage knew Patman and the House well and differentiated Patman's removal from his removal. Poage stressed Patman's political ideology, separation from mains-

---

117. Albert to McClendon, October 4, 1976, Folder 97, Box 7, Biographical Series, Albert Collection.

118. "Wright Patman's 1934th Weekly Letter," January 30, 1975, Folder: Wright Patman's Weekly Letter 1975, Box 1613A, Papers of Wright Patman.

119. Patman to constituent, February 4, 1975, Folder: 2 of 6, Box 162B, Papers of Wright Patman.

tream thought, and management of the Committee. In his "Oral Memoirs," Poage said:

"Because he couldn't get along with his own members. While it came at the same time I lost the chairmanship of the Agricultural Committee, I think it was entirely different situation. He had a candidate running against him--of his own committee--who was charging that Patman couldn't run the committee, and I think there was a good deal to that. Part of it was due to the fact that Patman always had some weird or extreme views that he was trying to put over in the committee all the time, and some of them were resenting the way he was pushing them over. They always do that. You always have some--the chairman--I had it and every other chairman has people resent the action of the chairman. But Patman's views were rather extreme on a good many things, and more and more members of his own committee felt that he was following a course completely contrary to their views and wishes."[120]

Poage interpreted his removal in terms of a liberal-conservative ideological clash. Poage discussed his removal in a constituent newsletter dated January 17, 1975. He wrote that he felt that the 144 who voted against him wanted to "do something to challenge the "Establishment'" and that they "felt that they must prove their liberalism by voting down the Leadership's recommendation." Poage wrote that "Many others just felt that they wanted a more free-wheeling administration of the Committee." Poage stressed that the Democratic majority

---

120. "Oral Memoirs Poage," volume 5, p. 90-91, Poage Papers.

had a philosophy that he rejected; he would not change his principles but would work with Foley.[121]

Poage also discussed his recollections of the removal in his "Oral Memoirs" and again stressed the liberal-conservative ideological clash. Poage described the reason for his removal in these terms: "And there were then some members who had served in Congress and who had been defeated and had come back again, and they, of course, were the more extreme or radical group. And they said to their colleagues--they had a number of caucuses before there was any official action. And I know some of them described certain members of Congress as being extremely reactionary and that they ought to be replaced, and I'm certain that I was one of them." He thought that his chances for reelection to the chair were automatically hurt because the Agriculture Committee chairmanship vote came so early; it was voted on first. The freshmen were eager to have an impact, and he felt the full brunt of their ambition. Poage stressed that the Agriculture Committee supported him.[122] In addition, Poage stated that he believed that he was seen as a "reactionary conservative" and as an "impediment to legislation" in his removal.[123]

Fowler West interpreted Poage's removal in terms of a liberal-conservative ideological clash. West stressed the role of the food stamps program as a source of tension between Poage and his critics: "But Poage didn't like it, said he didn't think there should be a food stamp program. So that, that made a lot of people upset. They really thought he was too conservative." West added that, "And I always thought that

---

121. Constituent newsletter, January 17, 1975, Poage Papers.
122. "Oral Memoirs Poage," volume 4, p. 1346-1351, Poage Papers.
123. "Oral Memoirs Poage," volume 5, p. 90-91, Poage Papers.

Poage probably ought to go on a little more with that and I think had he done even a little bit, he probably would have been able to get through. He did not go out of his way to help any of the urban liberals. And he didn't play ball with them, and it cost him." West thought that the way he treated other members was not the problem. The false perception that he cared about farmers and not the urban poor hurt him. West said: "But not so much the way he treated other members as much as it was his conservatism, his identification with trying to help farmers and not giving a damn about urban poor. Which wasn't really true, but nevertheless that was the perception."[124]

Tom Foley stressed conservatism, rather than management of the Committee, as the primary reason for Poage's removal. Foley wrote: "Mr. Poage had been singled out by a number of activists on the nutrition and food stamp issues as being insensitive and hostile. While it's true he was a critic of nutrition programs, I always thought he was fair in permitting them to be debated and voted on by the committee. While Chairman Poage's manner was somewhat autocratic, he listened to opposing views and allowed amendments to be offered. I didn't think he was guilty of the kind of abuse that I'd seen in other committees."[125]

Hebert interpreted his removal in terms of his characteristic independent streak. He wrote that without Richard Nixon on the political scene, the "Eastern Establishment" looked for new victims. They chose committee chairmen who were ideologically conservative; they had wanted

---

124. Fowler West, interview by author, January 19, 2000, telephone tape recording, T. Harry Williams Center for Oral History, Louisiana State University, Baton Rouge, LA.
125. Biggs, *Honor in the House*, 56.

to make this challenge for a long time. The chairmen were individualists who could not be controlled: "Most of these chairmen were the last of the individualists, men who had grown to maturity pulling on their own bootstraps and they would not be dominated by the powerbrokers of the Eastern Establishment whose money had bought and sold many a public officeholder, or at least frightened them into line."[126] Hebert thought that he was the main target due to his "outspoken, no-punches-pulled, stand on Vietnam and my conservative, individualistic philosophy."[127]

Hebert also interpreted his removal with a great stress on the role of the public interest group Common Cause, a notable public interest group in the 1970s. John Gardner had been a Republican but served as Secretary of Health, Education, and Welfare in the administration of Lyndon Johnson. In August 1970, Gardner announced the creation of a public interest group that became Common Cause. Within six months, the new group had over 100,000 members. In its early years, Common Cause addressed issues such as the Vietnam War, campaign finance reform, and government reform.[128] In a book entitled, *In Common Cause*, Gardner wrote that Common Cause made the reform of the seniority system one of its top priorities in 1970. He argued that the seniority system prevented committee chairs from being held accountable to the party and the public: "All of the attributes we seek in our political and governmental institutions--access, responsiveness,

---

126. Hebert, *Titans*, 437.
127. Hebert, *Titans*, 441.
128. "A Short History of Common Cause," Common Cause website, accessed March 21, 2011,
http://www.commoncause.org/site/pp.asp?c=dkLNK1MQIwG&b=474135
9.

accountability--are violated or made more difficult of achievement by the seniority system."[129] Andrew S. McFarland wrote about Common Cause in *Common Cause: Lobbying in the Public Interest*. McFarland argued that in the 1970s Common Cause exerted much effort to lobby members of the House to pass legislation that it favored. This legislation concerned issues such as campaign finance reform, seniority system reform, regulation of lobbyists, and public access to Congressional committees' and government agencies' meetings.[130]

Common Cause took an interest in the chairmen in 1975. Common Cause activists were outside the Caucus room during the days of the removal.[131] Common Cause released a pamphlet about the committee chairmen entitled "Report on House Committee Chairmen." This Common Cause pamphlet was dated January 13, 1975 and was 31 pages long.[132] The "Report" evaluated the chairmen's conduct using three criteria: compliance with House, Caucus, and committee rules; use of power; and personal and procedural fairness in the management of the committee. The "Report" claimed that Ray Madden of Indiana (Rules), Patman, and Harley Staggers of West Virginia (Interstate and Foreign Commerce) "show significant shortcomings." Mahon, Poage, and Hays "show a pattern of more serious abuses." Hebert "flagrantly violates all

---

129. John W. Gardner, *In Common Cause* (New York: W. W. Norton & Company, Inc., 1972), 61.

130. Andrew S. McFarland, *Common Cause: Lobbying in the Public Interest* (Chatham, NJ: Chatham House, 1984), 108-111.

131. "House Democratic Revolt Claims 3 Chairmen," *Congressional Quarterly Weekly Report*, January 25, 1975, 210-215.

132. "Report on House Committee Chairmen," January 13, 1975, File # 2, Box # 219, Poage Papers.

three standards." The "Report" also contained information on the voting habits of chairmen.[133]

The "Report" portrayed Patman as autocratic and ineffective. The "Report" claimed that, "Committee Members complain that he selectively ignores Members' calls for recognition and that debate is too often peremptorily cut off. Thus, meetings often degenerate into a chaotic atmosphere, lacking dignity and decorum." Members faulted the Committee for not completing work on important items. Patman failed to provide proper party ratios, as mandated by the Caucus, on subcommittees and failed to comply with Committee rules mandating semi-monthly meetings. In some matters, Committee rules did not comply with Caucus rules.[134]

The "Report" portrayed Poage as autocratic. It claimed that Poage violated the rules by maintaining only a minimal committee staff and by denying subcommittee chairs the right to any staff. Poage engaged in procedural abuses in order to promote positions that he supported, and significant legislation sometimes was not properly considered by the Committee. In addition, the Committee's rules violated Caucus rules in some matters.[135]

The "Report" gave a very negative evaluation of Hebert. It claimed that he denied subcommittee chairs the right to hire their own staff, harassed and discriminated against members with whom he disagreed, established additional subcommittees to evade Caucus rules, employed his chairmanship to oppose

---

133. "Report on House Committee Chairmen," p. 1-3, January 13, 1975, File 2, Box 219, Poage Papers.

134. "Report on House Committee Chairmen," p. 16-17, January 13, 1975, File 2, Box 219, Poage Papers.

135. "Report on House Committee Chairmen," p. 5-7, January 13, 1975, File 2, Box 219, Poage Papers.

Caucus policy regarding the war in Indochina, and failed to exercise his duty to use the Committee to provide oversight of the military. The "Report" stated that, "He violates the rules, he treats Members unfairly, and he abuses his power as Chairman."[136]

Hebert blamed Common Cause for his removal. He claimed that Common Cause had a "full-time staff of paid lobbyists patrolling the halls of Congress daily, harassing, encouraging, managing, and seeing to it that those representatives in their fold toed the line" when Congress convened in January 1975. He claimed that Common Cause held meetings to instruct members of Congress on how to vote. Hebert wrote that he realized that Common Cause wanted to end the seniority system and the committee system, make the party caucus supreme, and allow majority rule to dominate.[137] The Common Cause "Report" immediately caught Hebert's attention. As reported on January 14, Hebert said that the Common Cause "Report" was "'so ridiculous, misleading and distorted as not to justify a comment.'" Hebert said he followed the majority of his Committee, and his Committee supported him as chair. He said Common Cause was opposed to a strong national defense. Hebert said, "'If anybody can show where I have violated the majority vote of my committee, I'll step down.'"[138] As reported, Hebert discussed his removal on the NBC "Today" show and said, "'Common Cause started this thing in 1969 and they have conducted one of the most vicious and reprehensible campaigns that I've ever seen in my life.'"

---

136. "Report on House Committee Chairmen," p. 11-15, January 13, 1975, File 2, Box 219, Poage Papers.
137. Hebert, *Titans*, 440-441.

Hebert claimed that Common Cause used "'misrepresentation, downright lies, downright distortions.'" He warned that, "'The American people better wake up to what this outfit's doing because they can destroy this country.'" Hebert claimed that he declined an opportunity to chair the Committee on Standards of Official Conduct because the chairs were emasculated, "'They can't make a move without the approval of the (Democratic) caucus.'"[139]

There are diverse opinions regarding the role of Common Cause, and in addition to Hebert, other opinions stressed the role of Common Cause. In an anniversary publication, Common Cause claimed that it worked with the DSG and pro-reform Congresspersons from 1972 to 1975 to end the seniority system and establish elected committee chairs.[140] In his book about Common Cause, Andrew S. McFarland argued that the Common Cause pamphlet "played a major role" in the removal of Patman, Poage, and Hebert.[141] In 2011, the Common Cause website also claimed primary credit for the removal: "One of our first reform efforts was aimed at making the U.S. Congress more open and accountable by putting an end to the stultifying seniority system, pushing for public votes on legislation, and opening committee meetings to the public. The Watergate scandal and the influx of dozens of new, reform-minded Members of Congress in 1974 spurred these and other reforms, most of which would not have

---

138. Mary Russell, "Common Cause Report Hits Hebert," *Washington Post*, January 14, 1975, A4.

139. "Rep. Hebert Castigates Citizen Unit," *Washington Post*, February 6, 1975, A9.

140. Ruth MacKenzie Saxe, *1970-1980; A Decade of Citizen Action in Common Cause* (Washington, D. C.: Common Cause, 1980), 16.

141. McFarland, *Lobbying in the Public Interest*, 133.

occurred without the outside pressure and inside lobbying of Common Cause."[142]

Other persons closer to the removal discounted the role of Common Cause. John Gardner was more realistic about the role of Common Cause and thought that Hebert exaggerated Common Cause's role in the removal. Common Cause was one of many participants but lacked the ability for significant influence because it was outside government and did not have power.[143] Ottinger did not remember Common Cause having a role in the removal, especially not a critical role.[144] Reuss said Common Cause had no role in the removal.[145] Pat Schroeder did not remember Common Cause having a role in the removal.[146]

Patman, Poage, and Hebert were removed, but other conservatives and Southerners retained their committee chairmanships. Some reasons help explain this fact. Fowler West thought that chairmen such as George Mahon and Olin Teague were better aware of the changes of the era and adapted. They retained their positions by accommodating their

---

142. "A Short History of Common Cause," Common Cause website, accessed March 21, 2011, http://www.commoncause.org/site/pp.asp?c=dkLNK1MQIwG&b=474135 9.

143. John Gardner, interview by author, December 2, 1999, telephone tape recording, T. Harry Williams Center for Oral History, Louisiana State University, Baton Rouge, LA.

144. Richard Ottinger, interview by author, November 18, 1999, telephone tape recording, T. Harry Williams Center for Oral History, Louisiana State University, Baton Rouge, LA.

145. Henry Reuss, interview by author, January 27, 2000, telephone tape recording, T. Harry Williams Center for Oral History, Louisiana State University, Baton Rouge, LA.

critics and potential opponents.[147] Poage explained that power on the Appropriations Committee was more decentralized, and Mahon did not appear as conservative or autocratic as Poage did.[148] Jim Wright stressed personal qualities as aiding Mahon: "Apparently George had charmed the newcomers with his witty, conversational, noncondescending appearance before their group. He even invited the newcomers on a tour of the Appropriations committee rooms."[149]

Media coverage of the removal in newspapers and magazines showed great variation. For example, *Congressional Quarterly Weekly Report* consistently provided quality coverage of the events and the participants.[150] In contrast, the *Washington Post* provided a brief survey of the events and the participants but failed to provide thorough examination.[151] Also, the *New York Times* provided a brief survey of the events and the participants but failed to provide thorough examination.[152] The *Time* article on the removal was

---

146. Pat Schroeder, interview by author, March 27, 2000, telephone tape recording, T. Harry Williams Center for Oral History, Louisiana State University, Baton Rouge, LA.

147. Fowler West, interview by author, January 19, 2000, telephone tape recording, T. Harry Williams Center for Oral History, Louisiana State University, Baton Rouge, LA.

148. "Oral Memoirs Poage," volume 4, p. 1348-1349, Poage Papers.

149. Wright, *Balance of Power*, 238.

150. "Democrats Oust Hebert, Poage; Adopt Reforms," *Congressional Quarterly Weekly Report*, January 18, 1975, 111-119, 165-166; "House Democratic Revolt Claims 3 Chairmen," *Congressional Quarterly Weekly Report*, January 25, 1975, 210-215.

151. Richard L. Lyons and Mary Russell, "Democrats Oust House Chairmen Hebert, Poage," *Washington Post*, January 17, 1975, A1, A9; Richard L. Lyons and Mary Russell, "Patman Loses House Chair; Hays to Stay," *Washington Post*, January 23, 1975, A1, A19.

152. Richard D. Lyons, "2 More Chairmen Ousted; 4 House Panels Unsettled," *New York Times*, January 17, 1975, 1, 29; Richard D. Lyons,

very superficial and limited in scope and factual content.[153] The two *Newsweek* articles on the removal also were very superficial and limited in scope and factual content.[154]

After the removal, life continued for the chairmen, but their careers were near their conclusion regardless of the events of January 1975. Patman worked on his Committee and his preferred issues. He served as chair of the Subcommittee on Domestic Monetary Policy, chair of the Joint House-Senate Committee on Defense Production, and vice chairman of the Joint House-Senate Economic Committee.[155] He advocated an audit of the Federal Reserve System by the General Accounting Office.[156] On January 14, 1976, Patman announced that he would not seek reelection.[157] Patman died of pneumonia on March 7, 1976, at Bethesda Naval Medical Center in Maryland at age 82. At that time, his House career of forty-seven years ranked as the fourth longest in U. S. history.[158]

Poage remained in the House longer than Patman. Poage wrote that when the Agriculture Committee met, Foley, as the new chairman, nominated Poage as vice chair. The

"House Democrats Oust 3 Chairmen, But Retain Hays," *New York Times*, January 23, 1975, 1, 24.

153. "A Whiff of Rebellion in the 94th," *Time*, January 27, 1975, 26-28.

154. "Earthquake in the Congress," *Newsweek*, January 27, 1975, 27-28; "Humbling the Elders," *Newsweek*, February 3, 1975, 16-17.

155. "Wright Patman's 1935th Weekly Letter," February 6, 1975, Folder: Wright Patman's Weekly Letter 1975, Box 1613A, Patman Papers.

156. Marjorie Hunter, "4 Ousted House Chairmen Just Watch Parade," *New York Times*, October 22, 1975, 47, 74.

157. Rob Meckel, "Patman Will Not Run," *Texarkana Gazette*, January 15, 1976, 1-a, 2-a.

158. Eileen Shanahan, "Wright Patman, 82, Dean of House, Dies," *New York Times*, March 8, 1976, 1, 28.

whole Committee voted on him, and he was elected to that post. He held it for his last four years in the House.[159] Poage worked and served as chair of the Subcommittee on Livestock and Grains.[160] Poage later explained that he would have retired earlier but that the removal and a Republican opponent in 1976 persuaded him to run for reelection: "I wasn't going to let them say that they had run Poage out or that they got him where he couldn't win."[161] Finally, in 1977, Poage announced that he would not run for reelection. At that time, he ranked second in seniority in the House.[162] Poage died on January 3, 1987 at the age of 87 during heart surgery. He was a resident of Waco.[163]

Hebert displayed ambiguous conduct after the removal. In 1975, Hebert held the chair of the Armed Services Subcommittee on Investigations.[164] Hebert wrote that he was named unanimously to lead this subcommittee. He claimed that Price referred tough questions to him and consulted with him since he sat on Price's right side at meetings of the full Committee. He wrote: "For all intents and purposes, I had the power I had before. Only the title was missing--some of the time."[165] In contrast, Pat Schroeder recalled that Hebert

---

159. Poage, *85 Years*, 148.

160. Marjorie Hunter, "4 Ousted House Chairmen Just Watch Parade," *New York Times*, October 22, 1975, 47, 74.

161. "Oral Memoirs Poage," volume 4, p. 1371, Poage Papers.

162. "Poage Won't Seek Re-Election After 4 Decades on Hill," *Washington Post*, September 25, 1977, A7.

163. "Bob Poage Dies After Surgery," *Waco Tribune-Herald*, January 4, 1987, 1A, 10A.

164. "A Change of Style on House Armed Services," *Congressional Quarterly Weekly Report*, February 15, 1975, 336-341.

165. Hebert, *Titans*, 449-450.

resembled a "wounded lion" after the removal and did little public work for the Committee.[166]

Hebert continued a feud with Common Cause. In a *Washington Post* letter-to-the-editor, Hebert charged Common Cause and John Gardner with factual misrepresentation by claiming in a February 6, 1975 article that Hebert's colleagues removed him. Hebert explained that among 434 colleagues in the House, only 152 voted against him. Hebert wrote that Democrats who favored him faced threats; if they voted for him, they would lose their seniority and their committee assignments. The Republicans faced threats, too; they would face retaliation if they voted for him.[167] In an extension of remarks on February 25, 1975, Hebert criticized Common Cause and entered into the *Record* the ruling in *Common Cause et al. v. National Association of Manufacturers* from the U. S. District Court for the District of Columbia. The court dismissed Common Cause's suit against the National Association of Manufacturers to force it to register and to report according to the Federal Regulation of Lobbying Act. Hebert stated: "I have denounced Common Cause publicly in an effort to let the American people know what this anti-national-defense lobbying group is up to in this Congress. And I will continue to keep track of its operations because I feel the people have a right to know." He added that, "I do not object to Common Cause's promotion of liberal ideas, but I do object to its attempt to portray itself to the American people as an organization that

---

166. Pat Schroeder, interview by author, March 27, 2000, telephone tape recording, T. Harry Williams Center for Oral History, Louisiana State University, Baton Rouge, LA.

167. F. E. Hebert, "Rep. Hebert Replies," *Washington Post*, February 11, 1975, A15.

is fighting for the common man or so-called average citizen of all persuasions."[168]

Hebert's career ended quickly. In March 1976, he declared that he would not run for reelection. Hebert died on December 29, 1979 after a heart attack. He was 78 years of age. He served in the House longer than any previous Louisiana congressman.[169]

Wilbur Mills also ended his career quickly. After the removal, it was reported that Mills was not active in Ways and Means Committee work; he stated that he did not miss his chairmanship.[170] Mills announced on March 5, 1976 that he was not seeking reelection to the House in 1976.[171] Mills died on May 2, 1992 in Kensett, Arkansas.[172]

Many of the reformers and the freshmen had supported Wayne Hays, but the post-Watergate demand for accountability, which never disappeared from the nation, eventually overwhelmed him, too, in a sensational scandal in 1976. Elizabeth Ray told the *Washington Post* on May 23 that she had been employed as a secretary on the House Administration Committee since late April 1974. She claimed that she could not type, file, or answer the phone. She was not required to perform any official work and only came to the office once or twice a week for a few hours. She said her

---

168. *A Loss for Common Cause*, 94th Cong., 1st sess., *Congressional Record* 121 (February 25, 1975): 4313.

169. "Hebert Dies Following Long Illness," *Times-Picayune*, December 30, 1979, 1, 4.

170. Marjorie Hunter, "4 Ousted House Chairmen Just Watch Parade," *New York Times*, October 22, 1975, 47, 74.

171. David Speights, "Wilbur Mills Retires," *Congressional Quarterly Weekly Report*, March 13, 1976, 563-564.

172. Dennis Hevesi, "Wilbur Mills, Long a Power in Congress, Is Dead at 82," *New York Times*, May 3, 1992, L53.

responsibility was to have sex with Hays at her apartment once or twice a week. Her salary was $14,000 annually. Life was complicated for Hays. Hays obtained a divorce from his first wife on January 15. Hays then married his second wife on April 13; she worked in his Ohio district office. Hays admitted that he had a consensual relationship with Ray. Hays refused to invite Ray to the reception for his wedding and called the Capitol police to remove Ray from his office on April 6. Hays fired her. Therefore, Ray chose to inform the public about the affair.[173] On June 18, Hays resigned from the chairmanship of the House Administration Committee under pressure from the House Democratic Leadership, and House Democrats already had plans to remove Hays and to select a new chairman.[174] Tip O'Neill wrote that he demanded Hays resign his chairmanships or he would utilize the Caucus and have Hays stripped of his chairmanships.[175]

Elizabeth Ray took advantage of the opportunity provided by the scandal to write a novel, *The Washington Fringe Benefit*. The novel concerned corruption and scandals involving politicians as seen through the experiences of a woman named Elizabeth Ray. The novel was written in the first-person voice. The novel showed great similarity to Ray's real experiences in Washington, D. C. Yet, the short preface for the novel stated that: "This is a work of fiction. All characters, except my own and certain celebrities that I've met, are

---

173. Bruce F. Freed, "Democrats Fear Fallout From Hays Affair," *Congressional Quarterly Weekly Report*, May 29, 1976, 1331-1332, 1334.

174. Bruce F. Freed with David Speights, "Hays Resigns Post; Scandal Broadens," *Congressional Quarterly Weekly Report*, June 19, 1976, 1564, 1566, 1624.

175. O'Neill, *Man of the House*, 216.

composite people made up out of various bits and pieces of real men and women. Although readers may think they recognize actual people, there is no intended similarity."[176]

William "Fishbait" Miller noted the scandal and its significance. He stressed that Ray benefitted from the revelation of the scandal which was unusual: "The Hill crowd murmured that they had never seen anything like it--usually the girl who tells loses her job and slinks away in shame, and here was a girl who was striding away into the sunset in a storybook happy ending." Miller claimed that Hays was very antagonistic and abusive to others in the early part of 1976. Miller wrote that other House members were indifferent or happy about Hays' downfall because he had been difficult to work with and abusive and antagonistic for a long time.[177]

By late January 1975, the U. S. House of Representatives had been fundamentally altered. The removal of Patman, Poage, and Hebert was not simply a change in personnel in a few positions of authority. Rather, the removal was the final and necessary act in the overthrow of the seniority system and the entire Bipartisan House System. The Congressional reform movement had achieved incremental reforms over a period of years, and the implemented reforms strongly resembled the Bolling plan for reform presented in his books in the 1960s. The reforms needed to be utilized on significant matters to truly have an effect. The removal of the chairmen was a bold act with few precedents that directly struck the Bipartisan House System.

---

176. Elizabeth L. Ray, *The Washington Fringe Benefit* (New York: Dell Publishing Co., Inc., 1976), preface.
177. Miller, *Fishbait*, 176-179.

Chapter 9 - The Legacy

The removal of the triumvirate of Patman, Poage, and Hebert was a highly salient event with grand and profound ramifications. The Bipartisan House System was overthrown, and as a result, the new circumstances permitted the rise of the Partisan House System in the decades following 1975.

The removal of Patman, Poage, and Hebert can be explained in the following terms, and the larger context in which they served is highly significant. Patman, Poage, and Hebert all had long careers in Congress during the era of the Bipartisan House System. They exemplified the Bipartisan House System and all of its advantages and disadvantages. They amassed power through the seniority system and the autonomy of the committee chairs. Undoubtedly, they generated critics through their efforts to promote their ideology and their management of their Committees. Meanwhile, the Congressional reform movement sought to fundamentally alter the House. As a result, chairmen such as the triumvirate stood essentially as obstacles to reform, and the Congressional reform movement rose as a threat to the status quo and them. The freshmen bloc elected in 1974 possessed a genuine interest in reform and also altered the composition of the Democratic Caucus. With the demand for accountability sweeping the nation, entrenched chairmen occupied a precarious position. Within the House, a coalition of critics, reformers, and freshmen coalesced around the idea of reform and sought a salient victory for reform. Persons such as Phillip Burton and Richard Ottinger played critical roles in organizing and directing this diverse coalition during a volatile time in the House and the nation. The coalition reached a consensus on targeting the chairmen, the seniority system, and the entire Bipartisan House System.

The distinctive circumstances and experiences of Patman, Poage, and Hebert relative to the other committee chairmen require consideration. Only three chairmen lost their positions, and other conservative Southerners retained their chairmanships. It would be difficult to quantitatively rank all the chairmen based on management of their Committees or ideology, and therefore, it cannot be stated definitively that the triumvirate were any more or less autocratic than other committee chairs. Nonetheless, the triumvirate exemplified the characteristics of the Bipartisan House System, and the charge of autocratic management of the Committee became the general reason for the removal. The coalition specifically selected them for removal as the Ottinger interview revealed. Despite this commonality, the three chairmen displayed critical differences, and the specific reasons for their selection varied.

Despite his record of achievements and credentials as a reformer, Wright Patman fell to reform. He had an ideology that was outside mainstream thought, and his Committee seemed to have lost confidence in him because of his ideology and his management of the Committee. His Committee seemed ineffective. Patman's record of achievements and credentials as a reformer did not seem relevant in 1975. The combination of his ideology and the problems within the Committee made Patman appear to be an impediment to progress to many members in the House.

Bob Poage followed both conservative values and progressive values throughout his career, but the conservative values of Poage were the most salient by 1975. Poage's conservative ideology was not outside mainstream thought, but his ideological clashes with liberals intensified because of the general direction of public policy in the 1970s and the increasingly liberal orientation of the Democratic Caucus. Poage continued to manage the Committee autocratically while many other members favored the specific reforms and the general idea of reform. Despite these conflicts, Poage retained the confidence of his Committee. Poage's progressive nature and achievements from his early career did not seem relevant in 1975. Poage's work on behalf of rural America and the agriculture sector meant little to people not connected with either or both of them. The combination of the liberal-conservative ideological clash and the autocratic management style made Poage appear to be an impediment to progress to many members in the House.

Hebert stood in a liberal-conservative ideological clash, but personal characteristics such as his independent steak played a critical role in Hebert's removal. Hebert's conservative ideology was not outside mainstream thought, but he, too, found that ideological clashes with liberals became more salient because of the general direction of public policy in the 1970s and the increasingly liberal orientation of the Democratic Caucus. Hebert managed the Committee autocratically while many other members favored the specific reforms and the general idea of reform. The Vietnam War produced great controversy and division, and these byproducts were unavoidably associated with Hebert because of his position on the War. In addition, Hebert's demeanor and manners, as seen in the conflicts with Schroeder and Dellums, alienated people and made cooperation more difficult. The combination of the liberal-conservative ideological clash, the autocratic management style, and the personal characteristics made

Hebert appear as an impediment to progress to many members in the House.

The DSG had an ambiguous connection to the removal. As an organization, the DSG did not play a role in the removal. Tom Foley supported Poage's reelection as chairman and was a leading member of the DSG. Frank Thompson had great credentials as a reformer and was also a leading member of the DSG. Yet, the Caucus chose Hays over Thompson. By 1975, the DSG was very large and included members from the Southern states and members who were moderate in ideology, and some of those persons would likely have been sympathetic to the triumvirate. Yet, the DSG was the driving force for Congressional reform and made the removal possible. A coalition that included persons who were core DSG activists conducted the removal, and some of them played leading roles such as Phillip Burton and Henry Reuss. The removal cannot be credited to the DSG directly, but it is legitimate to see the removal as at least partly stemming from the DSG's ideology, goals, and actions. Therefore, it is legitimate to view the removal as at least partially a DSG achievement.

A few other issues are relevant to the explanation. Self-interest often overrides principle, and Patman, Poage, and Hebert could not find a quick and easy means to win support as Hays did. As a result, that autocratic chairman retained his position despite the coalition's basic principle of reform. The Caucus was not unanimous in the removal of the triumvirate, and Poage's removal rested on a three-vote difference. Yet, the majority of the Caucus favored removal. Regional bias did not play a role in the removal. Common Cause did not play a role in the removal. Hebert just seemed to be angry and wanted a scapegoat. The House Republicans did not play a role in any aspect of the removal. President Gerald Ford did not play a role in the removal.

The Bipartisan House System was completely overthrown. The removal showed that the reforms passed in the previous years would be utilized over significant aspects of the House and would not simply be formalities. Most obviously, the seniority system had not only been reformed but also had been overthrown, and the autonomy of the committee chairs was curtailed. The reforms and the removal itself fundamentally altered the other characteristics of the House. The Speaker and other party leaders had gained greater power through the DSPC and its new roles, and the DSPC was one of the two instruments used to carry out the removal. The Caucus gained power very quickly and served as one of the two instruments that removed the chairmen. It used majority rule. The Caucus' actions were partially a means of imposing party discipline. Patman, Poage, and Hebert had, in their own ways, served contrary to the preferences of the majority in the Caucus, and as a result, they were removed. The demand for accountability stemming from the Watergate Crisis had produced the freshmen bloc elected in 1974. They were assertive and impatient. Their assertiveness amounted to a rejection of the traditional House customs which shaped relations among members and the work of the House for decades. They chose to challenge the entrenched chairmen. Without party leaders with limited powers, autonomous committee chairmen, seniority, and weak party discipline, the ability to accommodate significant regional and ideological blocs and bipartisanship would be more difficult. The ability to promote or impose party unity was now stronger than it had been since the early twentieth century. Bolling's plans for reform were largely implemented. Now, the House was left to develop a new system based on the reforms and changes that had overthrown the Bipartisan House System.

Immediately after the removal in 1975, the House experienced an interregnum characterized by a lack of central direction, and this interregnum is frequently called an era of subcommittee government. Tip O'Neill saw the freshmen Democrats of both 1974 and 1976 as contributing to significant changes in the House. Initially, the House became more difficult to manage, and party discipline became weaker. These Democrats from 1974 and 1976 wanted to exert influence immediately. O'Neill wrote that, "With such a large group of outspoken new members, Congress became more difficult to control than ever before. Party discipline went out the window. These people were impatient, and they wanted to be part of the action right away. New members once were seen and not heard, but now it seemed that even the lowliest freshman could be a power in the House."[1] Jim Wright described the House in the late 1970s. There was less partisanship. There was weak party discipline among Democrats, and it was common to need Republican votes to pass Carter's programs. Wright wrote that, "We had what might be called a floating majority for most of the Democratic program. New coalitions would have to be formed around each issue."[2] Pat Schroeder explained that after the reforms and the removal, subcommittee chairmen became more important, committees became more democratic in terms of the influence members possessed and the division of resources, and chairmen were restrained and had to work with

---

1. O'Neill, *Man of the House*, 283-285.
2. Wright, *Balance of Power*, 312.

members.[3] In a November 1978 constituent newsletter, Poage claimed that the reformers had relaxed discipline in the House and made the House more open and democratic at the expense of efficiency.[4] One of the freshmen of 1974 and a later U. S. Senator, Paul Simon of Illinois, noted the legacy of the reforms: "In retrospect we served the House and the nation poorly with some of our reforms. While each of the changes individually is defensible, the net result reduced the ability of the House leaders and committee chairs to exercise restraint on a body that sometimes needs it."[5]

During this era, the House Democrats acquired new leadership. Carl Albert retired, and Tip O'Neill continued his rise similar to previous Majority Leaders. On December 6, 1976, House Democrats unanimously chose Tip O'Neill as the Democratic nominee for Speaker.[6]

O'Neill was a fitting choice to be Speaker for the Democrats. He was liberal but was not an ideological extremist. He was conventional in his personal beliefs and practices. He understood the customs of the House and therefore understood the potential and limitations of party authority. Under the appropriate circumstances, he could increase party authority without generating inherent opposition to the change.

Due to O'Neill's rise, there was a volatile and close contest for Majority Leader. Jim Wright described the Majority

---

3. Pat Schroeder, interview by author, March 27, 2000, telephone tape recording, T. Harry Williams Center for Oral History, Louisiana State University, Baton Rouge, LA.

4. Constituent newsletter, November 17, 1978, Poage Papers.

5. Paul Simon, *P. S.: The Autobiography of Paul Simon* (Chicago: Bonus Books, 1999), 136.

6. Thomas P. Southwick, "House Democrats Elect Leaders, Slow Reforms," *Congressional Quarterly Weekly Report*, December 11, 1976, 3291-3295.

Leader contest in 1976. Whip John McFall of California wanted the position, but some people thought that he was not sufficiently aggressive to be Majority Leader. In addition, some people thought that he was too moderate ideologically. Phillip Burton sought the position and therefore divided the California delegation. Bolling sought the position, too. Bolling and Burton had a bad relationship. McFall, Burton, and Bolling began campaigning in the first months of 1976. Then, some members began asking Wright to run for Majority Leader, but Wright took no action on the possibility. McFall became embroiled in a scandal, and more members began asking Wright to seek the position. Finally, Wright began campaigning for Majority Leader.[7] The contest arrived. On the first ballot, the totals were: Burton, 106; Bolling, 81; Wright, 77; and McFall, 31. McFall withdrew, and on the second ballot, the totals were: Burton, 107; Wright, 95; and Bolling, 93. On the third ballot, Wright defeated Burton, 148-147.[8] Burton's biographer noted that Burton had alienated many people with his tactics and had experienced personal disagreements with other members. Any of these few individuals could have changed the outcome of the Majority Leader contest.[9]

Jim Wright exercised increasing power in the House. Wright was a moderate in ideology, and his Texas background made him acceptable to conservatives and traditionalists. He was conventional in his personal beliefs and practices. He understood the customs of the House and therefore understood the potential and limitations of party authority. Under the

---

7. Wright, *Balance of Power*, 259-260.

8. Thomas P. Southwick, "House Democrats Elect Leaders, Slow Reforms," *Congressional Quarterly Weekly Report*, December 11, 1976, 3291-3295.

appropriate circumstances, he could increase party authority without generating inherent opposition to the change.

The Caucus asserted itself in early 1975 but faced a quick and strong reaction, and this development contributed to the lack of central direction. Bob Carr of Michigan used the rules to hold a special meeting of the Caucus on March 12 to consider his resolution expressing opposition to additional U. S. military aid for Indochina. The resolution was a "sense of the caucus" resolution and was non-binding. The resolution passed, 189-49. Afterwards, liberals worried that the Caucus might be overused and cause trouble, and conservatives feared that the Caucus might become too powerful. In addition, there was concern that the Caucus could infringe on the committees' jurisdiction, and many members still wanted to preserve the committees' traditional jurisdiction.[10] On September 9, the House Democratic Caucus made two major changes to its rules. The Caucus approved, by voice vote, opening most Caucus meetings to the public. The Caucus would be open and public unless a majority voted to close it. The Caucus would be closed during debate on Caucus rules changes; elections of House leaders, committee chairmen, and committee members; and consideration of miscellaneous matters. The Caucus approved, by voice vote, the elimination of Caucus Rule 8 which provided that the Caucus, through a two-thirds vote, could bind members on a floor vote on legislation. Foley led the

---

9. Jacobs, *Rage for Justice*, 325-327.
10. Bruce F. Freed, "House Democrats: Dispute Over Caucus Role," *Congressional Quarterly Weekly Report*, May 3, 1975, 911-912, 914-915.

effort to eliminate this rule. The rule had rarely been used in recent years.[11]

As a result of the changes, the Caucus lost its assertiveness and declined. The Caucus became ineffective as seen in the Caucus from August 20, 1980. The Caucus convened at 9:04 a.m. in the Hall of the House of Representatives for the regular monthly meeting. Foley, as Caucus Chairman, presided. He announced that since this meeting was noticed to Democrats as pro forma without any business on the agenda, he was adjourning the Caucus. The Caucus adjourned at 9:05 a.m.[12]

The presidents of this era, Gerald Ford and Jimmy Carter, observed the changes and labored under them. Ford wrote that when he was in Congress, he believed Congress performed its job properly. After he became president, his view changed: "It seemed to me that Congress was beginning to disintegrate as an organized legislative body. It wasn't answering the nation's challenges domestically because it was too fragmented. It responded too often to single-issue special interest groups and it therefore wound up dealing with minutiae instead of attacking serious problems in a coherent way."[13] Jimmy Carter expressed a similar opinion. Carter argued that reforms in the House and the Democratic Party had severely weakened the strength of party leaders. He argued that this arrangement was different from the era of Lyndon Johnson's presidency. During that era, Johnson, the Speaker of the

---

11. Bruce Freed, "House Democratic Caucus," *Congressional Quarterly Weekly Report*, September 13, 1975, 1956.

12. Caucus minutes, August 20, 1980, p. 1-2, Folder: Foley Papers Democratic Caucus Minutes--June 18/July 2/August 20- & Sept. 17/November 19 1980, Box 185, Foley Papers.

13. Ford, *Heal*, 150.

House, and the Ways and Means Committee chair could reach a consensus on a tax or welfare position and be sure that the House would ratify their position. Carter argued that, "The absence of discipline or consensus within the Democratic party strengthened the influence of special-interest lobbies on the legislative process--a highly dangerous development."[14] Carter wrote, concerning Tip O'Neill and the House during his presidency, that, "He had a nearly impossible job trying to deal with a rambunctious Democratic majority that had been reformed out of almost any semblance of discipline or loyalty to him, and on many occasions he and I were to commiserate about the almost anarchic independence of the House."[15]

The years from the mid-1970s to the present featured many changes for the nation, but some were more politically relevant than others. The post-War economic boom ended, and the nation experienced alternating periods of growth and recession and new economic problems. The nation suffered from outsourcing in which U. S. companies removed jobs from America and relocated them to foreign nations. The U. S. began a fiscal crisis in the 1970s that continued to worsen in the ensuing decades in which the federal government borrowed unusually large and growing sums of money to function, posted increasingly large deficits, and grew the national debt to gargantuan levels. The federal government had a balanced budget in only four fiscal years after fiscal year 1969 (fiscal years 1998, 1999, 2000, and 2001). Immigration continued to make America more diverse. The Hispanic population greatly increased and greatly impacted some states such as Texas and California, and the Asian population also increased. Many

---

14. Carter, *Keeping Faith*, 84.
15. Carter, *Keeping Faith*, 77-78.

communities and areas of the U. S. became identified with the label "minority-majority" to indicate that the majority of the local population was not White.

In the late 1970s, there was dissatisfaction with the status quo, and much of the dissatisfaction was directed towards Liberalism which had dominated public policy since the 1930s. A revived Conservatism emerged that tapped into this dissatisfaction, offered genuine conservative alternatives to Liberalism, and reshaped the Republican Party. The Republican Party became more conservative and homogeneous and presented an ideological challenge to the Democratic Party and Liberalism. The ideological divisions among liberals, moderates, and conservatives continued within the Democratic Party, and the Democrats struggled to preserve the policies and ideas of Liberalism while also responding to the public dissatisfaction with the status quo which often entailed a critique of Liberalism. In the South, the Republicans continued to become more competitive, and the number of people identifying themselves as conservative Democrats declined. The South became competitive between Democrats and Republicans in local, state, and federal elections and then transformed into a Republican-dominated region. In other regions, Democrats again lost support among some traditional White Democratic constituencies. Overall, minorities seemed to favor the Democratic Party. Black Americans continued to be a solid Democratic constituency, but the growing Hispanic population showed greater political diversity. Republicans had more support from Hispanic voters, overall, than from Black voters, but Democrats still saw them, in many situations, as a solid Democratic constituency. The liberal-conservative paradigm gained even more influence and had the effect of homogenizing or nationalizing local politics and people's viewpoints on issues and partisan identification. Increasing numbers of people adopted the stereotypical liberal or conservative ideology and positions with little variation. National issues became more significant in local politics. Increasing numbers of states and electoral districts became seen as safe for one party or the other. Secure Democratic areas were "blue," and safe Republican areas were "red." Only a minority of the states were seen as truly competitive in presidential elections. Nonetheless, many of the landmark achievements of Liberalism remained popular, and the public reacted negatively to extreme conservative ideas and extreme actions by conservatives that seemed to threaten these achievements and the status quo. As a result, the political parties enjoyed rough parity overall, frequent changes in control of government, and frequent periods of divided government.

In the years after the removal of the chairmen and the overthrow of the Bipartisan House System, a new centralized system of management based on strong party authority emerged, the Partisan House System. This new system emerged in the early 1980s and became institutionalized in the ensuing decades. It continues to the present. Although the Democrats and the Republicans experienced changes in control of the House, large shifts in the partisan lineup, and changes in party leaders, the characteristics of the Partisan House System endure, and both parties follow similar practices. The Partisan House System is characterized by stronger party leaders and institutions, a greater stress on party unity and discipline, greater uniformity among party members regarding ideology and voting, and a more partisan approach towards the work of the House. With these characteristics, bipartisanship suffers, and there is less ideological diversity. The Partisan House System is a natural and logical consequence of the Congressional reform movement and the removal of the chairmen. The vision for the House expressed in Bolling's books was fully implemented. In addition, the larger political trends that characterized the United States since the Watergate Crisis created circumstances favorable to the characteristics of the Partisan House System. Jim Jones of Oklahoma served as the House Budget Committee chairman in the 1980s. In 2002, he succinctly identified the early 1980s as the origins of a drastically more partisan era: "The combination of the very high partisanship, no-give policy of the Reagan White House in '81-82 coupled with the Democrats pounding the Republicans on Social Security in the '82 elections, and becoming very partisan on that issue, was really the start, in my judgment, of what has been the most partisan two decades in my lifetime."[16]

Tip O'Neill and Jim Wright guided the House Democratic Leadership for several years before and during the beginnings of the Partisan House System. These years featured the rise of Ronald Reagan to the presidency, the articulation of a revived conservative ideology, a challenge to the New Deal-Great Society ideology and policies, and the growth of the Republican Party in the South. Faced with the lack of direction in the House and these national circumstances, the House Democrats under O'Neill and Wright responded with efforts to increase party authority as a means to immediately promote their policies and to address electoral challenges. The actions of the Democrats

---

16. Jim Jones, interview by author, July 12, 2002, telephone tape recording, T. Harry Williams Center for Oral History, Louisiana State University, Baton Rouge, LA.

and the Republicans, the Congress and the presidency, and the public all resulted in the Partisan House System.

In response to the national political conflicts of the 1980s, the House Democratic Leadership promoted stronger party authority in a policy outlined by Jim Wright at a meeting of the Democratic Caucus on September 16, 1981. Wright identified four points. First, the House Democrats offered amnesty for past actions and votes. Second, there was a distinction between rewards and punishments. Seats on the four leadership committees (Ways and Means, Appropriations, Rules, and Budget) and chairmanships of committees were treated as rewards that also carried obligations or responsibilities; they were awarded by the Caucus. Third, the DSPC designated certain votes as key votes, and members' records on these votes were used to help determine who received seats on the four leadership committees. Finally, there was an effort to distinguish "between the occasional aberration and consistent, steady record of defection and conniving with the opposition."[17]

After years of decay, the Caucus was again revived, but in the 1980s, the Caucus was used to build stronger party authority through consensus rather than coercion. Gillis W. Long of Louisiana served as Caucus Chairman in the Ninety-seventh and Ninety-eighth Congresses (1981, 1982, 1983, and 1984) and implemented a Caucus program to strengthen the Democratic Party. Long explained his rationale for the Caucus in a 1984 letter to Tip O'Neill. Long argued that House reforms decentralized authority in the House, thus depriving the

---

17. Caucus minutes, September 16, 1981, p. 72-77, Folder: Foley Papers Democratic Caucus Minutes--September 16/October 7, 21 November 18/December 15 1981, Box 185, Foley Papers.

Leadership of the mechanisms to pressure members on votes that it earlier exercised. In response, the Leadership needed to build consensus using other tactics. Long stressed the practice of "consulting a large number of Members in an orderly way that both allows Members to understand an issue better and to feel involved in the Leadership's strategic decision." Long saw the Caucus as "fast becoming a constructive and effective arm of the Leadership."[18]

Long's assistant and advisor, Al From, served as executive director of the Caucus during Long's Caucus tenure. From explained that Long and his Caucus associates tried to execute their Caucus program in venues or areas outside the normal work of the House in order to avoid direct conflict with powerful House leaders. Long's Caucus associates typically did not hold positions of great authority in the House. Long and his Caucus associates did not try to influence roll call votes or legislation.[19]

The Caucus became very active in the early 1980s. The Caucus was closed to the media and the public. Caucus rules called for a regularly scheduled gathering at least once a month. Attendance improved at Caucus meetings. The meetings generally had 137 members or more present; 137 members were needed for a quorum. Special meetings could be held with the collection of at least fifty signatures. In the previous six years of open gatherings, attendance by

---

18. Long to O'Neill, September 17, 1984, Folder: Kelley's files--Thank you to Speaker 1984, Staff Files Eleanor Kelley Files Box 8, Thomas P. O'Neill Papers, Congressional Archives, John J. Burns Library, Boston College, Chestnut Hill, MA.

19. Al From, interview by author, May 16, 2003, telephone tape recording, T. Harry Williams Center for Oral History, Louisiana State University, Baton Rouge, LA.

Democrats was low.[20] Much of the Caucus program was promoted by the Committee on Party Effectiveness. This group was a collection of thirty-seven members representing the various ideologies and regions in the Caucus, and it included the leaders of the DSG, the Conservative Democratic Forum, the Congressional Black Caucus, and the Rural Caucus. The Committee began work in early 1981 and held frequent meetings with the goal of reviving the Democratic Party.[21] The Caucus completed the codification of the Caucus rules. The work began under Phillip Burton as Caucus Chairman and was continued by Tom Foley as Caucus Chairman. In September 1982, the Caucus adopted the codified rules. Previously, the Caucus rules were in two parts: the Standing Rules of the Caucus and a Caucus Manual. Additions were made to the Manual over time, and the rules became problematic.[22]

The Caucus offered ideas to the nation. In September 1982, the Caucus issued *Rebuilding the Road to Opportunity: A Democratic Direction for the 1980s,* a book that contained statements on economic policy, housing, small business, women's economic issues, the environment, and national security prepared by Caucus task forces. These statements were not official party positions or dogma. They were policy

---

20. "Secret Meetings Restore Vigor: Democratic Caucus Renewed as Forum for Policy Questions," *Congressional Quarterly Weekly Report,* October 15, 1983, 2115-2119.

21. "Caucus Report for the 97th Congress" and letter from Long and Ferraro to Hightower, November 29, 1982, Folder: Caucus Corr--82, Box 26-JEH 360, Jack E. Hightower Papers, Baylor University Collections of Political Materials, Baylor University, Waco, TX.

22. "Caucus Report for the 97th Congress" and letter from Long and Ferraro to Hightower, November 29, 1982, Folder: Caucus Corr--82, Box 26-JEH 360, Jack E. Hightower Papers, Baylor University Collections of Political Materials, Baylor University, Waco, TX.

ideas that reflected consensus positions and that presented alternatives to Republican policies. The task forces were appointed by the Speaker and the Caucus Chairman. The statements were reviewed and approved by the Committee on Party Effectiveness.[23]

Conservative Democrats from the South exercised great influence for decades in the Democratic Party and in the House, but the Partisan House System and the changes in the nation posed new challenges to them in the years after the removal. A group of conservative Democrats formed the Democratic Conservative Forum in 1980 in order to gain a greater role in the Democratic Party in the House. They called for better committee posts for themselves and a more moderate position by the House Democratic Party. Texan Charles W. Stenholm took the lead in organizing the group.[24] The group officially became the Conservative Democratic Forum (CDF). Stenholm served as the coordinator of the CDF; the CDF had no leaders per se.[25] Stenholm explained that the CDF had regular meetings to discuss issues facing the House and to inform its members about the issues. The CDF focused

---

23. "Caucus Report for the 97th Congress" and letter from Long and Ferraro to Hightower, November 29, 1982, Folder: Caucus Corr--82, Box 26-JEH 360, Jack E. Hightower Papers, Baylor University Collections of Political Materials, Baylor University, Waco, TX.

24. Richard L. Lyons, "Conservative House Democrats Seeking Larger Role in Party," *Washington Post*, November 20, 1980, A3.

25. Stenholm to Nichols, January 31, 1983, Folder: 32-Z-2 Democratic Caucus, Box 28 of 32, Accession # 87-4, William F. Nichols Papers, Special Collections and Archives, Auburn University, Auburn, AL.

primarily on budget and fiscal issues. The CDF did not take official positions on issues.[26]

By the 1980s, conservative Southern Democrats and the traditional House customs with which they were associated faced new circumstances and challenges resulting from national social and economic changes. With the success of the Civil Rights Movement, civil rights ceased to be a divisive issue for Southerners, and the South experienced economic development and population growth. Black voters became a core constituency for Democrats against Republicans in general elections and could critically influence Democratic primaries. In many Democratic primaries in the South, liberal-leaning constituencies became the main constituencies. Conservative constituencies became less prominent in the Democratic primaries in the South, and there was a noticeable decline in the number of conservatives voting in the Democratic primaries in the South. Because of these changes, the South began electing many more Republican Congressmen than it had elected in past decades when most Southern Congressmen were Democrats. Many younger Southern Democrats were ideologically closer to the national Democratic Party than were the older conservative Southern Democrats. After facing strong Republican opponents in general elections, some southern Democrats became less inclined to view Republicans in Congress as potential allies. Southern Democrats were struck by Texas Democrat Jack Hightower's defeat in 1984 by a Republican opponent. Hightower became bitterly partisan as a result. Some southern Democrats believed

---

26. Charles W. Stenholm, interview by author, June 11, 2002, telephone tape recording, T. Harry Williams Center for Oral History, Louisiana State University, Baton Rouge, LA.

that Republicans in Congress were not interested in compromise and Conservative Coalition cooperation. Some Southern Democrats thought that Republicans engaged too frequently in partisan and obstructionist tactics. There were fewer conservative Southern Democrats in Congress, and their decline precipitated the decline of a set of folkways in Congress which conservative Southern Democrats participated in and perpetuated for many decades. The Conservative Coalition experienced decline and rarely appeared on votes. Democrats voted more as a united bloc both in the House and in the Senate, and the Republicans became more united, too.[27]

The removal of Patman, Poage, and Hebert established a precedent that chairmen could and would be removed if they lost majority support. This precedent shaped the Armed Services chairmanship in the mid-1980s. On January 4, 1985, the Democratic Caucus removed Melvin Price as chair of the Armed Services Committee and elevated Les Aspin of Wisconsin to the post. Price lost on a vote of 121-118 despite O'Neill's call to retain Price as chair for one more term. Price had the support of the House Democratic Leadership, the Congressional Black Caucus, senior members, and about half of the members of the Armed Services Committee. The Caucus passed over several more senior members to elect Aspin. He was seventh in seniority on the Committee and had the support of junior Democrats of various ideological positions. Although Aspin supported and compromised with Reagan on defense

---

27. Alan Ehrenhalt, "Changing South Perils Conservative Coalition," *Congressional Quarterly Weekly Report*, August 1, 1987, 1699-1705.

issues, he had liberal leanings and was critical of the Department of Defense on some occasions.[28]

Despite these events, the chairmanship remained unsettled for two more years. Ron Dellums continued as a member of the Armed Services Committee and wrote that Aspin angered many Democrats; Aspin utilized the Armed Services chair to impede the Caucus in its attempts to end the MX missile and supported the Contras as Reagan favored. Many Democrats wanted the House Democrats to take greater action to restrain Reagan's foreign/military policies.[29]

The controversy surrounding Aspin created the circumstances for Bob Poage's successor from the Eleventh District of Texas, Marvin Leath, to challenge Aspin for the chairmanship using the chairmen selection process established years earlier. Leath was first elected to the House in 1978 and was generally regarded as conservative. Leath explained his reasons for the challenge and his plans for the Committee starting in 1986. He stood for a strong defense, consensus, and realization of fiscal constraints: "We must be perceived as a party that stands for a strong defense, yet a party where all members, from conservative to liberal, are determined to give the Pentagon the extreme scrutiny and oversight necessary to insure the strength to deter aggression without bankrupting our economy."[30] The steering committee that worked for Leath's election to the chairmanship included members regarded as

---

28. Margaret Shapiro, "Democrats Remove Price as Chairman," *Washington Post*, January 5, 1985, A1, A6.

29. Dellums, *Lying Down*, 153-156.

30. Leath to Wright, July 17, 1986, Folder: Leath, Marvin (Texas), Box 3-35 of 42, Jim Wright Papers of Jim Wright Collection, Mary Couts Burnett Library, Texas Christian University, Fort Worth, Texas.

conservative, moderate, and liberal. Melvin Price and Dellums were members of the steering committee.[31]

At the start of the One Hundredth Congress, the House Democrats elected their committee chairs and resolved the Armed Services chair issue. On January 7, 1987, the Caucus voted 124-130 to reject Aspin for the chairmanship. On January 8, the DSPC nominated Charles Bennett of Florida for the chairmanship by a vote of 16-11. He ranked second in seniority on the Committee among Democrats. Also, Nicholas Mavroules of Massachusetts indicated that he might compete for the chairmanship.[32] The Caucus met on January 22, 1987, and there were four contestants: Bennett, Leath, Aspin, and Mavroules. Dellums delivered the speech nominating Leath for the chairmanship in the Caucus.[33] The results of the first ballot were: Bennett, 44; Leath, 69; and Aspin, 96. Mavroules was eliminated from the contest due to finishing last in votes.[34] The results of the second ballot were: Leath, 91 and Aspin, 108. Bennett was eliminated because he finished last.[35] A vote between Aspin and Leath was reached, and Aspin won, 133-

31. Steering committee to Foley, January 5, 1987, Folder: Foley Papers Leadership Files/100th Cong.--Steering & Policy Cte Requests, 1986-1987, Box 168, Foley Papers.

32. Jacqueline Calmes, "Aspin Ousted as Armed Services Chairman," *Congressional Quarterly Weekly Report*, January 10, 1987, 83-85.

33. Caucus minutes, January 22, 1987, p. 16-20, Folder: Foley Papers Democratic Caucus Minutes--January 22, 29/February 4, 19/March 11, 18-1987, Box 187, Foley Papers.

34. Caucus minutes, January 22, 1987, p. 51, Folder: Foley Papers Democratic Caucus Minutes--January 22, 29/February 4, 19/March 11, 18-1987, Box 187, Foley Papers.

35. Caucus minutes, January 22, 1987, p. 53, Folder: Foley Papers Democratic Caucus Minutes--January 22, 29/February 4, 19/March 11, 18-1987, Box 187, Foley Papers.

116.[36] Dellums wrote that after retaining the chair, Aspin reformed his ways to manage the Committee more openly and with more input from Committee members.[37]

O'Neill was succeeded by Jim Wright as Speaker, and Jim Wright became the first institutionally powerful Speaker since Joseph Cannon and managed the House as a strong Speaker in the One Hundredth Congress and in the One Hundredth and First Congress. Wright thought that Sam Rayburn influenced his development as a representative. Wright believed that he did several things that he had witnessed Rayburn doing years earlier. Wright noted a difference between him and O'Neill concerning the relative position of committee chairs. O'Neill believed the committee chairs should receive wide latitude in formulating legislation on account of their expertise in their committee's area of jurisdiction. In contrast, Jim Wright believed the direction for legislation should come from the Democratic Caucus majority. Wright described himself in this way: "I guess if people think of me as a strong Speaker it's because I was more direction-oriented, more goal-oriented."[38]

Wright espoused his belief in a strong Speaker to the nation. In a speech to the Democratic Caucus on December 8, 1986, Wright called for Congress to take the initiative and to act as an equal partner/branch of the government in relation to the executive branch as the Constitution mandated. He wanted Congress to "renew its rightful role in this 100th Congress as a

---

36. Caucus minutes, January 22, 1987, p. 62-64, Folder: Foley Papers Democratic Caucus Minutes--January 22, 29/February 4, 19/March 11, 18-1987, Box 187, Foley Papers.

37. Dellums, *Lying Down*, 153-156.

38. Jim Wright, personal interview recording by author, March 20, 2002, Fort Worth, Texas.

prime initiator of policy."[39] After his election as Speaker by the House, Wright gave a speech and discussed the important and Constitutional-based role Congress should play in the operation of government. He stressed that Congress and the Presidency were partners in government, equal partners, and depended upon cooperation with one another. He warned that Congress would act as an equal partner under his Speakership.[40]

Wright recalled the start of the One Hundredth Congress (1987 and 1988). The DSPC issued a resolution, passed by the Caucus, calling for the implementation of an agenda. The agenda contained bills that were numbered one through twenty to emphasize their importance. Wright held a conference with the committee chairs in order to receive the chairs' agreement for a specific schedule, or timetable, for each important bill to be reported by the relevant committee. Members could know the rough outlines of the House's work schedule and be ready for the important bills. The committee chairs were cooperative and did not oppose Wright's plan for the agenda and schedule. Rostenkowski was the only chairman who showed any tendencies to work independently, but this trait was not a serious problem and did not occur regularly.[41] The important bills Wright cited were listed in the *Congressional Record* starting with HR 1.[42]

---

39. Wright speech to Democratic Caucus, December 8, 1986, Folder: Democratic Caucus, Box 3-26 of 42, Jim Wright Papers.

40. *Election of Speaker*, 100th Cong., 1st sess., *Congressional Record* 133 (January 6, 1987): 4-5.

41. Jim Wright, personal interview recording by author, March 20, 2002, Fort Worth, Texas.

42. *House Bills*, 100th Cong., 1st sess., *Congressional Record* 133 (L-Z and History of Bills): 3267-3268.

Tom Foley served as Majority Leader under Wright and noted Wright's strong Speakership. Foley wrote that Wright believed in a strong, involved Speaker that diligently, rather than casually, managed the House. This belief was based on the Sam Rayburn practice and image, and the rest of the House was supposed to accept and to implement the Speaker's direction. Foley wrote that "There ought to be decisions from the top, there ought to be direction from the top, there ought to be organization from the top, there ought to be follow-through and obedience."[43]

Wright's strong Speakership was noticed by the public and the media. It was reported that Wright had good relations with some chairs such as Jack Brooks (Government Operations), John Dingell (Energy and Commerce), and James Howard (Public Works). They willingly accepted Wright's use of an agenda with close management by the Speaker. Wright's relations with Rostenkowski were different. Rostenkowski preferred the O'Neill strategy of not advocating tax increases unless Reagan also advocated tax increases. In contrast, Wright made the House Democrats take the lead in promoting a tax increase. Wright was viewed as having immersed himself in the details of legislation and its progression through the House. He was viewed as being a strong Speaker who used his authority to push his agenda which was viewed as consistent with the concerns and beliefs of the majority of Democrats.[44] Also, Wright appointed the DSPC members for the freshmen, the women members, and the Black members

---

43. Biggs, *Honor in the House*, 92.
44. Janet Hook, "Speaker Jim Wright Takes Charge in the House," *Congressional Quarterly Weekly Report*, July 11, 1987, 1483-1488.

instead of letting these groups elect their own representatives as O'Neill had done.[45]

Under Wright, the decline of the Conservative Coalition was noted in different forms. Statistically, the Conservative Coalition as a voting phenomenon declined in the One Hundredth Congress. In the House, it appeared on 8.4% of the votes in 1988 and on 8.8% of the votes in 1987.[46] An internal packet from the House Democrats' Whip Organization from the One Hundredth Congress discussed the increasing Democratic unity and stressed the House Democratic Leadership's efforts to include conservative Democrats in the formulation of policy. The packet stated that, "Conservatives are more willing than in the early days of the Reagan Era to 'make their deal' inside the Democratic Party, creating new opportunities for the House Democratic Leadership when the Leadership gives them a real policy role." The packet also stated that, "No conservative will work with the Leadership on every issue. But the Leadership does not need them all each time. A Member can work with the Leadership and remain a tough conservative."[47]

As a strong Speaker, Wright used his authority over the Rules Committee and the rules for debate over legislation to advance his Party's agenda. Wright recalled that he worked with the Rules Committee to get rules to protect the bills from obstructionist tactics which had been used significantly in the

---

45. Janet Hook, "House Leadership Elections: Wright Era Begins," *Congressional Quarterly Weekly Report*, December 13, 1986, 3067, 3070-3072.

46. Macon Morehouse, "Conservative Coalition: Still Alive, but Barely," *Congressional Quarterly Weekly Report*, November 19, 1988, 3343-3346.

47. Whip Packet, Folder: Foley Papers Leadership Files/100th Cong.-- Whip Organization [1987-1988], Box 168, Foley Papers.

Ninety-ninth Congress. Such tactics included requesting a recorded vote for every amendment and offering pointless/trivial amendments which required a certain amount of time for debate and voting.[48] Wright worked more closely with the Rules Committee as Speaker than O'Neill did. Wright saw the Rules Committee as a leadership tool and sought restrictive rules for top bills in 1987. House Republicans were angry at the Democratic Leadership's use of the Rules Committee and its rules to restrict floor debate and floor amendments. On some occasions, some Democrats felt the impact of the Rules Committee's restrictions and fought the tactics. The House Democratic Leadership claimed the Rules Committee's restrictions were needed to effectively manage the House, and such restrictions increased.[49]

On May 24, 1988, the Republicans made speeches for two hours on the House floor covered by C-SPAN that accused the Democrats of autocratic behavior. According to the Republicans, the Democrats brought more bills to the floor without committee consideration and brought more bills to the floor under restrictive rules. Often, the rules prevented amendments from being offered. The Democrats denied a fair share of staff to the Republicans. The Democrats allowed nearly 50% of the bills passed by the House to be commemorative as opposed to substantive legislation. Republicans claimed these trends grew under both O'Neill and Wright as Speakers.[50]

---

48. Jim Wright, personal interview recording by author, March 20, 2002, Fort Worth, Texas.

49. Janet Hook, "GOP Chafes Under Restrictive House Rules," *Congressional Quarterly Weekly Report*, October 10, 1987, 2449-2452.

50. Don Phillips, "House GOP Says Rights Are Denied," *Washington Post*, May 25, 1988, A3.

Jim Wright's tenure as Speaker was short due to the increasingly high partisan tensions. Wright believed that his efforts for peace in Nicaragua inflamed extreme conservatives. They responded with media attacks against him and became motivated to target him. At this point, the House Republicans had not won on any significant votes in the One Hundredth Congress. They were unable to cooperate with the conservative Democrats as they did in the early 1980s. Wright recalled that scuttlebutt emanating from the Republican Conference indicated that Republican extremists were calling for a direct attack on Wright. Newt Gingrich led the charge against Wright.[51] Gingrich filed a complaint with the Committee on Standards of Official Conduct alleging that Wright had improper conduct concerning investments in oil and gas properties and royalties from a book published by someone who had financial ties to Wright's reelection committees. Seventy-two Republicans, including most of the Republican leadership, issued a letter to the Committee's chair, Julian C. Dixon of California, urging the Committee to investigate Wright. Minority Leader Bob Michel did not sign the letter.[52]

The effort against Wright proved successful in 1989. The Committee on Standards of Official Conduct issued a report on April 17. The Committee announced that it believed Wright violated House rules in sixty-nine instances, but Wright refuted the charges. Yet, the Committee voted to begin a preliminary inquiry into Wright and hired a trial lawyer, Richard J. Phelan, to lead the inquiry. The circumstances in national politics also affected Wright's predicament. The Senate rejected Republican

---

51. Wright, *Balance of Power*, 473-474.
52. Tom Kenworthy, "72 Republicans Ask Panel to Probe Wright's Finances," *Washington Post*, May 27, 1988, A1, A5.

John Tower for Defense Secretary, and rumors spread of Republicans targeting Wright for revenge. The press greatly publicized Wright's problems, and the problems of Wright's aide, John P. Mack, worsened Wright's problems. Mack eventually resigned. On May 31, Wright announced that he would resign as Speaker on June 6.[53]

Tom Foley presided as Speaker for over five years in an increasingly partisan environment. Foley wrote that when Jim Wright resigned in 1989, the general atmosphere in the House was very partisan and antagonistic. There was a general feeling among Republicans that the Democrats had disrespected and mistreated them. There was a general feeling among Democrats that the opposition to Wright was a purely partisan effort for partisan gain. There was a lot of animosity towards Newt Gingrich. Foley wrote: "There was a feeling in the House that things had gotten impossibly tense and bitter. While there were members in both parties that desperately wanted to return to a more civil and cooperative environment, the general atmosphere was poisonous."[54] Foley noted the intensified partisan attitude among many in his Party: "In their eyes I was failing in my partisan duty if I didn't get up every morning with a fresh attack on the administration. Any kind of cooperation was suspect."[55]

Foley witnessed the House's historic shift in 1994 that fundamentally altered the status quo, but the circumstances for the House Democrats had already been altered in 1992 due to the election of Bill Clinton as president. Foley bluntly explained

---

53. Janet Hook, "Passion, Defiance, Tears: Jim Wright Bows Out," *Congressional Quarterly Weekly Report*, June 3, 1989, 1289-1294.
54. Biggs, *Honor in the House*, 107-108.
55. Biggs, *Honor in the House*, 126-127.

the significance of Clinton to House Democrats. He wrote that, "During the first two years, the House did more than the White House might admit in subordinating ourselves to the President's agenda. It was on the theory that we'd been out of office for twelve years, and with a Democratic President we had a duty to do whatever we could to advance those programs that his administration wanted."[56] There were consequences: "My own view, and it's not intended to be critical of President Clinton, is that a number of Democratic members, including my own case, despite all my other problems, would have been reelected with President George Bush still in the White House."[57]

The elections for the One Hundredth and Fourth Congress in 1994 and the emergence of a Republican majority in the House continued and entrenched the Partisan House System that began after the removal. The Republicans won control of the House in the 1994 elections. They gained fifty-three seats, and five seats were still unresolved immediately after the election. The new lineup for the House tentatively included 231 Republicans, 203 Democrats, and 1 Independent. The Republicans used Bill Clinton as a campaign issue and tried to link Democratic Congressional candidates to Clinton.[58]

The South played a critical role in the Republicans' success in the 1994 elections, and the year 1994 was a pivotal year for the South. By the mid-1990s, great changes in the South were easily noted. Because of the elections, the Republicans would tentatively hold a majority of southern

---

56. Biggs, *Honor in the House*, 196.
57. Biggs, *Honor in the House*, 243-244.

governorships, a majority of the South's U. S. House of Representatives seats, and a majority of the South's Senate seats. The lineup for Southern House seats would change from an 83-54 Democratic majority to a tentative 73-64 Republican majority. Population growth in the South brought in many new people, and many of them were Republicans or Independents. The South's historic Democratic heritage held less influence over young Southern voters. Republicans challenged Democrats more often in Southern states.[59]

Once in power in 1995, House Republicans made changes to the House that were similar to the reforms of the Congressional reform movement of the 1960s and 1970s. House Republicans passed a package of rules changes on January 4. Many Democrats supported the package, and there was an absence of strong opposition to the package. Some of the minor rules changes made certain customs official that had been practiced for several years.[60] More importantly, the package of rules changes had significant effects on the House power structure. Three committees were eliminated: the District of Columbia Committee, the Merchant Marine and Fisheries Committee, and the Post Office and Civil Service Committee. Some committees were renamed, and some committees' jurisdictions were changed. The Speaker was limited to no more than four consecutive two-year terms. The chairs of

58. Dave Kaplan and Juliana Gruenwald, "Longtime 'Second' Party Scores a Long List of GOP Firsts," *Congressional Quarterly Weekly Report*, November 12, 1994, 3232-3239.

59. Rhodes Cook, "Dixie Voters Look Away: South Shifts to the GOP," *Congressional Quarterly Weekly Report*, November 12, 1994, 3230-3231.

60. David S. Cloud, "Organization: GOP, to Its Own Great Delight, Enacts House Rules Changes," *CQ Weekly*, January 7, 1995, 13-15.

committees and subcommittees were limited to no more than three consecutive terms beginning in 1995. The Office of the Doorkeeper was terminated, and its responsibilities were assigned to the Sergeant at Arms. Support of legislative service organizations with House office space and money was abolished.[61]

Partisanship reached new peaks in the middle of the 1990s. The year 1995 produced a new record high for party unity since Congressional Quarterly began analyzing data in 1954; the House experienced party unity votes on 73.2% of its roll call votes. There were still a few Democrats with low party unity scores, but there were even fewer Republicans with low party unity sores. Moderate Republicans became more conservative and partisan in their votes in order to pass a Republican program/agenda and maintain Republican control of the House. Freshmen Republicans (numbering seventy-three) gave Speaker Newt Gingrich strong support and enabled him to suppress and prevent challenges from Republican dissidents or potential Republican dissidents. Meanwhile, opposition to the Republican agenda helped rally the Democrats in both the House and the Senate.[62]

With a Republican Congress and a Democratic President, gridlock resulted. The Clinton administration sought to impede the Republican agenda rather than promote its own agenda, and the Republicans implemented only a limited portion of their agenda. Only eighty-eight bills were signed into law by January 3, 1996. This number of bills was the lowest

---

61. "Rules Changes Open the Process but Strengthen the Reins of Power," *CQ Weekly*, January 7, 1995, 14-15.

62. Dan Carney, "As Hostilities Rage on the Hill, Partisan-Vote Rate Soars," *CQ Weekly*, January 27, 1996, 199-201.

number since 1933. Clinton's success rate with Congress (how frequently the president won his way on roll call votes on which he took a clear position) was 36.2% in 1995. In his first two years, it was 86.4%. Clinton's 1995 percentage was the lowest percentage since Congressional Quarterly started analyzing data in 1953. Meanwhile, Clinton's public support increased during 1995 as a result of his conflicts with the Republicans.[63]

Amidst the partisanship, Gingrich acted as a strong and highly partisan Speaker. Gingrich exercised great authority over the House Republicans in 1995. He at times usurped authority from committee chairs, and the committee chairs accepted the usurpations because of the desire/need to pass the Republican agenda. Gingrich directly interfered in issues such as Medicare, management of the District of Columbia, tax breaks, telecommunications, content of appropriations bills, and farm subsidies. Gingrich maintained control of the legislative schedule.[64] In 2002, Charles Stenholm discussed the partisanship that grew in the 1990s and intensified in the next decade: "But in the end, the Gingrich Revolution has given us the Congress we have today, that has become and is becoming even more so a pure partisan animal in which it is Democrats versus Republicans on almost every issue. The country does not do well under that approach, but that's where we are because right now the country through the ballot box is saying, 'That's what kind of government we want.'"[65]

---

63. Jon Healey, "Clinton Success Rate Declined to a Record Low in 1995," *CQ Weekly*, January 27, 1996, 193-198.

64. Jackie Koszczuk, "Gingrich Puts More Power Into Speaker's Hands," *CQ Weekly*, October 7, 1995, 3049-3053.

65. Charles W. Stenholm, interview by author, June 11, 2002, telephone tape recording, T. Harry Williams Center for Oral History, Louisiana State University, Baton Rouge, LA.

The growing partisanship and gridlock left conservative Democrats in unfortunate circumstances. The CDF had fifty-four members in 1994 before the elections but was set to lose twenty-one members for the next Congress.[66] In 1995, Republicans rarely needed conservative Democrats because of their majority numbers. Republicans, especially House Republicans, were uninterested in altering their legislation to attract conservative Democrats. Stenholm explained that: "'The extreme element of the Republican Party didn't want any part of compromise.'" The Conservative Coalition appeared only 11.4% of the time in House and Senate votes. When it appeared, it generally was successful. In addition, Southern Democrats continued to change in the 1990s. Some long-time Southern Democrats lost to Republicans or switched parties. Because the South continued to change socially and economically, Southern Democrats became more diverse with more Black members and Hispanic members.[67]

During the challenging years of the 1990s, the conservative Democrats became known as Blue Dogs. The Blue Dog Coalition was organized after the 1994 elections by "fiscally conservative and moderate Democrats." The group stated its founding principles: "Their goals were to hold both parties accountable to promises of fiscal restraint and, by working with both parties, to stop legislation from going too far right or too far left." The name "Blue Dog" emerged from several influences. Artist George Rodrigue of Louisiana frequently painted blue dogs. For many decades, many

66. Karen Foerstel, "Democratic Leaders Seek Support," *Congressional Quarterly Weekly Report*, November 12, 1994, 3224.
67. David Hosansky, "Southern Democrats Not Needed for Republicans to Win Votes," *CQ Weekly*, January 27, 1996, 202-204.

Southerners claimed that they would rather vote for a yellow dog over a Republican. In addition, some members felt "'choked blue'" by the extremes of both parties. The Blue Dogs officially announced their formation on February 14, 1995.[68] G. V. "Sonny" Montgomery of Mississippi was a conservative Democrat who served in the House for many years and served as chairman of the Veterans' Affairs Committee. He felt the Blue Dogs were more liberal, overall, than the conservative Democrats of previous decades but still believed in bipartisanship.[69]

The DSG experienced profound change in the 1980s and 1990s. Jim Wright recalled that the DSG's impact or influence on Congress was lessened in the 1980s because Reagan served as president and possessed the initiative. The Democrats were forced to impede Reagan's agenda and were unable to make great liberal advances.[70] Then, the rules changes adopted in 1995 changed the DSG's role significantly. In 1994, twenty-eight caucuses received recognition from the House Administration Committee and held the status of legislative service organization (LSO). These LSOs included groups such as the DSG, the Republican Study Committee, the Congressional Black Caucus, the Hispanic Caucus, the Sunbelt Caucus, and the Women's Issues Caucus. These LSOs received office space and equipment, and the House permitted their members to use money from their office funds to finance

---

68. "History," Blue Dog Coalition website, accessed July 11, 2012, http://ross.house.gov/BlueDog/history.htm.

69. G. V. "Sonny" Montgomery with Michael B. Ballard and Craig S. Piper, *Sonny Montgomery: The Veteran's Champion* (Starkville, MS: Mississippi State University Libraries, 2003), 123-124.

70. Jim Wright, personal interview recording by author, March 20, 2002, Fort Worth, Texas.

the LSOs' staffs and activities.[71] In response to the rules changes for LSOs, members of the House began assigning work formerly done by LSO staffs to their House office staffs. In addition, rules changes required the DSG to privatize their publications. Congressional Quarterly bought DSG Publications.[72]

In the twenty-first century, partisanship and Republican electoral success significantly struck one of the pillars of the Democratic Party, the state of Texas. In 2004, the Republican-controlled Texas legislature approved a mid-decade redistricting plan designed to benefit Republicans. The plan and the strategy for its approval was orchestrated by U. S. House of Representatives Majority Leader Tom DeLay of Texas who traveled to Austin to promote the plan. Democratic state legislators traveled en masse to Oklahoma and New Mexico on separate occasions to impede the redistricting plan's approval. Under the plan, several incumbent Democrats were placed in new districts. In some cases, incumbents were placed in the same district. The old Eleventh District of Bob Poage and Marvin Leath was divided, and the number was assigned to a different area of Texas. The current Texas lineup was then 17 Democrats and 15 Republicans.[73] The Texas redistricting plan benefited Republicans in the 2004 elections. Republicans gained five seats in Texas by beating Democratic incumbents and winning in some redrawn districts with open seats.

71. David S. Cloud, "GOP's House-Cleaning Sweep Changes Rules, Cuts Groups," *CQ Weekly*, December 10, 1994, 3487-3489.

72. Jonathan Salant, "LSOs Are No Longer Separate, But the Work's Almost Equal," *CQ Weekly*, May 27, 1995, 1483.

73. Gregory L. Giroux, "Texas Completes Unusual Redistricting and Readies for GOP Stampede Next Year," *CQ Weekly*, October 11, 2003, 2502-2503.

Republicans won six of the seven seats that they wanted to gain in Texas. Republicans possessed a tentative 21-11 edge in the Texas delegation.[74]

In the 2000s, the Partisan House System seemed to be institutionalized. By 2004, Minority Leader Nancy Pelosi of California, a Democrat, and Speaker Dennis Hastert of Illinois, a Republican, did not consult with one another regularly about House work. The House possessed strong partisan parity with the majority party holding a relatively small majority, and therefore, the minority party remained a persistent threat. This parity spurred the parties to sharpen their differences, instead of seeking consensus, as a means to galvanize their supporters for the elections. Over the previous thirty years, redistricting of House districts created more party-safe districts and fewer competitive districts. These party-safe districts were more likely to elect partisan members. In party-safe districts that resulted from redistricting, members tended to drift towards their political base (left/liberal or right/conservative) and away from the ideological center. House work became less personal, and members spent more time in their districts. Therefore, members did not form the friendships typical for members of the House in previous decades. Both parties' members seemed less interested in compromise and accommodation. Within this political environment, members were less interested in policing their own members and holding them accountable to ethics standards for fear of electoral consequences. Many rank-and-file members in both parties did not seem to want House leaders to consult with one another and compromise. Ultimately, many people felt that the House's increased

74. Peter E. Harrell, "A Slightly Redder Hue," *CQ Weekly*, November 6, 2004, 2621-2623.

partisanship and negative style reduced the House's effectiveness and prestige.[75]

The Parties showed great similarity in their conduct. By 2006 and 2007, the House Democrats and the House Republicans followed the same practices, and these practices applied to years of Democratic majority control and Republican majority control. Typically, the majority party tried to limit the minority party's ability to exercise influence by offering amendments to legislation, and the minority party argued that the majority governed unfairly.[76]

The Democrats regained control of the House following the 2006 elections, and the nation gained its first woman Speaker of the House, Nancy Pelosi. Yet, the change was accompanied by continuity in some important instances. With a new Democratic majority and Speaker, the House convened on January 4, 2007. Pelosi was elected Speaker over John Boehner of Ohio, 233-202. The House addressed H Res 6, a rules package of five parts. Republicans were not permitted to offer any significant amendments to the rules package, and some Republicans complained about the restriction. Title I, passed 426-0, extended the rule on term limits for committee chairs.[77]

Ideologically, Pelosi and the Democrats still showed some of the diversity characteristic of the Party in previous decades. Yet, the distribution of authority and numbers differed. The House Democrats were described in the following manner.

---

75. John Cochran, "Disorder in the House--And No End in Sight," *CQ Weekly*, April 3, 2004, 790-791, 793-797.

76. David Nather, "Same Rules Squabbles, Different Majority," *CQ Weekly*, January 8, 2007, 99.

77. Martin Kady II, "New Majority, New Rules," *CQ Weekly*, January 8, 2007, 122-124.

The New Democrat Coalition was an organized bloc of members favoring a pro-business agenda. The Blue Dogs were regarded as fiscal conservatives or deficit hawks. Fourteen Democrats were in both groups. The Congressional Progressive Caucus was an organized bloc of members favoring traditional liberal values. Approximately seventy members were unaligned Democrats not affiliated with any of the three blocs; these unaligned members represented all ideological positions and included rank-and-file members and leaders. The moderates (New Democrats and Blue Dogs) and the unaligned members constituted a majority of the House Democrats.[78]

Pelosi's Speakership reflected the Partisan House System. She was partisan and deeply involved with House affairs. She was willing to avoid controversial issues in order to avoid intra-party fights and to maintain good prospects for the Party in the elections. She stressed personal loyalty. She consulted regularly with the different factions or blocs among the House Democrats and opposed liberal Democrats on some salient issues. Under her, the Democrats continued the use of restrictive rules limiting the minority's influence. [79]

Partisanship was normative. For example, the year 2008 displayed great partisanship as seen in party unity votes. House Democrats voted, on average, with their Party majority on 92% of party unity votes. This average tied the record set in 2007 for Democrats. The Blue Dogs' average was 91%. For the

---

78. Alan K. Ota, "Pelosi Trip Begins in Center Lane," *CQ Weekly*, November 13, 2006, 2977-2981.

79. Edward Epstein, "Her Key to the House," *CQ Weekly*, October 29, 2007, 3158-3165.

Republicans, their average was 87%. The Republicans' record was 91% which was reached in 1995, 2001, and 2003.[80]

In the 2010 elections, the Republicans won control of the House, and the Democrats experienced severe setbacks. The new Congress would feature 242 Republicans and 193 Democrats. The Republicans gained sixty-three seats. There were eighty-seven Republican freshmen and nine Democratic freshmen.[81] Democrats had significant defeats in rural and suburban districts, and these defeats/districts included some of the Blue Dogs. In the elections, fourteen of the twenty-eight Democrats on the Agriculture Committee lost reelection. Also, three Democrats who were committee chairs were defeated for reelection.[82] In 2010, twenty-eight Blue Dog members retired or lost reelection. The Blue Dogs, as of January 2011, had twenty-six members.[83]

Seniority, once a pillar of the Bipartisan House System, received little respect in the Partisan House System, but the Democrats showed greater respect for it than the Republicans. In 2007, the Democrats still used seniority as a factor; the DSPC recommended the most senior member on each committee for the chairs of the sixteen committees over which it exercised selection authority.[84] In 2009, when the House convened, the House passed a package of rules changes, H

80. Shawn Zeller, "2008 Votes Studies: Party Unity--Parties Dig in Deep on a Fractured Hill," *CQ Weekly*, December 15, 2008, 3332-3335.

81. Sam Goldfarb, "GOP Goes to Work on Agenda," *CQ Weekly*, January 10, 2011, 120-122.

82. Alan K. Ota, "The House: New Majority, New Challenges," *CQ Weekly*, November 8, 2010, 2528-2532.

83. Alan K. Ota, "Blue Dog Democrats Scratching to Get In," *CQ Weekly*, January 10, 2011, 88.

84. Rebecca Kimitch, "CQ Guide to the Committees: Democrats Opt to Spread the Power," *CQ Weekly*, April 16, 2007, 1080-1083.

Res 5, along party lines. The package included a measure eliminating the six-year term limit for committee chairs.[85] The One Hundredth and Twelfth Congress began work on January 5, 2011. The House passed a rules package, H Res 5, along party lines, 238-191. The rules package reestablished the six-year term limit for committee chairmen.[86]

By the second decade of the twenty-first century, the House of Representatives, the political system, and the nation had experienced great changes. The Bipartisan House System naturally had its advantages and its disadvantages, and these advantages appear more significant when compared to the characteristics of the Partisan House System. The Congressional reform movement achieved its immediate goals but unintentionally acted as a catalyst for other changes. The creators had created a monster that possessed its own will and that could not be controlled. The Partisan House System emerged, developed, and matured quickly, and other trends in the nation supported the partisanship of the Partisan House System. Overall, the House, the political system, and the nation were receptive to the most salient characteristic of the Partisan House System, intense partisanship. The Congressional reform movement sought to make the majority party be effective in governing and accountable to the nation. Unfortunately, the partisanship of the Partisan House System dominated, and the reformers' goal of effectiveness and accountability was relegated in priority. The House, the Congress, the entire federal government, and the entire political system displayed

---

85. Bennett Roth, "House Adopts Package of Rule Changes," *CQ Weekly*, January 12, 2009, 75-76.

86. Sam Goldfarb, "GOP Goes to Work on Agenda," *CQ Weekly*, January 10, 2011, 120-122.

periods and instances of extreme inefficiency and negligence regarding the fundamental responsibilities of governing the nation. Empty rhetoric and symbolic gestures occupied too much of the federal government's time and effort. Too little time and effort was applied to real problems and constructive solutions. Problems were ignored and allowed to worsen. The trends that began in the late twentieth century and persisted in the early twenty-first century are poised to continue for the near future. The current status quo features a plethora of ugly partisanship but still lacks the ability to be consistently effective. Therefore, the Republic is vulnerable and threatened.

Bibliography

Archival Sources

Albert, Carl. Collection. The Carl Albert Congressional Research & Studies Center, University of Oklahoma, Norman, OK.

Bolling, Richard W. Collection. Dr. Kenneth J. LaBudde Department of Special Collections, Miller Nichols Library, University of Missouri-Kansas City, Kansas City, MO.

Foley, Thomas S. Congressional Papers. Manuscripts, Archives, and Special Collections, Holland/New Library, Washington State University, Pullman, WA.

Hightower, Jack E. Papers. Baylor University Collections of Political Materials, Baylor University, Waco, TX.

Long, Gillis W. Papers. Hill Memorial Library, Louisiana State University, Baton Rouge, LA.

Nichols, William F. Papers. Special Collections and Archives, Auburn University, Auburn, AL.

O'Neill, Thomas P. Papers. Congressional Archives, John J. Burns Library, Boston College, Chestnut Hill, MA.

Patman, Wright. Papers. Lyndon Baines Johnson Library, Austin, TX.

Poage, W. R. Papers. Baylor Collections of Political Materials, W. R. Poage Legislative Library Center, Baylor University, Waco, TX.

Rayburn, Sam. Papers. Dolph Briscoe Center for American History, University of Texas at Austin, Austin, TX

Reuss, Henry S. Papers, 1839-1982. Milwaukee Manuscript Collection 112, Wisconsin Historical Society Milwaukee Area Research Center, Golda Meir Library, University of Wisconsin-Milwaukee, Milwaukee, WI.

Wright, Jim. Papers. Jim Wright Collection, Mary Couts Burnett Library, Texas Christian University, Fort Worth, TX.

Interviews

From, Al. Interview by author, May 16, 2003, Baton Rouge, Louisiana. Telephone tape recording. T. Harry Williams Center for Oral History, Louisiana State University, Baton Rouge, Louisiana.

Gardner, John W. Interview by author, December 2, 1999, Baton Rouge, Louisiana. Telephone tape recording. T. Harry Williams Center for Oral History, Louisiana State University, Baton Rouge, Louisiana.

Jones, Jim. Interview by author, July 12, 2002, Baton Rouge, Louisiana. Telephone tape recording. T. Harry Williams Center for Oral History, Louisiana State University,   Baton Rouge, Louisiana.

Ottinger, Richard. Interview by author, November 18, 1999, Baton Rouge, Louisiana. Telephone tape recording. T. Harry Williams Center for Oral History, Louisiana State University, Baton Rouge, Louisiana.

Poage, Bob. Oral History Collection, Lyndon Baines Johnson Collection, Lyndon Baines Johnson Library, Austin, Texas.

Reuss, Henry. Interview by author, January 27, 2000, Baton Rouge, Louisiana. Telephone tape recording. T. Harry Williams Center for Oral History, Louisiana State University, Baton Rouge, Louisiana.

Schroeder, Pat. Interview by author, March 27, 2000, Baton Rouge, Louisiana. Telephone tape recording. T. Harry Williams Center for Oral History, Louisiana State University, Baton Rouge, Louisiana.

Stenholm, Charles W. Interview by author, June 11, 2002, Baton Rouge, Louisiana.Telephone tape recording. T. Harry Williams Center for Oral History, Louisiana State University, Baton Rouge, Louisiana.

Teicher, Oren. Interview by author, November 23, 1999, Baton Rouge, Louisiana. Telephone tape recording. T. Harry Williams Center for Oral History, Louisiana State University, Baton Rouge, Louisiana.

West, Fowler. Interview by author, January 19, 2000, Baton Rouge, Louisiana. Telephone tape recording. T. Harry Williams Center for Oral History, Louisiana State University, Baton Rouge, Louisiana.

Wright, Jim. Personal interview recording by author, March 20, 2002, Fort Worth, Texas.

Periodicals

Congressional Quarterly Weekly Report.
CQ Weekly.
New Republic.
New Orleans States.
New York Times.
Newsweek.
Redbook.
Texarkana Gazette.
Time.
Times-Picayune.
Waco Tribune-Herald.
Washington Post.

Primary Source Books

Albert, Carl, and Danney Goble. *Little Giant: The Life and Times of Speaker Carl Albert*. Norman, Oklahoma: University of Oklahoma Press, 1990.

American Bankers Association. *Comments on Mr. Patman's ABC's of Money*. New York: privately printed.

Battistella, Annabel "Fanne Foxe", and Yvonne Dunleary. *Fanne Foxe*. New York: Pinnacle Books, 1975.

Biggs, Jeffrey R., and Thomas S. Foley. *Honor In The House: Speaker Tom Foley*. Pullman, Washington: Washington State University Press, 1999.

Bolling, Richard. *House Out of Order*. New York: E. P. Dutton & Co., Inc., 1965.

_____. *Power in the House: A History of the Leadership of the House of Representatives*. New York: E. P. Dutton & Co., Inc., 1968.

Brownson, Charles B., ed. *1975 Congressional Staff Directory*, 17th ed. Alexandria, Virginia: The Congressional Staff Directory, 1975.

Carter, Jimmy. *Keeping Faith: Memoirs of a President*. Fayetteville: The University of Arkansas Press, 1995.

Congressional Quarterly Almanac, 93rd Congress 1st Session 1973. Washington, D. C.: Congressional Quarterly, 1974.

Congressional Quarterly Almanac, 93rd Congress 2nd Session 1974. Washington, D.C.: Congressional Quarterly, 1975.

Dean, John W., III. *Lost Honor*. Los Angeles: Stratford Press, 1982.

Dellums, Ronald V., and H. Lee Halterman. *Lying Down With the Lions: A Public Life From the Streets of Oakland to the Halls of Power.* Boston: Beacon Press, 2000.

Ford, Gerald R. *A Time to Heal: The Autobiography of Gerald R. Ford.* New York: Harper & Row, 1979.

Gallup, George H., ed. *The Gallup Poll: Public Opinion 1972-1977. Vol. 1, 1972-1975.* Wilmington, Delaware: Scholarly Resources, 1978.

Gardner, John W. *In Common Cause.* New York: W. W. Norton & Company, Inc., 1972.

Hebert, F. Edward, and John McMillan. *Last of the Titans: The Life and Times of Congressman F. Edward Hebert of Louisiana.* Lafayette, Louisiana: Center for Louisiana Studies at the University of Southwestern Louisiana, 1976.

Martin, Joe, and Robert J. Donovan. *My First Fifty Years in Politics.* New York: McGraw-Hill Book Company, Inc., 1960.

Miller, William "Fishbait" and Frances Spatz Leighton. *Fishbait: The Memoirs of the Congressional Doorkeeper.* Englewood Cliffs, NJ: Prentice-Hall, Inc., 1977.

Montgomery, G. V. "Sonny", Michael B. Ballard, and Craig S. Piper. *Sonny Montgomery: The Veteran's Champion.* Starkville, MS: Mississippi State University Libraries, 2003.

O'Neill, Tip, and William Novak. *Man of the House: The Life and Political Memoirs of Speaker Tip O'Neill.* New York: Random House, 1987.

Patman, Wright. *Bankerteering, Bonuseering, Melloneering.* Paris, Texas: Peerless Printing, 1934.

_____. *Our American Government and How It Works*, 7th ed. New York: Barnes & Noble, 1974.

_____. *The Robinson-Patman Act: What You Can and Cannot Do Under This Law*. New York: The Ronald Press Company, 1938.

Poage, W. R. *My First 85 Years*. Waco, Texas: Baylor University Press, 1985.

Ray, Elizabeth L. *The Washington Fringe Benefit*. New York: Dell Publishing Co., Inc., 1976.

Reuss, Henry S. *When Government Was Good: Memories of a Life in Politics*. Madison, Wisconsin: University of Wisconsin, 1999.

Rhodes, John, and Dean Smith. *I Was There*. Northwest Publishing, Incorporated, 1995.

Schroeder, Pat. *24 Years of House Work... and the Place Is Still a Mess: My Life in Politics*. Kansas City, Missouri: Andrews McMeel, 1998.

Simon, Paul. *P. S.: The Autobiography of Paul Simon*. Chicago: Bonus Books, 1999.

Udall, Morris K., Bob Neuman, and Randy Udall. *Too Funny to Be President*. New York: Henry Holt and Company, 1988.

West, Fowler. *He Ain't No Lawyer! Memories from My Years with Congressman Bob Poage*. Waco, TX: Baylor University, 2009.

Wright, Jim. *Balance of Power: Presidents and Congress From the Era of McCarthy to the Age of Gingrich*. Atlanta: Turner Publishing, Inc., 1996.

Government Publications

Congressional Record.

Ford, Gerald R. *Public Papers of the Presidents of the United States: Gerald R. Ford, 1974-1977*.

Galloway, George B. *History of the United States House of Representatives.* Washington, D. C.: U. S. Government Printing Office, 1965.

Nystrom, Duane, ed. *Biographical Directory of the United States Congress, 1774-1989*, Bicentennial Edition. Washington, D. C.: Government Printing Office, 1989.

U. S. Congress. House. Committee on Armed Services. *Investigation of the My Lai Incident: Hearings of the Armed Services Investigating Subcommittee of the Committee on Armed Services.* 91st Cong., 2nd sess., April 15, 16, 17, 23, 24, 27, 28, 29, 30, May 8, 9, 12, 13, June 9, 10, 22, 1970.

U. S. Congress. House. Committee on Armed Services. *Investigation of the My Lai Incident: Report of the Armed Services Investigating Subcommittee of the Committee on Armed Services.* 91st Cong., 2nd sess., July 15, 1970.

U. S. Congress. House. Committee on the Judiciary. *Charges of Hon. Wright Patman Against the Secretary of the Treasury: Hearings Before the Committee on the Judiciary.* 72nd Cong., 1st sess., January 13, 14, 15, 18, 19, 1932.

Secondary Source Books

Goodman, Walter. *The Committee: The Extraordinary Career of the House Committee on Un-American Activities.* New York: Farrar, Straus and Giroux, 1968.

Jacobs, John. *A Rage for Justice: The Passion and Politics of Phillip Burton.* Berkeley, California: University of California Press, 1995.

Kutler, Stanley I. *The Wars of Watergate: The Last Crisis of Richard Nixon.* New York: Alfred A. Knopf, 1990.

McFarland, Andrew S. *Common Cause: Lobbying in the Public Interest.* Chatham, New Jersey: Chatham House, 1984.

Olson, James S., and Randy Roberts, eds. *My Lai: A Brief History With Documents*. The Bedford Series in History and Culture. Boston: Bedford Books, 1998.

Saxe, Ruth MacKenzie. *1970-1980; A Decade of Citizen Action in Common Cause*. Washington, D. C.: Common Cause, 1980.

Schlesinger, Arthur M., Jr. *The Age of Roosevelt: The Crisis of the Old Order, 1919-1933*. Boston: Houghton Mifflin, 1957.

Young, Nancy Beck. *Wright Patman: Populism, Liberalism, & the American Dream*. Dallas: Southern Methodist University Press, 2000.

Zelizer, Julian E. *Taxing America: Wilbur D. Mills, Congress, and the State, 1945-1975*. New York: Cambridge University Press, 1998.

Internet Sources

Baylor Collections of Political Materials, accessed March 8, 2007,
http://www3.baylor.edu/Library/BCPM/Poage/poage_biogr aphy.html.

Blue Dog Coalition website, accessed July 11, 2012,
http://ross.house.gov/BlueDog/history.htm.

Common Cause website, accessed March 21, 2011,
http://www.commoncause.org/site/pp.asp?c=dkLNK1MQI wG&b=4741359.

Uniformed Services University of the Health Sciences website, accessed February 5, 2015, https://www.usuhs.edu/.

Index

The ABC's of America's Money System, 38-41

Agnew, Spiro 136

Agricultural and rural policy and legislation, 60-70, 211-212, 215-217

Albert, Carl, 4-8, 10, 13-14,18-19, 21-22, 97-99, 103, 109, 114, 120, 122-133, 147, 157, 161, 162, 165-166, 172-174, 178-181, 183-184, 188, 190, 193-194, 196, 200, 212-213, 237

American Bankers Association, 41

Anderson, John 172-173

Animal rights legislation and policy, 64-65

Annunzio, Frank, 123, 211

Anti-Old Regulars or Reformers, 83

Armed Services Investigating Subcommittee of the Committee on Armed Services and its *Report* on My Lai, 89-93

Ashley, Thomas, 44, 185-186

Aspin, Les, 250-253

Bank Holding Company Act of 1956 and Amendments of 1969, 43-44

Bank Merger Act of 1960 and Amendments of 1966, 42

Banketeering, Bonuseering, Melloneering, 28-29, 38

Barrett, William, 179

Battistella, Annabel or Fanne Foxe the "Argentine Firecracker", 148-150, 165-166

Bennett, Charles, 252

Bergland, Bob, 198

Bevill, Tom, 178

Bingham, Jonathan, 178-179

Bipartisan House System, 1-3, 26, 231-236

Blatnik, John, 101, 104-105, 114-115

Blue Dog Coalition, 264-265, 269-270

Board of Education, 6-7, 15-16, 109

Boehner, John, 268

Boggs, Hale, 6, 15, 18-19, 124, 126, 180

Boland, Edward, 206-207

Bolling Committee or Select Committee on Committees and its plan, 129-132

Bolling, Richard, 3, 5-8, 10, 13, 15, 17-19, 22-23, 29-30, 105, 107, 109-114, 119, 129-130, 140, 165 ,178, 180, 185, 187-188, 190, 200-202, 231-236, 238, 244

Bolling's Congressional reform plan, 111-114, 231-236, 244

Bonus or adjusted-service certificates, 32-34

Bonus Expeditionary Force, 32-33

Bowles, Chet, 101

Brademas, John, 119, 178-179

Brasco, Frank, 46

Brodhead, William, 179

Brooks, Jack, 190-191, 255

Budget and Impoundment Control Act, 140-141

Burleson, Omar, 20

Burton, John, 188

Burton, Phillip, 114, 119, 123, 129, 152-155, 157, 172-174, 178, 183-184, 202, 205, 231-236, 238, 247

Calley, William, 88

Cannon, Clarence, 25

Cannon, Joseph, 1-2, 128, 165, 253

Carr, Bob, 239

Carter, Jimmy and/or Carter administration, 139, 236, 240-241

Casey, Bob, 206-207

Caucus, 1-2, 7-8

Chambers, Whittaker, 86-87

Chappell, Bill, 46

Chisholm, Shirley, 123, 157

Civil Rights Act of 1964, 47-48, 74-75, 96

Civil Rights Act of 1966, 108-109

Civil Rights legislation and Civil Rights Movement, 11, 74-75, 95-96, 108-109

Clark, Frank, 161

Clinton, Bill and/or Clinton administration, 259-260, 262-263

Colmer, William "Bill", 19-20, 24, 158

Committee Chairmen, 1, 2, 9-11, 13, 18-20, 23-24, 110-112, 114-118, 123-132, 162-165, 167-171, 174-180, 182-191, 194-202, 207-208, 217, 219-220, 231-237, 245, 250-255, 261-262, 270-271

Committee System, 1, 2, 8-11, 18-20, 110-112, 114-118, 122-132, 162-165, 174-176, 231-237, 239, 250-253, 261-262, 270-271

Committee on Agriculture (House), 16-17, 60-72, 170, 183-184, 192, 194-195, 203-204, 208, 211-212, 214-217, 220, 225, 232-233

Committee on Appropriations (House), 25, 164-165, 205-207, 223-224, 245

Committee on Armed Services (House), 84-85, 88-93, 96-99, 171, 184, 192,

195-196, 204, 208, 212, 233-234, 220, 226, 250-253
Committee on Banking and Currency and/or Committee on Banking, Currency and Housing (House), 27-29, 44-46, 131, 167, 169-170, 179-180, 184-188, 192, 196-199, 208, 211, 219-220, 224-225, 232
Committee on the Budget (House), 163, 245
Committee on Committees (House Democrats), 8-9, 14, 97, 112, 121-122, 125-126, 162-163, 178-180, 182-183, 192-193
Committee on Committees (House Republicans), 8-9
Committee on Commerce (House), 210
Committee on the District of Columbia, 126, 261
Committee on Education and Labor (House), 116-118, 120-121
Committee on House Administration (House), 118, 180-182, 188-189, 192, 199-202, 205, 208, 228-229
Committee on the Judiciary (House), 137, 142
Committee on Merchant Marine and Fisheries, 261
Committee on Party Effectiveness, 247-248

Committee on Post Office and Civil Service Committee (House), 261
Committee on Rules (House), 1-2, 11, 13, 15, 22-23, 165, 190, 245, 256-257
Committee on Standards of Official Conduct (House), 258
Committee on Un-American Activities (House), 86-88, 95
Committee on Ways and Means (House), 8-9, 14, 147-148, 163-164, 166, 179, 189-190, 208, 245
Committee Reform Amendments of 1974, 106, 130-132
Common Cause, 218-223, 226-227, 234
Congressional Black Caucus, 97
Congressional Progressive Caucus, 269
Congressional Quarterly and *Congressional Quarterly Weekly Report*, 23-24, 59, 202, 208-210, 224, 256, 262-263, 264, 269-270
Congressional reform and Congressional reform movement, 100-134, 155-156, 160, 162-165, 174-176, 182-183, 231-236, 244
Conlon, Richard, 114, 119, 129
Connally, John, 57

Conservative Democrats and/or Southern /Democrats, 11, 17-24, 55-58, 85-86, 101-104, 107, 110-112, 123, 132-133, 192-194, 202, 248-250, 256, 264-265

Conservative Coalition, 17, 21-24, 101-103, 112, 192-194, 208-210, 249-250, 256, 264

Conservative Democratic Forum, 248-249, 264

Conyers, John, 124-126

Cooley, Harold, 16-17, 64, 70-71

Corman, Jim, 97

Cox, Archibald, 136

Cox, Eugene, 22

Cross, Oliver Harlan, 52-53

Culver, John, 129

Davis, Mendel, 179

Dean, John, 47

Delaney, James, 190

DeLay, Tom, 266

Dellums, Ronald, 97-98, 204, 212, 233, 251-253

Democratic Caucus (House), 7-8, 114-116, 118-123, 128-129, 154-155, 157-158, 160-165, 178, 182-191, 194-202, 205-207, 231-236, 239-241, 245-248, 252-254

Democratic Congressional Campaign Committee, 154-155, 189, 201, 205

Democratic Party or Democrats, 2, 13-24, 55-58, 83-86, 100-104, 107, 110-112, 132-133, 135-136, 141-146, 192-194, 231-238, 248-250, 254-256, 269

Democratic Solid South, 55-57

Democratic Steering and Policy Committee, 128, 162-163, 178-180, 192, 193, 231-236, 245, 254, 255

Democratic Study Group, 100-110, 114-115, 118-119, 121-123, 128-129, 174-176, 231-236, 265-266

Dent, John, 178

Deschler, Lewis, 7

Dickinson, William, 91

Diggs, Charles, 190-191

Dingell, John, 160, 255

Dixiecrats, 56-57, 88, 95-96, 101, 159

Dixon, Julian, 258

Doorkeeper (House), 158-162

Eisenhower, Dwight and/or Eisenhower administration, 24, 57, 58, 116

Elections of 1974, 141-146, 189

Elections of 1994, 259-261

Elections of 2006, 268

Elections of 2010, 270

Ervin, Sam, 47

Evans, Frank, 185

Evins, Joe, 206-207, 191

Federal Elections Campaign Amendments of 1974 and Federal Election Campaign Act of 1971, 140-141
Federal Reserve System, 38-41, 45
Flood, Daniel, 206-207
Foley, Tom, 10, 12, 16-17, 69-70, 72, 114, 146, 162-163, 183, 192, 194-195, 203-204, 208-212, 215, 217, 225, 234, 239-240, 247, 255, 259-260
Food Stamp Program, 67-70, 170, 211-212, 215-217
Ford, Gerald and/or Ford administration, 129-130, 136-137, 139, 141-142, 162, 212, 235, 240
Fraser, Don, 114, 119, 156, 164, 181, 188-189
Frelinghuysen, Peter, 129
Freshmen of Ninety-fourth Congress, 141-142, 144-146, 154-158, 160, 167-171, 174-176, 183, 189, 202-205, 213, 215-216, 223-224, 231-237
From, Al, 246-248
Fulton, Richard, 179

Gallup Poll, 138-139, 143
Gardner, John, 218, 222-223, 226-227
Garner, John Nance, 6, 20
Gettys, Tom, 46

Giaimo, Robert, 164-165, 178
Gibbons, Sam, 105
Gingrich, Newt, 258-259, 262-263
Ginn, Ronald "Bo", 197
Goldwater, Barry, 115
Great Depression, 28-30, 32-34
Griffin, Charles, 46
Gubser, Charles, 91

Haley, James, 190-191
Halleck, Charles, 91
Hanna, Richard, 46
Hansen Committee or Committee on Organization, Study, and Review and its plan, 122-123, 125-128, 130-132, 182-183
Hansen, Julia Butler, 123
Harding, Kenneth, 158, 172
Hardy, Porter, 91
Hastert, Dennis, 267
Hays, Wayne, 123, 124, 127, 154-155, 162, 180-182, 188-189, 192, 200-202, 205, 208, 219, 228-230, 234
Hebert, Felix Edward "Eddie", 1, 29, 77-99, 127, 143, 160, 167, 168, 171, 175-176, 180, 184, 187, 192-196, 202, 204, 205, 208-210, 212, 213, 217-223, 226-227, 231-236
Henderson, David, 191
Hicks, Floyd, 198
Hightower, Jack, 249

Hiss, Alger, 86-87
Holifield, Chet, 127
Holt, Marjorie, 171
Hoover, Herbert and/or
Hoover administration, 31-33,
56
House Democratic
Leadership, 6, 8,12, 14, 15,
22, 24, 83-84, 88, 97, 103,
125, 128-129, 193-194, 229,
257, 244-245, 254-256
House Out of Order, 109-112
Howard, James, 255
Hullabaloo, 78

In Common Cause, 218,

Jacobs, Andrew, 155, 160
Jarman, John, 210-211
Jaworski, Leon, 136
Jennings, W. Pat, 158, 171-
173
Johnson, Lyndon and/or
Johnson administration, 7,
24, 73, 103, 114-115, 118-
119, 218, 240-241
Joint Committee on Defense
Production, 28
Joint Economic Committee,
28
Jones, Edward, 123
Jones, Jim, 244
Jones, Robert, 191
Jones, Sam, 82, 83
Jordan, Barbara, 179, 185,
186

Katzenbach, Nicholas, 108
Kennedy, Edward, 47
Kennedy, John F., 15, 118-
119
Kennedy, Robert, 105, 145
King Caucus, 2
Kirwan, Michael, 12
Koch, Edward, 188, 200
Krueger, Robert, 198, 202

LaFalce, John, 176, 200
Landrum, Phil, 123, 197
Latch, Edward, 158, 172, 173
Leath, Marvin, 251-253, 266
Levitas, Elliot, 188-189
Liberal Manifesto, 100-101
Long, Earl, 82, 83
Long, Gillis, 185, 190, 245-
248
Long, Huey, 29, 81
Long political machine, 81-82
Longworth, Nicholas, 6
Louisiana, state of and/or
government and politics, 77-
83
Louisiana State University,
81-82

MacArthur, Douglas, 33
Mack, John, 259
Madden, Ray, 190-191, 219
Maguire, Gene, 188
Mahon, George, 20, 24, 127,
190, 191, 206, 207, 219, 223-
224

Majority Leader (House), 11-12, 18-19, 237-238
Maloney, Paul, 84
Manhattan Project, 24-25
Marcantonio, Vito, 19-20
Marshall, George, 25
Martin, Dave, 129, 130
Martin, Joseph, 4, 13, 22, 24, 25
Matsunaga, Spark, 179, 190
Mavroules, Nicholas, 252
McCormack, John, 6-8, 12, 15, 25, 119-122, 159
McFall, John, 178, 206, 207, 238
McGovern, George, 57, 140
McMillan, John, 126
Meeds, Lloyd, 129, 185, 200-201
Mellon, Andrew, 30-32
Metcalf, Lee, 101, 102
Metcalfe, Ralph, 179
Michel, Robert, 172, 208, 258
Mikva, Abner, 114, 155, 188
Miller, George, 171
Miller, J. Irwin, 156-157
Miller, William "Fishbait", 19-20, 45-46, 148, 158-162, 181-182, 229-230
Mills, Wilbur, 24, 96-97, 127, 146-150, 165-166, 179, 227-228
Mink, Patsy, 157
Minority Leader (House), 22, 24
Moakley, Joseph, 190

Moffett, Anthony, 171, 205
Molloy, J.T., 161, 172-173
Monahan, John, 161
Montgomery, G.V. "Sonny", 194, 265
Moorhead, William, 185, 187, 197-198
Morgan, Thomas, 158, 188, 190, 191
Moss, John, 178, 210
Mundt, Karl, 87
Murphy, Morgan, 190,
Murtha, John, 188
My Lai Massacre, 88-93

Natcher, William, 206, 207
National Association of Manufacturers, 227
National Committee for an Effective Congress, 156-157
Neal, Stephen, 176, 200
New Deal, 53-55, 59, 61-62
New Democrat Coalition, 269
New Orleans, Louisiana, 77-83
New Orleans States, 78, 80-83
New Republic, 138
New York Times, 200, 224
Newsweek, 224
Nixon, Richard and/or Nixon administration, 45-47, 85, 87, 106, 118, 136-142, 145, 169, 217
Noe, James, 82
Nolanville, Texas, 53-54

Oberstar, James, 188
O'Hara, James, 105, 114, 119, 123, 124, 182-183, 165, 188
Old Regulars, 78, 81-83
O'Neill, Thomas "Tip", 6-7, 11-12, 15, 97, 114, 124, 126, 127, 137-138, 145, 152, 157, 161, 163-164, 171-174, 178-179, 180, 207-208, 229, 236-237, 241, 244-245, 250, 253, 255, 257
Ottinger, Richard, 144, 147-148, 153-156, 160, 168-169, 174-176, 205, 223, 231-236

Partisan House System, 243-245, 267-268
Passman, Otto, 205-207
Patman, Wright, 1, 6-7, 20, 24, 27-48, 123, 127, 142, 146, 167-170, 172, 175-176, 178-179, 183, 185-187, 192, 196-199, 202-203, 205, 208-210, 211, 213-215, 219-220, 224-225, 231-236
Patten, Edward, 200
Pattison, Edward, 200
Pelosi, Nancy, 267-269
Pepper, Claude, 190
Perkins, Carl, 190-191
Phelan, Richard, 258
Poage, Bob, 1, 16, 20, 23, 28, 49-76, 127, 142-143, 167-168, 170, 175-176, 180, 183-184, 187, 192-195, 202-205,

208-217, 219-220, 223-226, 231-237, 251, 266
Powell, Adam Clayton, 116-118
Power in the House, 109-110, 112-114
Price, Melvin, 178, 191-193, 195-196, 208-210, 212, 226, 250

Rangel, Charles, 200
Rankin, John, 88, 95
Rarick, John, 120
Ray, Elizabeth, 228-229
Rayburn, Sam, 4-8, 10, 12-16, 20, 22, 24, 25, 83-84, 109, 160, 165, 253, 255
Reagan, Ronald and/or Reagan administration, 244-245, 251, 255, 256, 265
Rebuilding the Road to Opportunity: A Democratic Direction for the 1980s, 247-248
Redbook, 98-99
Rees, Thomas, 185, 187
"Report on House Committee Chairmen", 219-221
Republican Party or Republicans, 2, 11, 17, 21-24, 55-58, 85-86, 101-103, 112, 132-133, 135-136, 142-143, 192-194, 208, 234-235, 249-250, 257-259
Reuss, Henry, 29, 45, 101, 119, 123-124, 166-167, 174-

175, 178-179, 184-185, 187, 188, 196-199, 202-203, 208-210, 223, 231-236
Rhodes, George, 101
Rhodes, John, 142, 172, 173, 208
Ridenhour, Ronald, 88-90
Rivers, L.M., 23-24, 84-85, 89-91
Roberts, Ray, 191
Robinson, Joseph, 36
Robinson-Patman Act and price discrimination, 34-36
Rockefeller, Nelson, 137
Rodino, Peter, 190-191
Rodrigue, George, 264
Roosevelt, Franklin and/or Roosevelt administration, 22, 24-25, 29, 34, 52-53
Rosenthal, Benjamin, 127
Rota, Robert, 158, 173
Rostenkowski, Dan, 254-255

Sabath, Adolph, 36-37
Sarbanes, Paul, 129
"Saturday Night Massacre", 136
Scheuer, James,155, 185
Schroeder, Pat, 96-99, 204, 223, 226, 233, 236-237
Select Committee on Small Business, 28
Seniority system and seniority in general, 9-19, 110-112, 114-132, 156, 160, 168, 174-

176, 218-219, 222, 231-236, 270-271
Shivers, Allan, 57
Sikes, Robert, 206-207
Simon, Paul, 237
Sirica, John, 46, 136-137
Sisk, B.F. "Bernie", 101, 124, 157-158, 190
Slack, John, 206-207
Small business legislation, 36-38
Smith, Al, 56
Smith, Howard, 11, 22
Smith, Neal, 123
Solomon, Oscar, 77-78
Speaker of the House, 1-6, 8, 11-13, 24, 128, 131, 162-165, 235-236, 253, 255, 261
Spellman, Gladys, 185
Staggers, Harley, 190-191, 210, 219
Stanton, James, 161-162, 188, 200, 201
Steed, Tom, 207
Steiger, William, 129
Stenholm, Charles, 248-249, 263-264
Stephens, Robert, 46, 129, 178, 196-199
Stevenson, Adlai, 57
Stimson, Henry, 25
Stokes, Louis, 188
Stratton, Samuel, 91
Strauss, Robert, 154
Era of Subcommittee Government, 236-241

Sullivan, John, 78
Sullivan, Leonor, 157, 179, 185, 190-191, 199, 211

Taber, John, 25
Tangeman, Clementine, 156-157
Teague, Olin, 20, 24, 123, 127, 157, 191, 223
Teicher, Oren, 144-145, 155-156
Texas delegation (House), 15, 20-21, 202, 266-267
Texas, state of and/or government and politics, 27-28, 49-52, 55-58, 60, 266-267
Thomas, Albert, 73
Thompson, Frank, 101, 105, 108, 115, 117, 119, 121, 123, 178, 180, 188, 189, 200-202, 234
Thornberry, Homer, 6
Time, 224
Times-Picayune, 78, 80, 82
Tirey, Frank, 53-55
Tower, John, 259
Treen, David, 193
Truman, Harry and/or Truman administration, 56-57
Tulane University, 78-79
Two-party system, 57-58

Udall, Morris, 12-13, 89, 118-120, 124, 138, 161-162, 178, 188
Ullman, Al, 191

Uniformed Services University of Health Sciences, 93-95
United States v. Richard M. Nixon, 136-137

Vanik, Charles, 123-124, 163
Vietnam War, 85, 88-93, 135-136, 145, 171, 217-218, 233-234
Voting Rights Act of 1965, 48, 74-75, 96
Wallace, George, 120
War Powers Act, 140
The Washington Fringe Benefit, 229
Washington Post, 224, 226-228
Watergate Crisis, 46-47, 135-146, 235-236
Watson, Albert, 115-116
West, Fowler, 70-73, 145-146, 170, 203, 204, 216-217, 223
Whip, 11-12, 126-127, 153
Whitten, Jamie, 160, 205-207
Wiggins, Charles, 129
Williams, John Bell, 115-116
Wilson, Charles, 200-201
Wirth, Timothy, 168
World War I and World War I veterans, 2, 32-34
World War II, 24-25, 36-38, 73
Wright, Jim, 8, 11, 15-16, 20-21, 24, 29, 60, 109, 125, 133,

140, 145, 152, 154-155, 158,
167-168, 171, 179, 185, 186,
198-199, 203-204, 223-224,
236-239, 244-245, 253-259,
265

Yates, Sidney, 206-207
Young, Andrew, 190
Young, C.W. Bill, 129
Young, John, 190

Index